The Imperial School for Tribes

The Imperial School for Tribes

Educating the Provincial Elite in the Late Ottoman Empire

Mehmet Ali Neyzi

I.B. TAURIS
LONDON · NEW YORK · OXFORD · NEW DELHI · SYDNEY

I.B. TAURIS
Bloomsbury Publishing Plc
50 Bedford Square, London, WC1B 3DP, UK
1385 Broadway, New York, NY 10018, USA
29 Earlsfort Terrace, Dublin 2, Ireland

BLOOMSBURY, I.B. TAURIS and the I.B. Tauris logo
are trademarks of Bloomsbury Publishing Plc

First published in Great Britain 2023
Paperback edition published 2025

Copyright © Mehmet Ali Neyzi 2023

Mehmet Ali Neyzi has asserted his right under the Copyright, Designs
and Patents Act, 1988, to be identified as Author of this work.

For legal purposes the Acknowledgements on pp. xiii–xv constitute
an extension of this copyright page.

Series design by Adriana Brioso
Cover image: Students of Mekteb-i Aşiret-i Humayun (Imperial Tribal School).
(© History and Art Collection/Alamy Stock Photo)

All rights reserved. No part of this publication may be reproduced or
transmitted in any form or by any means, electronic or mechanical, including
photocopying, recording, or any information storage or retrieval system,
without prior permission in writing from the publishers.

Bloomsbury Publishing Plc does not have any control over, or responsibility for,
any third-party websites referred to or in this book. All internet addresses given
in this book were correct at the time of going to press. The author and publisher
regret any inconvenience caused if addresses have changed or sites have ceased
to exist, but can accept no responsibility for any such changes.

A catalogue record for this book is available from the British Library.

A catalog record for this book is available from the Library of Congress.

ISBN: PB: 978-0-7556-4977-8
ePDF: 978-0-7556-4975-4
eBook: 978-0-7556-4976-1

Typeset by Integra Software Services Pvt. Ltd.

To find out more about our authors and books visit www.bloomsbury.com
and sign up for our newsletters.

To the dear memory of my advisor, mentor and friend
Professor Abdurrahim Abu Husayn
who sadly passed away on 23 June 2022

'It has been customary to conceive of the history of the Arab Middle East in the Ottoman period mostly in terms of cities which were centers of imperial administration. Rural and tribal areas away from these cities were treated, for the most part, as though they did not exist.'

Kamal S. Salibi, 'Middle Eastern Parallels: Syria-Iraq-Arabia in Ottoman Times', in *Middle Eastern Studies*, Vol. 15, No. 1, 1979.

'In the cause of fitting the ungainly body of late Ottoman history to the Procrustean bed of modernization theory, many purported anomalies have been rather elegantly amputated. This study seeks to account for some of the truncated parts of the corpus of late Ottoman history.'

Benjamin C. Fortna, 'Imperial Classroom, Islam, the State, and Education in the Late Ottoman Empire', Oxford, 2000.

Contents

List of figures	x
List of tables	xii
Acknowledgements	xiii
Introduction	1
1 The school for tribes: A chronology	11
2 Recruitment and placement	35
3 Educators and curriculum	75
4 Life stories – Greater Syria	91
5 Life stories – Libya	123
6 Life stories – Iraq	149
Conclusion	163
Notes	177
Bibliography	201
Index	216

Figures

1.1 Announcement of the establishment of the school, *Tercüman-ı Hakikat*, 8 July 1892, Mekteb Tesisi — 15
1.2 Official notice of the inauguration date of the school as October 4, *Tercüman-ı Hakikat*, 8 July 1892, Tebligat-ı Resmiye — 16
1.3 Cover letter for charter and curriculum signed by the council of ministers, Ottoman Archives, I.MMS 131-5641-1, 22 July 1892 — 17
1.4 Some photos of the students in their native attire — 20
1.5 Photos of students in their new uniforms — 20
1.6 Official Stamp of The School for Tribes, Ottoman Archives Y-MTV-79-182-2-1, 8 July 1893 — 24
1.7 Royal picnic organized for The School for Tribes, 4 June 1893, Istanbul University rare documents collection — 25
1.8 Fresh graduates in Erzurum, *Tercüman-ı Hakikat*, 7 June 1898 — 30
3.1 Decorative booklet sent to the palace containing exam results, Ottoman Archives, Y-EE.-D 962, 14 Aug 1894 — 79
4.1 Photo of Shallash in Ghouta — 100
4.2 *Filistin* newspaper, 2 February 1926 — 102
4.3 Ramadan Shallash and the French High Commissioner Jouvenel — 103
4.4 *Al-Yarmouk* newspaper, 14 February 1926 — 104
4.5 Photo of Fahd al-Atrash, Sharifa Zuhur, *Asmahan's Secrets, Woman, War and Song,* University of Texas at Austin, 2000, p. 166 — 108
4.6 Asmahan, Second photo shows her attending the speech of General De Gaulle at the American University of Cairo, wearing a brooch of the Croix de Lorraine, symbol of Free France, 1941, Zuhur, p. 167 — 112
4.7 Aboud Abd al-Razzak Merhebi in his uniform — 115
4.8 Three graduates: Aboud, Mouin and Ibrahim with the French Consul in 1928 — 116
4.9 Photo of Mustafa Adib during the road construction in Konya, 1913 — 118

4.10	Ottoman and Arab. Sultan's decree praising Abdel Fattah and Collage of members of the Syrian Congress	119
4.11	The Merhebı Family in Hotel Royal, Tripoli, circa 1920	120
5.1	Map of 146 Sanussi lodges (Africa and Hijaz), E.E. Evans-Pritchard, *The Sanussi of Cyrenaica,* Oxford, 1949 (reprint 1973), p. 24	125
5.2	Photograph of first page of Omar Mansour's memoirs	127
5.3	Photograph of Omar Mansour's civil service academy diploma	130
5.4	Omar Mansour as a young Ottoman Paşa	133
5.5	Book written by Orhan Koloğlu about his father's life	137
5.6	Sadullah Koloğlu in Ankara	139
5.7	Photograph of funeral, Orhan Koloğlu, *Arab Kaymakam*, Aykırı, 2011, p. 200	141
5.8	The two Zafır mansions in the 1950s and today	144
6.1	Abdulmuhsin and Abdulkarim as aide-de-camps of the sultan (*yaver-i hazret-i şehriyari*)	154
6.2	Abdulmuhsin, Prime Minister of Iraq	160
6.3	Suicide note of Abdulmuhsin Saadun, Abd al-Razzaq Al-Hasani, *Tarikh al-Wizarat al-Iraqiya,* II, Dar al-Shuyun al-Thakafiya, Iraq, 1988, p. 284	161
7.1	*Vakit* newspaper, 28 May 1933 and Turkish Republic Cabinet memorandum regarding mobile training for tribes, 23 October 1933, from the Republican Archives	167
7.2	The Aşiret Mektebi building today – Restored according to original drawings	173

Tables

1	Quotas and actual recruitment figures	61
2	Breakdown of 333 students by region and year	61
3	Number of students who graduated from the military and civil service academies	62
4	List of names of 363 students	62
5	Merhebi family tree – *Students highlighted*	121

Acknowledgements

In August 2015, I was awed by the 150-year aura of College Hall at the American University of Beirut and finally discovered the office of Professor Abu Husayn. He knew I was interested to work on Sultan Abdulhamid II, but asked me what I would like to do more specifically for my dissertation. I said I would like to explore the one and only trip of an Ottoman ruler to Europe in 1867. Sultan Abdulaziz visited Paris, London, Brussels, Berlin and Vienna and took his nephews Murat and Abdulhamid with him. They met Napoleon III, Queen Victoria, King Leopold, Kaiser Wilhelm and Emperor Franz Joseph. Abdulhamid fell ill in Vienna on the return journey and remained there for an additional two months for recovery. He was twenty-five years old. I believe this experience must have left an indelible mark on the future Sultan.

My professor said this was interesting but would be more appropriate as a paper topic. He then asked me whether I knew of the Aşiret Mektebi (The School for Tribes). Although I had been reading on the Hamidian period for almost thirty years I had not heard about this school. Abu Husayn briefly summarized the rationale of the institution and emphasized that very little research had been done regarding this unique project of Sultan Abdulhamid. I was excited and we discussed the idea of exploring the future careers of the graduates, which would shed some light on the results of this investment. So that is how it all started.

I cannot sufficiently express my gratitude to Professor Abu Husayn who guided me throughout my six years of studies at AUB. He was an amazing scholar and had a very deep understanding of the Middle East and Turkey. Born in Nuba, Palestine, he earned a scholarship at AUB and was a student of Kamal Salibi. In 2013, he was chosen as an honorary member of the Turkish Historical Society. He diligently analysed and questioned my work, his English was impeccable and I had to rewrite many sections several times.

There is one more person without whose companionship my doctoral degree and this book would never have been possible – my wife and best friend for half a century. Fahrünisa left her position as professor of physics at Boğaziçi University and agreed to migrate to Beirut with me in 2015. We spent the fall semester of 2017 together in Cairo, where I attended the American University of Cairo. She supported me during my periods of research, transcription, writing and rewriting. We were very lucky that our three grandchildren were born during these exceptional years.

The third important figure who acted as my wise guide is Hasan Kayalı, my dear friend. Back in 2010 when I was travelling to Beirut to develop wind energy projects (which are sadly still not realized), Hasan suggested that I go to AUB and meet his friend Professor Abu Husayn. After this visit I decided to pursue my doctoral degree in Lebanon rather than the United States. Hasan followed my progress throughout and diligently read and commented on all my first and later drafts. I cannot thank him enough.

I was very fortunate to have wonderful scholars on my dissertation committee. I would like to express my sincere gratitude to the chairman, John Meloy, to my friend Michael Provence, to Tariq Tell from AUB who was also my tutor for two wonderful courses and supported me greatly in my research, and finally Tufan Buzpınar.

Very special thanks go to Mansour al-Kikhia, son of Omar Mansour, who was one of the outstanding graduates of the School for Tribes. Professor Kikhia sent me a copy of his father's handwritten and unpublished memoirs of twenty-six pages from 1919. Professor Kikhia visited Istanbul several times providing me also with pictures and documents related to his father. Sadullah Merhebi from England kindly shared his research on his family tree as well as many pictures and documents related to the Merhebi students from Akkar, Lebanon. Nasser al-Sadoun from Jordan sent me a book and many photos of Abdulmuhsin Saadun, who served as Prime Minister in Iraq. I was fortunate to meet Orhan Kologlu before he passed away, who wrote the life story of his father Sadullah, Prime Minister of Libya. Finally, I would like to thank Güngör Tekçe for his support and his amazing book on the Zafir family, who sent four students to the School for Tribes.

Hiba Turman assisted me tremendously in all my Arabic research. She scanned the *Thamarat al Fünun* newspaper of Beirut for fifteen years and found many references to the School for Tribes. Later she searched the Palestine newspapers and identified several clippings about Ramadan Shallash.

Hiba also did a meticulous translation of Omar Mansour's memoirs. Habibe Çıkılıoğlu scanned the *Tercüman-ı Hakikat* newspaper for the duration of the school and discovered hundreds of articles about the School for Tribes, which I later transcribed. Budak Kayabek and Ekrem Sırma supported me in deciphering some difficult texts in the Ottoman script. Several friends read my manuscript and gave useful comments. I am indebted particularly to Charles Allen from California, who improved my writing style significantly. Special thanks to Turgay Bayındır and Samira Shami. I am very grateful to my final readers Deniz Akyüz and Jean and Barry Robinson.

Finally, my mother, Professor Olcay Neyzi, who passed away on 3 February 2022, was my great supporter and read all my draft chapters. She was an ardent Kemalist (Ataturk fan) and this project allowed us to have long discussions on our Ottoman past.

Introduction

The Auspicious Event was the term adopted by the Ottomans for the bloody abolition of the traditional Janissary Corps in 1826. The Ottoman state was determined to centralize its power in Istanbul and remove all impediments towards this objective. A new structure named The Mohammedan Victorious Army was established, modelled on the Napoleonic example.[1] Over the previous centuries, the Janissaries had become a strongly entrenched and privileged group, becoming the terror of subjects and statesmen instead of being the terror of enemies. This landmark event paved the way for the social, fiscal, legal and educational reforms known collectively as the *Tanzimat*, which continued unabated until the First World War.

With increased centralization, the tentacles of the empire began to extend even to the remotest corners of the realm. Like the Habsburgs in Austria and the Romanovs in Russia, the Ottomans strived to realize 'a transition to a modern imperial model infused with national imagery and identity',[2] hence the concept of Ottomanism was introduced along with centralization. The land law of 1858 and the provincial reform law of 1864 laid out the legal foundations for the penetration of the state into the countryside. The new system of government was gradually introduced into the provinces, Syria (1866), Libya (1867), Hijaz (1868), Eastern Arabia (1871) and Yemen (1872). Carefully picked governors were charged with building local administrative councils to control their regions, boost agricultural output and maximize tax revenues. 'Ottoman modernity involved a process of mediation and translation to adapt new ideas from the West to radically different settings across the Empire.'[3]

During this period, the government began to intervene more directly in the lives of individual Ottoman subjects. The first census was carried out in most parts of the empire in 1831, and censuses were repeated throughout the century.

However, the census was regarded by the provinces as groundwork for forced conscription in the army and resisted by much of the population. Meanwhile, the nineteenth century witnessed a constant increase in international trade. The development of cash crops encouraged the merchant classes to participate in the state's project of centralized rule and helped to integrate the countryside with the cities. The relationship between the capital and economic centres like Aleppo, Damascus and Beirut was bolstered.[4]

Midhat Paşa can probably be described as one of the most effective pioneers in building the 'soft power' of the Ottoman Empire. In this new world, the state accepted to provide services for its citizens, with the population contributing to the welfare of the fatherland. Midhat Paşa was appointed to lead the Danube Province, newly created as a role model in 1864. During his governorship, he developed the infrastructure: building schools, hospitals, roads and bridges, and urging local notables to support these investments. In 1869, he was sent to Baghdad, where he was able to replicate the Balkan experience. He reformed the 6th Army and opened a military school to train local recruits, also establishing commercial sea traffic between Basra-Suez and Istanbul. A special fleet like the one on the Danube was constructed to boost transportation on the Euphrates and Tigris rivers. By applying the new land law, Midhat Paşa issued countless deeds to supporters of the regime and at the same time increased the tax base. He was able to extend the Ottoman state apparatus to Kuwait and Qatar and into the Arabian Peninsula.

A similar drive to extend the administration of the empire was executed in the area known as today as Jordan, a frontier zone between the state and the nomadic tribes. In this region, the Ottomans led a systematic effort to fortify and expand the towns, starting from Ajlun in the north in the 1850s and gradually moving south to Maan in 1895.[5] Around 25,000 Circassian refugees who fled the Russian army were settled in these locations, and the city of Amman was populated and made into a regional centre during this process.

One of the outstanding characteristics of the nineteenth century was the creation of national education systems worldwide. In order to build unified and homogeneous populations, the Europeans developed methods of pedagogy and centrally defined curricula which were utilized to create 'model citizens'. The Ottomans emulated the West by first revamping the military academy in 1834, a school which produced many future leaders of the country, including

Ataturk.[6] In 1838, a group of top-level bureaucrats proposed to build new high schools with a modern curriculum all around the country, which would cater to bright students who had completed their primary education. Uniforms, the class system and textbooks were novelties introduced into these schools.

The imperial edict of 1839 stipulated that education was one of the duties of the state and subsequently the first department of education in the Ottoman Empire was established.[7] It was announced in 1846 that primary education would be reformed, the modern high schools would be multiplied, and a university would be opened. This structure evolved into a Ministry of Public Education in 1857, which was charged to educate and train students in the Western sciences.[8] The Civil Service Academy[9] was established in 1859 to produce qualified bureaucrats for administrative positions in the state apparatus, and in 1863 the first university was opened,[10] while many new high schools were established in the provinces.

Abdülaziz was the first Ottoman sultan to visit Europe in 1867, where he was taken to a tour of several schools in Paris, which impressed him. The French minister of education, Jean Victor Duruy, acted as a consultant to the sultan to prepare the Ottoman Regulation of Public Education issued in 1869.[11] This regulation declared that education was the correct path to join the community of civilized nations and was an important milestone in the history of education in the Ottoman Empire.[12] It is significant that in the same year the Russian Empire introduced a similar educational reform based on the French model, and in 1870 Japan announced a major national blueprint for state education.[13]

In 1876, Sultan Abdülhamid II, one of the most controversial figures in Ottoman history, found himself unexpectedly on the throne. 'There is a strong tendency among historians to describe nineteenth century Ottoman political development in terms of a dichotomy between Westernizing reformers and traditionalist reactionaries. Sultan Abdülhamid II is a particularly good case to illustrate the inadequacy of this approach.'[14] Abdülhamid continued the modernization drive of the *Tanzimat*, while he simultaneously embraced and promoted the Islamic heritage of the empire. After losing much of the Balkan territories in the early days of his reign, Sultan Abdülhamid came to rule a largely Muslim population. The Arab provinces had always had particular significance for the Ottoman state for varied reasons. The Pan Islamism that Abdülhamid espoused and the emphasis he placed on his caliphal role rendered the significance of these largely Muslim parts of the empire even greater in the last quarter of the nineteenth century. Moreover, the Ottoman state feared that the infectious nature of nationalism which had resulted in the loss of the Western provinces would soon make its appearance in the Arab regions. Hence, the attempt to better integrate the Arabs into the empire acquired critical urgency and called for unconventional methods.

The two areas of remarkable success of Sultan Abdülhamid's reign were the implementation of the planned reforms of the *Tanzimat* in infrastructure and education. Both of these areas involved significant projects directly related to the Arab subjects of the sultan. Hijaz and Yemen were moved up the administrative hierarchy to become the top-level provinces of the empire. Sultan Abdülhamid was staunchly pacifist, and consequently, some years after his accession, the Ottoman Empire achieved a balanced budget and honored its debt payments. This policy allowed the state to divert its resources to infrastructure investments, particularly in the Arab provinces. Telegraph lines were extended to Hijaz and Basra, and the Hamidian clock towers became a symbol of the state in all the provincial capitals, with the Hijaz railway perhaps one of the most ambitious projects to be realized in the area of infrastructure.

The Hijaz railway has received ample scholarly and other types of attention, whereas the less visible Ottoman investments in education are not much celebrated. For the Ottomans, the encroachment of the West was not only a military and economic threat, but it was also ideological. In the area of education, the foreigners attacked the empire on several fronts. The missionaries multiplied their efforts in the empire in the nineteenth century, presenting an example where science and religious training could be applied side by side. The Ottoman minorities endowed their schools with funds; thus, the level of literacy as well as attendance in higher education of the non-Muslim subjects of the empire was far superior to that of the Muslims. Russia, Bulgaria, Serbia and Greece opened schools in the Balkan regions and lured students to study abroad. Iran penetrated the Eastern borders to promote Shiite teachings. These developments urged the religious institutions to support the sultan in promoting an Islamic education with a modernized curriculum.

Abdülhamid had visited the Western capitals in the grand tour of Europe with his Uncle Abdülaziz, and he appreciated the benefits of science and technology. He had observed the rigorous, widespread education system in the West. It was clear that the *Tanzimat* efforts in the field of education mostly remained ink on paper. The literacy rate was low, primary schooling was still dominated by the religious schools, and the modern high schools were few and far between.

There were two main causes for the slow development of public education in the Ottoman Empire. The first was the resistance of the religious institutions which still dominated this sphere. Sultan Abdülhamid led a strong drive to combine Western technology and science with an Islamic education. His approach allowed the religious elites and the populace to accept the new schooling system, which helped the establishment of new schools in all parts of the Empire. The second reason the development of public education in the Ottoman Empire stalled during was financial. Upon the suggestion of the grand viziers Kamil Paşa and Sait Paşa, a new tax was instituted in 1884, which was added to the traditional tithe tax.[15] The new tax was collected in the provinces, and half of the proceeds were used to finance the new high schools in these regions. This steady income allowed Sultan Abdülhamid to go down in history as the sultan who built the highest number of schools in the empire. In addition to this tax, Abdülhamid and his ministers devised many other schemes to contribute to the education budget.

Sultan Abdülhamid boosted all levels of education defined in the regulation of 1869. The primary schools were either converted from the classical religious format or were built anew. High schools were multiplied, reaching a total of 619 around the empire with approximately 40.000 students by the end of the sultan's reign in 1909. Midhat Paşa, who had become Governor of Syria in 1878, opened thirty-five schools in two years. Sait Paşa was another champion of education, and he claimed to have opened 156 high schools during his tenure as minister of education and later as grand vizier. He also introduced French as a mandatory course in all high schools. Another important agent of change was Münif Paşa, who served as minister of education four times. Münif Paşa reorganized, upgraded and spread schools to train teachers to all the provinces,[16] a very critical addition to the system. Also, several schools were opened to educate and train women as students and teachers.

In this book I examine one of the most ambitious, but little-known educational projects of Sultan Abdülhamid II, the *Aşiret Mektebi*, School for

Tribes. The tribes were a constant problem for the Ottoman Empire; they neither paid taxes, nor were willing to join the army. Their raids on urban areas and the *Hajj* (pilgrimage) caravans caused significant economic losses for the empire and undermined the legitimacy and prestige of the sultan. While continuing to utilize the classical Ottoman methods of co-opting Arab urban notables, Abdülhamid made a special effort to reach out to the Arab tribes. He frequently invited local leaders of the Arab provinces to the capital. It is also known that during his reign some of the powerful tribal chiefs could communicate directly with the palace by private telegraph codes.[17] In 1891, when the Governor of Syria tried to block the visit of one of the minor tribal leaders to Istanbul, the palace stated that 'any sheikh who wanted to visit the sultan could not be refused'.[18]

There are numerous references to the School for Tribes in the scholarly literature dealing with Ottoman history; however, most of these references consist of one or two lines, just noting the existence of the school or some specific aspect of it. The first short article about the school appeared in a Turkish historical journal in 1972, the result of preliminary archival research.[19] Interestingly, the only other two works dedicated to the school were written concurrently, one in England and the other in Turkey. Eugene Rogan's article appeared in 1996,[20] while Alişan Akpınar's small booklet was completed in 1997.[21] In 2001, Rogan's article was translated into Turkish and was published in conjunction with Akpınar's booklet. In his foreword to this edition, Akpınar states that the two scholars used much of the same archival material but were unaware of each other's research.[22] There have been no other specific publications on the School for Tribes for over two decades.

Scholars have speculated about several features of the Aşiret Mektebi. One interpretation of the purpose of the school is based on the controversial theory of Ottoman Orientalism. In this reading, the school is labelled as an effort to bring civilization to the 'savages' of the empire.[23] Other scholars theorize that one of the reasons for founding the school was to keep sons of tribal leaders as hostages in the capital, which would prevent any potential revolt.[24] Furthermore, Orhan Koloğlu draws a parallel between the school and the janissary system as a method to recruit promising youngsters to the management of the empire. Michael Provence describes the arduous journey of these young students to the capital, which could sometimes take over one month, and adds that they were 'virtually imprisoned within the school compound'.²⁵ Despite the challenges of the experience, Provence regards the school as one of the more noteworthy vehicles utilized by Sultan Abdülhamid to modernize the empire.

Benjamin Fortna describes the career of Hacı Recai Efendi, the first Director of the School for Tribes, who promoted the expansion of religious training in the modern schools of the Ottoman Empire. Recai Efendi was one of the authors of the curriculum reform report of 1887, which stated that: 'The establishment of matters of belief truly depends on being led and guided on that path in the beginning stages of adolescence.'²⁶ The School for Tribes began recruiting twelve-year-old students who were trained in keeping with the tenets of this report. Another principle promoted by Recai was the necessity of having students perform their prayers as a congregation, a ritual which was strictly applied in the school. As Fortna summarizes: 'Here is a Hamidian education policy in microcosm: a moving away from the more overtly secular aspects of the *Tanzimat* conception of Ottoman education toward a consciously Islamic basis.'²⁷

Several sources state that there was a riot in the school in 1907 resulting from the poor quality of the food, and therefore the school was closed, yet many scholars question this simplistic explanation and suggest other possible reasons for the rather abrupt termination of the school. One view is that the students were politicized with the growing Young Turk and Arab nationalist movements. Others emphasize the high cost of the school, which became an insupportable drain on the budget. One of the aims of this book is to attempt to elaborate on the achievements and the failures of the school and assess the reasons for its closure.

Corinne Blake investigated the careers of the Syrian graduates of the civil service academy, some of whom had studied earlier at the School for Tribes. Her conclusion was that until the end of the First World War, most of these Arab graduates supported the continued existence of a multi-ethnic, polyglot Ottoman Empire.²⁸ The examples provided by Benedict Anderson from Europe, Russia and the Far East illustrate that experiments similar to the School for Tribes were conducted in all parts of the globe. In Anderson's words: 'The interlock between particular educational and administrative pilgrimages provided the territorial base for new "imagined communities" in which natives could come to see themselves as "nationals".[29] Indeed, in the transition from empires to nation states, ruling elites worldwide attempted to use educational institutions to mould their subjects into citizens.

I attempt to analyze the School for Tribes through the discourse of its founders, the acts and ideology of its administrators/teachers, and the future lives and actions of its graduates. As with other institutions, not all the realities on the ground conformed to the assumptions made at the beginning of this initiative. The reactions of the students to this presumably transformative experience were contradictory and complex. However, the archival evidence suggests that the school was generally well-received, the institution and its graduates were held in high esteem, and the Arab graduates maintained close ties with the Ottomans even after the end of the First World War. In summary, I conclude that the Aşiret Mektebi can provide a unique perspective to re-evaluate the late Ottoman struggle for modernity.

A chronology of the school is presented in Chapter 1. The proposal to establish the school was drafted in June 1892 and specified that students between the ages of twelve and sixteen, who were physically fit, intellectually gifted and belonged to prestigious tribal families, would be trained in the capital for five years. In July, Sultan Abdülhamid decreed that the school be opened on the auspicious date of the Prophet's birthday, October 4, with fifty students from the Arab provinces. The inauguration was realized as planned, albeit with only twenty-five students, of whom only three could speak Turkish. In 1896, it was decided to further train the graduates in the military and civil service academies for one year to better prepare them for their future careers. Finally, in 1898, the first graduates were sent to their posts in their provinces. This system was to continue; for instance, in 1904, thirty-eight captains and fourteen district governors were posted to their provinces to serve the empire as qualified and loyal Ottoman officers. The school was terminated at the end of 1907, at which time the remaining students were sent to high schools close to their hometowns.

The recruitment of students to the School for Tribes and their placement processes are examined in Chapter 2. The difficulty of attracting the sons of tribal leaders became evident from the start. Having filled only half the projected quota at the time of inauguration, the administration agreed to admit

Kurdish tribal students whose fathers were commanders in the army and were clamouring to get in. Already in the first year, the mission of the school was diluted. In 1902, Sultan Abdülhamid decided that twenty Albanian students should be recruited to the school. The student composition was further complicated in the following year when seven Javanese were admitted. Overall, the recruitment process was cumbersome and inconsistent; many applicants were rejected. In addition, several students failed the rigorous programme and were expelled or left on their own accord. The graduates who were assigned to military and administrative posts frequently demanded promotions and transfers. Nevertheless, the school continued to attract tribal students until it was closed in 1907.

The preparation and evolution of the curriculum and some of the prominent educators of the school are presented in Chapter 3. At the time of foundation, the Hamidian regime had already added a strong Islamic flavour to the curriculum of state schools. As mentioned, one of the proponents of the new religious emphasis on education was Hacı Recai Efendi, who was appointed as the first director of the school. The administration realized that the first mission of the school would be to teach the students Ottoman Turkish, starting with the Arabic alphabet. The next task was learning to read and recite the Quran. In the following years religious training was complemented with Turkish grammar, vocabulary, reading and writing skills as well as mathematics, geography and French. The five-year curriculum included an explicit instruction that loyalty to the exalted office of the caliphate should be properly cultivated by the educators. There is no doubt that the students received a rigorous education and the experience transformed them from the sons of nomadic tribesmen into an elite corps of Ottomans. However, the specific roles the graduates played in the Ottoman and the post-Ottoman contexts are almost unknown. One of the best methods to judge the effectiveness of the school would be to study the careers of the graduates.

Chapter 4 is dedicated to several colourful graduates from Greater Syria, the region that sent the highest number of students to the school. Ramadan Shallash from Deir ez-Zor, a town on the Euphrates river, was a rebellious student, who continued his education at the military academy and served in the Ottoman army for many years. He has been described in Syria both as a national hero as well as a collaborator with the French. The second part of Chapter 4 is dedicated to Jabal Druze in Hawran. The most distinguished student among the Druze contingent was Fahd al-Atrash, whose family was recognized by the Ottoman government as the leaders of their region. Fahd's children, Asmahan and Farid al-Atrash became well-known artists in the Arab world. The final group of students presented in this chapter are from Akkar in northern Lebanon. The Merhebi's were the local strongmen and managed to send nine of their sons to the school, probably the highest incidence in one family.

A study on the Libyan graduates is presented in Chapter 5. Omar Mansour, who graduated in 1897 and continued his studies at the civil service academy, left his son a hand-written and unpublished diary dated 1919, which covers his years at the school and his early career. Omar Mansour had an illustrious life both as a member of the Ottoman Parliament as well as during the foundation of Libya in 1949, where he served as prime minister. Another prominent Libyan graduate is Sadullah Kologlu, who entered the school with Omar Mansour and graduated from the civil service academy. After a long career in Anatolia, Sadullah became a governor of the Turkish Republic, the highest provincial post. Later he returned to Libya and was supported by King Idris, who appointed him as minister and briefly prime minister. The life stories of twenty other Libyan graduates of the School for Tribes are briefly examined in the last part of the chapter.

The impressive career of Abdulmuhsin Saadun from Iraq is presented in Chapter 6. The Saadun family were leaders of the powerful Muntafiq confederation of the Basra region, who originated from Mecca and were distinguished as descendants of the Prophet. The brothers Abdulmuhsin and Abdulkarim Saadun graduated from the School for Tribes and then completed their studies at the military academy. Abdulmuhsin Saadun served in the Ottoman Army and Parliament, and upon his return to Iraq became prime minister four times between 1923 and 1929. He committed suicide during his fourth term and the imprint of his education at the school can be seen in the farewell note he left behind for his son, which was written in Ottoman Turkish.

In light of the research carried out on the Aşiret Mektebi and the careers of its graduates, it is clear that the school produced unique leaders who found a niche for themselves in the different political milieus of the Middle East.

1

The school for tribes: A chronology

In 1873, Münif Paşa, posted as ambassador to Tehran, sent a comprehensive treatise on government to his grand vizier.¹ Münif Paşa had been a leading proponent of the *Tanzimat* reforms, and in 1862, he began to publish the first popular science journal of the Ottoman Empire in Istanbul.² He wrote many articles in this journal about modernizing education. Münif Paşa was to serve as Sultan Abdülhamid's minister of education for three separate terms for a total of close to nine years ending in 1888. The treatise he penned in Tehran provided a roadmap for action in most areas of government, which foreshadowed many policies later adopted by Sultan Abdülhamid.³

Significantly, a key reform recommended by Münif Paşa was none other than the establishment of schools for the Arab tribes in an effort to enhance their dubious loyalty to the state. He further suggested that the sons of tribal chiefs should be brought to the capital so that the experience in the metropolitan setting would complement their formal education. Afterwards, they were to be assigned to their homelands to serve their respective communities as well as the empire. Most probably, this was the first time the concept of a school for the tribes was officially articulated. Thus, the credit for conceiving this project must go to Münif Paşa.

In 1886, during his term as minister of education, Münif Paşa recruited forty-eight sons of tribal chiefs from the provinces of the Hijaz, Yemen and Tripoli (Libya) to attend the military academy of Istanbul. Upon their arrival, Sultan Abdülhamid received the new students in person in the palace and expressed his conviction in their mission. Three and a half years later, the completion of their training was again marked by an audience with the sultan. Two of them (from Mecca) were given posts in Istanbul, while the others were sent to serve as lieutenants in the Ottoman army in their respective localities.

In his address, Sultan Abdülhamid impressed upon them the importance of setting an example in their provinces, so that other young men of their regions would also aspire to receive the education provided by the state and become loyal subjects. Ahmed Midhat, the editor of the major newspaper *Tercüman-ı Hakikat*, commented on this project as follows:

> The best education is received in military service. Although less than fifty years have passed since the *Tanzimat*; what has transformed the Ottoman population is the modern army. Whichever province has sent young men to be trained and serve in the military has progressed the most. Hijaz, Yemen and Tripoli have just started to be included in this mission, and these soldiers will now carry the torch of civilization to all their villages.[4]

It appears that recruiting sons of the tribal chiefs to the military academy was given up in favour of a more exclusive school for younger students. In 1891, the last cohort of fifty-five Arab tribal students graduated and were sent to their military posts. From then on, such students from the outer realms of the empire were to join the School for Tribes, which was established instead.[5]

In the spring of 1892, Sultan Abdülhamid asked one of his aides to prepare a treatise on the establishment of a school for tribes. Most historians credit this document to Osman Nuri Paşa (known as Hacı/Topal), who graduated from the military academy and after a successful military career, was appointed governor of Hijaz in 1882. In 1885, he wrote a detailed memorandum on the status of Arabia, in which he clearly underlined the distinction between nomadism (*bedeviyet*) and civilization (*medeniyet*).[6] In 1886, he became governor of Aleppo, then Yemen and returned to Mecca for his second term as Governor of Hijaz in 1890. Osman Nuri is known to have paid special attention to tribal affairs, and he had therefore commissioned the drawing of detailed maps of the locations of the tribes of Arabia and attempted consistently to lure the sons of tribal leaders to the Rüşdiye school in Mecca.[7] One of his notable projects was the building of telegraph lines from Damascus to Hijaz and on to Yemen.

Osman Nuri Paşa's intimate involvement in Arab tribal affairs, as well as his name, seems to have resulted in some confusion about the identity of the author of the treatise on the School for Tribes commissioned by the sultan. What needs to be highlighted in connection with the available documents related to the treatise and to the treatise itself is that the author is referred to by rank as Ferik (lieutenant general) Mehmed Nuri Paşa or just Nuri Paşa. It seems reasonable to assume that whoever wrote the treatise was in Istanbul in 1892. Osman Nuri Paşa, however, was probably in Hijaz in that year. More importantly, Osman Nuri was already promoted to the rank of Müşir (field marshal) in 1884, while all the documents clearly mention the author's rank as Ferik. Although it has not been possible to find much information about Mehmed Nuri, it is reasonable to deduce that he must have been one of the many aides of Sultan Abdülhamid at the time and prepared this document according to the instructions given to him, possibly by the sultan himself.

Whoever the author ultimately may have been, this comprehensive treatise was endorsed by the sultan. The text confirms this with the expression: 'Based on the wise directives and instructions of the Caliph.'[8] The document was officially presented to the grand vizier on 22 June 1892, and it incorporated a detailed blueprint for the School for Tribes. The aim was to eradicate the calamity of ignorance[9] of the Arab tribes and to serve as a model for future schools to be founded in the provinces. The school would train tutors who would later serve in these rural institutions. Physically and intellectually gifted sons of prominent families between ages twelve and sixteen would be recruited and brought to the capital escorted by government officers. High-calibre educators with knowledge of Arabic would be assigned to the school.

The treatise presented a tentative curriculum which included Ottoman Turkish, religious training, mathematics, history, geography, biology, chemistry and some training in agriculture and animal husbandry. It is worth noting that the author suggested including a history of Andalusia, where the Muslims were persecuted, thereby emphasizing the tolerance and justice of the Ottomans to their minorities. In addition, he proposed describing the state of Egypt before and after the Ottoman conquest to underline the grandeur of the Ottomans within the realm of Islam.[10]

The school was not replicated in the provinces and the eventual curriculum was not prepared to train tutors, but rather to develop young men for careers in the military or bureaucracy. However, the vocabulary and philosophy articulated in this treatise were adopted for the coming fifteen years of the school's existence.

Upon receiving the treatise, Sultan Abdülhamid proceeded promptly. Only one week later, on 29 June 1892, the Sublime Porte sent a memorandum to the Ministry of Interior, which included the sultan's decree to open a new school in Istanbul dedicated to train and educate the sons of Arab tribal leaders.[11] An announcement about the inauguration of the School for Tribes was also attached, and the ministry was instructed to organize the publication of this announcement in the newspapers of the following day.[12] In the *Tercüman-ı Hakikat* newspaper dated 30 June 1892, the first news item on page one was about the new school.[13] The text stated that the sultan had decided to establish a school for the Arab tribes which would be located in the royal apartments in Akaretler, which were quite close to the palace.[14] The minister of interior sent telegrams to the relevant provinces on 3 July 1892, to inform them about the establishment of the school.[15]

On 7 July 1892, the sultan decided that the school should be inaugurated on the auspicious date of the Prophet's birthday, 4 October 1892.[16] In other words, Sultan Abdülhamid decided to open this new school in the short time span of three months. The Ministry of Education was required to quickly prepare a charter for the school and to refurbish the apartments in Akaretler; the ministry was also tasked with preparing a report on its progress as soon as possible.

On July 8, two consecutive articles appeared in the *Tercüman-ı Hakikat*. The first one was titled Establishment of a School and was a slightly revised version of the original announcement. Below is a summarized version of this article:

> The sultan, who always acts with beneficence, has ordered the establishment of a new school called 'Aşiret Mektebi' to train and educate the sons of Arab tribal leaders living within his well-protected domains. A couple of royal buildings in Akaretler, Beşiktaş will be refurbished for this school, which will be under the protection of the Caliph to whom we are eternally indebted.

There was no longer any mention of future schools being established in the provinces, as had been considered earlier. On the next page of the same issue, there was a second article which informed the public that the school would be inaugurated on the Prophet's birthday. There was no turning back.

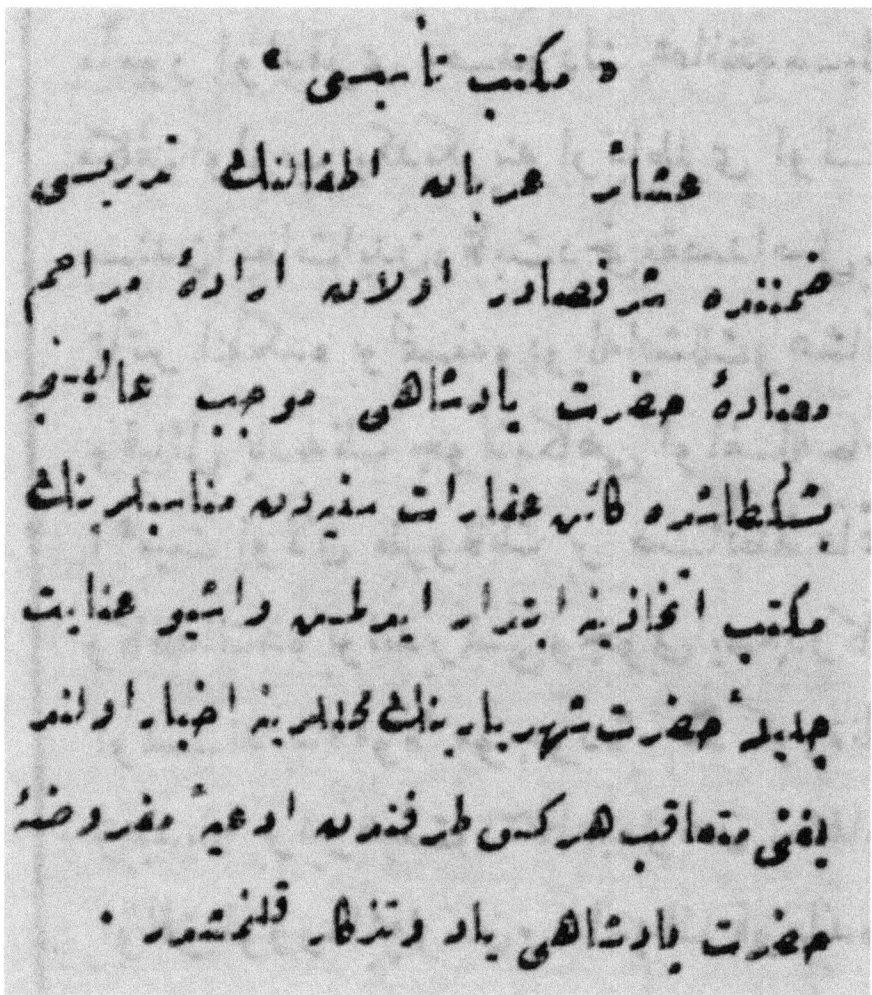

Figure 1.1 Announcement of the establishment of the school, *Tercüman-ı Hakikat*, 8 July 1892, Mekteb Tesisi.

On 11 July 1892, Zühdü Paşa, minister of education, sent a draft of the school charter and the curriculum for the first two years to the grand vizier, Kamil Paşa, confirming also that the necessary furniture and equipment were being procured to open the school on the appointed date. Kamil Paşa convened a meeting of the council of ministers, which endorsed the charter and the curriculum on 22 July 1892 and sent it to the palace for final approval.

Figure 1.2 *Tercüman-ı Hakikat*, 8 July 1892, Tebligat-ı Resmiye, Official notice of the inauguration date of the school as October 4, column 4.

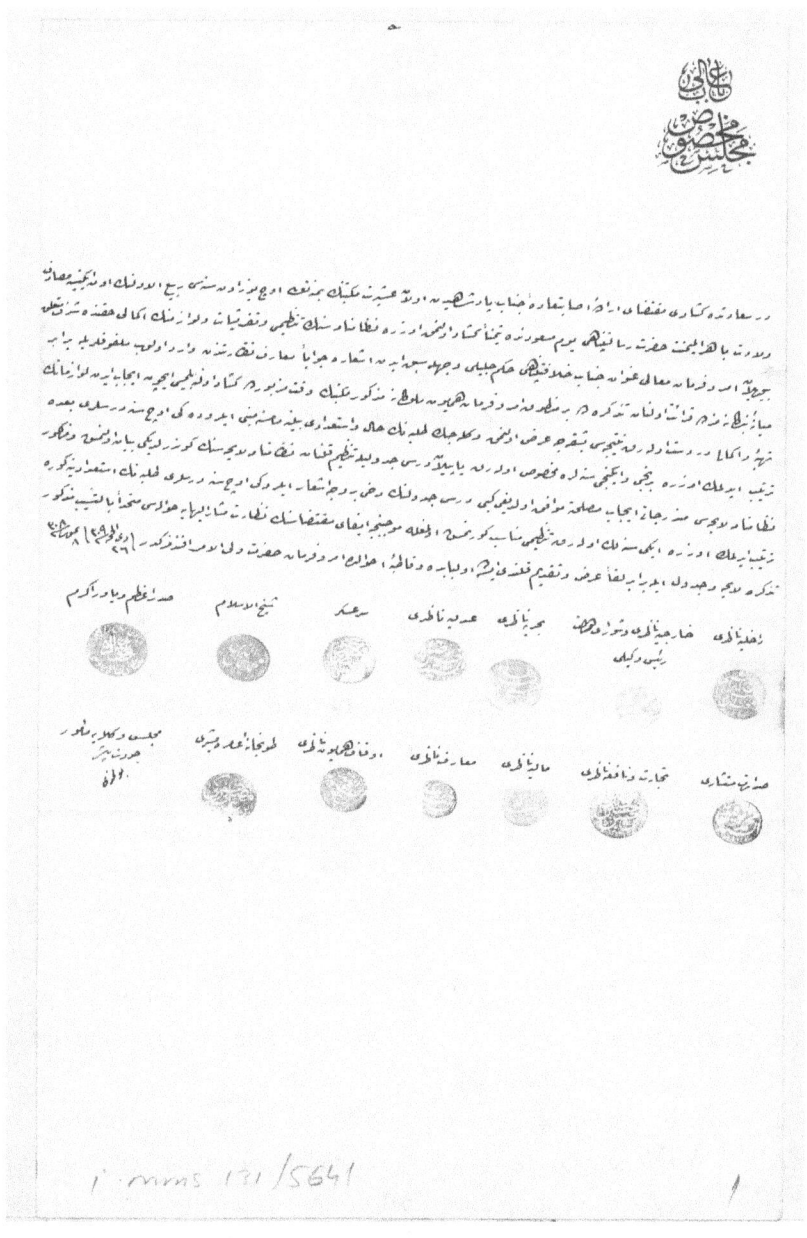

Figure 1.3 Cover letter for charter and curriculum signed by the council of ministers: Grand Vizier, Sheikh al-Islam, Ministers of Interior, Foreign Affairs, Navy, Justice, Army, Commerce and Public Works, Finance, Education, Charitable Foundations, Commander of the Tophane-i Amire (Artillery), Ottoman Archives, I.MMS 131-5641-1, 22 July 1892. The sultan's decree No. 1013, was issued on 25 July 1892, Ottoman Archives I.MMS-131-564-5-1.

The charter of the school comprised twelve articles which are summarized below:[17]

1. A boarding school named the School for Tribes has been established in Istanbul to educate and train the sons of Arab tribes.
2. The sultan has generously accepted to be the patron of the school.
3. The school will have five classes. In the first year fifty students will be admitted, and in the following years forty, to reach a total of 210 in the fifth year.
4. The students will be selected from among the physically and intellectually gifted sons of respected and venerable Arab tribal families who are between twelve and sixteen years of age.
5. The government will cover board and clothing and all other expenses as well as pay a monthly stipend of 30 kuruş for each student.
6. Three months prior to commencement of every academic year, the Ministry of Education will notify the provinces of Syria, Aleppo, Baghdad, Basra, Mosul, Tripoli, Yemen, Hijaz and Diyarbakir as well as the autonomous regions of Benghazi, Deir ez-Zor and Jerusalem to select and send students with appropriate qualifications.
7. The school will have a headmaster and an assistant as well as the necessary number of teachers and staff. The curriculum and administration will be governed by the regulation pertaining to boarding high schools.
8. The Ministry of Education will be responsible for appointing and dismissing teachers and staff as well as for defining and revising the curriculum as needed and selecting the textbooks.
9. The primary goal of establishing the school is to allow the tribes to benefit from the fruits of knowledge and civilization and increase their loyalty and affection towards the caliphate and the sultanate. The headmaster and the teachers will instruct the students on the religious duties incumbent upon them by the *Sharia* and civil laws.
10. Upon graduation the students will return to their tribes and will work as teachers in schools to be established in their environs or will be assigned other appropriate duties.

11. The students will be dressed in the school uniform.
12. The Ministry of Education will execute this charter.

On the day the charter was issued, 25 July 1892, the sultan's chief scribe, Süreyya Paşa, sent a note to the grand vizier suggesting that Esma Sultan's palace in Kabataş be assigned to the school. This palace was deemed inconvenient for the royal family due to its location on a slight hill. The sultan proposed that the ministry of finance procure a seaside mansion for Esma Sultan.[18]

On 15 August 1892, *Tercüman-ı Hakikat* published an article praising the sultan for establishing such a school, emphasizing his interest in the provinces and the potential of the future graduates to serve as well-trained commanders of the Hamidiye regiments:

> It is now well known that our venerable sultan will be inaugurating a special school for tribes on the birthdate of our Holy Prophet. We are delighted to report that several students from the provinces are already on their way to the capital to attend the school. Most of the nomadic tribes are far away from the enlightened urban areas. In this school, they will be introduced to the benefits of an education and will serve as examples to their peers. When these educated youngsters are placed in the very successful Hamidiye regiments, the value of this school will be even better understood.[19]

The grand vizier sent telegrams to the governors of the concerned provinces instructing them to send appropriate officers to prominent tribal chiefs to recruit students for the School for Tribes. The students were to travel in the company of a civil servant and arrive in Istanbul as soon as possible.[20] The minister of interior reported to the palace that 'the tribal leaders appreciate the value of this new school and are sending their children with great enthusiasm and gratitude.'[21]

The school was opened on October 4 as planned. The sultan asked the fresh arrivals to attend the celebration festivities for the Prophet's birthday in their native attire. The photographs of the students in their indigenous outfits were included in the famous albums of Sultan Abdülhamid, which were later sent to Western capitals.

Classes began the next day with the students dressed in their specially designed uniforms. A comparison of the photograph of the first group of

Figure 1.4 Some photos of the students in their native attire.

Figure 1.5 Photos of students in their new uniforms.

students in Akaretler with their original appearance conveys the significance of this social experiment.

Omar Mansour, described the uniform in detail in his memoirs:

The school's uniform was a formal suit, jacket and pants made of green material. The jacket had a red collar made of silk decorated with the school's logo. The logo consisted of two crescents facing each other with the name of the school Aşiret Mektebi inscribed in the middle. The buttons were golden colored with a crescent in the center.[22]

Two different autobiographies refer to these special uniforms, which became easily identified by the local population. Hagop Mıntzuri, a well-known Armenian writer, described the students as follows:

> Every Friday the Sinan Paşa Cami in Beşiktaş became packed.... Among the crowd you could discern the students of the School for Tribes with their olive-green uniforms embroidered with the insignia of the school. Their school was across the pier in Kabataş. They were rather dark-skinned sons of tribal chiefs and sheikhs. They were brought to Istanbul to learn Turkish.[23]

Ismayıl Hakkı Baltacıoğlu, a Kemalist educator who went to another nearby high school, the Şemsülmekatip in Kabataş, wrote that:

> There was a rather strange school called the School for Tribes close to us. We would recognize the students of this school from their special uniforms and their dark features. They were known to be rebellious and rumored to attack their supervisors from time to time.[24]

In the following months, the first class of the school reached a total of sixty-two, exceeding the original quota by twelve students. An adjacent building was refurbished to serve as an infirmary. Yusuf Zeki Bey, a medical doctor and colonel from the palace, was ordered to go to the school every morning and evening to attend to the medical needs of the students. Emin Bey, the chief surgeon of the palace, was charged with vaccinating the students.[25] On 17 October 1892, the students were paid their first stipends of 30 kurus each. Below is a vivid description of this affair:

> The students were lined up in an orderly fashion, and the director Ali Nazima Bey delivered a speech and then presented them the pouches which arrived from the Ministry of Education. The students were delighted and as a gesture of gratitude placed their pouches on their heads and then jointly prayed for the well-being and longevity of the sultan: 'Padişahım Çok Yaşa'.[26]

On 3 January 1893, Zühdü Paşa, minister of education, prepared a detailed internal directive,[27] defining the rights and responsibilities of the school's management and the rules of instruction. The document comprised seventy-four articles in eight sections, as summarized below:[28]

1. The introduction lists the basic characteristics of the school as defined in the charter.
2. The second section describes the duties of the director in minute detail. He is to be on campus seven days a week and alternate with his assistant during the night. The director is expected to enter classes randomly to check on the performance of the tutors and students. Every evening after classes, he must gather the students for communal prayers and communicate important developments of that day. He is expected to inspect and sign the report book every day. Every Thursday, he must summarize the weekly events and mete out required demerits to the students. The director has sole authority to allow students to leave the campus. He has also been charged with maintaining the cleanliness and sanitation of the school.[29]
3. The third section lays out the duties of the assistant director, accountant and scribe. In addition to his expected responsibilities, the scribe was charged to read and correct all letters to be sent by the students to their parents and present them to the director.
4. The fourth section, describing the tutors' responsibilities, is the longest. Students are to be treated equitably, and tutors must conduct their classes in Turkish. In case students cannot understand a term, an Arabic translation should be provided, but the Turkish version should then be repeated. The tutors are expected to spend four to five nights at the school.
5. The superintendents are to supervise the students during the breaks and study hours as well as in their dormitories. They will escort the students to the Friday prayers and may organize excursions after leaving the mosque. During these outings, the students are not to interact with anyone outside the school. The superintendents should preferably speak Arabic.
6. The sixth section addresses other personnel, including medical staff, warehouse officer, cooks and servants. The cook is charged with serving the students delicious meals and keeping the kitchen clean.

7. This section deals with awards and punishments. The names of students who earn an award were to be written in a decorative script and posted in the classroom. The punishments were ranked into six categories from a demerit to detention.
8. The final section concerns the examination system. In addition to daily and weekly tests, there were to be three examinations during the school year and one final general exam at the end.

During the month of Ramadan, on 3 April 1893, the results of the general examinations for the first year were sent to the palace. While a detailed analysis of these will be presented in Chapter 3, it is worth noting the reply sent by the sultan five days later. The school had failed some students and proposed that they do not return the following school year. The sultan responded that this may disillusion their families and their regions and demanded that the school 'strive to build students who are successful in all aspects, and if they are unable to do so, the authorities of the school will be responsible for the results'.[30] Nevertheless, those students did not return to the school, and the educators maintained their high standards in the coming years. The only example in the archival documents where the official stamp of the School for Tribes is clearly displayed also dates from this period.

On 2 June 1893, the students, tutors and staff were invited to a royal picnic on the pastures next to the Golden Horn.[31] After a sumptuous feast, speeches were delivered before the students returned to the school. Below are highlights of two of the speeches delivered on that day:

> Ali Nazima, Director: Our sultan has invited you to the Abode of Felicity for you to benefit from the fruits of knowledge and civilization. In return, you must all work very hard and be loyal and faithful to our Sovereign. You should forever act as veterans and lieutenants of our sultan. As long as you follow his footsteps, his bounty will always be with you. Let us repeat our oath of loyalty: *Padişahım Çok Yaşa!*
>
> Speech of a student: We were children wondering aimlessly and in ignorance in the outer realms of your sultanate, when we were allowed to attend this prestigious institution to discover the tenets of our religion and civilization. In the desert, we knew of no other place but our constantly travelling tents. During our trip to the capital, we were amazed by the many large towns

Figure 1.6 Official Stamp of The School for Tribes – Aşiret Mektebi, Ottoman Archives Y-MTV-79-182-2-1, 8 July 1893.

and cities that are part of our empire. Upon arrival to the Abode of Felicity, we all pledged our infinite allegiance to your Lofty Highness, the Caliph of Islam. All our needs are taken care of, and now we have had the additional honor to visit this beautiful pasture of Kağıthane to enjoy the royal banquet. We could not sufficiently express our gratitude, even if we could speak one thousand languages.

Several photographs of that day were taken by the royal photographer, Abdullah Freres.

The royal picnic became a tradition of the school; below are excerpts from the following year's speeches:[32]

Ali Nazima, Director: Science and knowledge are what make a man. Our Caliph has consistently struggled to save his subjects from the darkness of ignorance. We should always express our gratitude for living in the times of such a visionary ruler. As you are aware, in other countries people need to pay to educate their children, whereas in our country our sultan has ensured

Figure 1.7 Royal picnic organized for The School for Tribes, 4 June 1893, Istanbul University rare documents collection.

that as many youngsters as possible can receive a good education provided freely by the state. You have been included among these fortunate souls, and the first thing to do is to thank our sultan for his generosity. In order to be worthy of his beneficence, each of you should work hard and always repeat: *Padişahım Çok Yaşa!*

Speech by Sayyid Abdullah Efendi, student from Yemen: Dear friends. Last year we were also honored to be invited to such a royal picnic on these beautiful grounds. Our grand Caliph is even more caring than our mothers and fathers. He established a school dedicated to his tribal subjects in his grand capital. He has invested significant amounts to provide us with a superior education. We must repay our debts by working with all our might. Our parents and families who were not able to reach these fruits of civilization appreciate our good fortune. Our knowledge and experience fascinated our relatives and friends when we went home for our holidays last summer after passing our exams. Even on the route to our homes, the people we met on the way were impressed with our achievements and good luck. Our brothers are all hoping to attend our school.

Another speech was delivered by Azat Efendi, and the final speaker was Ahmad Efendi, who gave his speech in Arabic.

Meanwhile, it was clear that the Akaretler apartments could not accommodate the second group of incoming students. As per the previous suggestion by the sultan, on 12 June 1893, the grand vizier wrote to the minister of finance informing him that an agreement had been reached to purchase the seaside mansion of Khayreddin Paşa in Kuruçeşme for Esma Sultan.[33] This allowed the spacious Esma Sultan Palace and its gardens in Kabataş to be allocated to the School for Tribes.[34] On October 11, the grand vizier informed the minister of education that the palace was at his disposal. The minister promptly visited the premises and reported on 13 October 1893 the following:

> I visited the new premises yesterday morning. There is need for some refurbishment; however, I initiated the movement of the students' beds and furniture as well as the desks, the belongings of the teachers and staff as well as the kitchen equipment to the new location. The stoves and the wood for the stoves will be transported tomorrow. We will be presenting plans for the construction of new classrooms, dining hall and kitchen for your approval in the coming days.[35]

It is indicative of the significance the sultan attached to the school that the minister and the grand vizier were personally involved down to these minute details.

On 8 February 1895, an important change occurred in the position of the School for Tribes within the Ottoman administrative hierarchy. Tahsin Paşa, chief scribe, announced the decree of the sultan that the management of the school was transferred from the education ministry to the ministry of military schools.[36] The ministry of education would still supervise the academic activities of the school; however, all other matters would be handled by Zeki Paşa, general and minister of military schools. Another document from one day earlier informs us that there was a fight among the students and that a few policemen were permanently stationed on the premises.[37] The document states that one of the culprits was Ramadan from Deir ez-Zor, who will be discussed in Chapter 4. This was the culmination of the disciplinary problems encountered in the school, which led the sultan to intervene and bring in Zeki Paşa, one of his most trusted generals, to maintain order and security.

As the population of the school increased, so did the expenses. The apportioning of the travel expenses of the students frequently became a source of contention between the provincial authorities. One example was the extended conflict between Aleppo, Deir ez-Zor and Baghdad. On 12 July 1896, the head of the education commission of Deir ez-Zor sent a telegram to the minister of education stating that they had incurred travel expenses of 2.104,5 kuruş for the students of the school and notified Aleppo about the payment on 8 September 1895. Despite repeated requests, they were not reimbursed, and in the meantime had incurred an additional expense of 1.592 kuruş; hence, their budget was suffering significantly. They pleaded urgently for the ministry to instruct Aleppo to reimburse them.[38] The ministry instructed Aleppo to clear these accounts immediately.[39]

After the school had been operational for some years, the administration decided that it would be beneficial to further train the students for military or administrative careers. A special one-year programme[40] was established in the military and civil service academies, and on 1 October 1896, the palace instructed the school to transfer twenty-six graduating students and twenty-five students who had passed to the fifth class to these institutions. The group was to be supposed to be divided into two equal halves; however, a majority of the students chose to pursue a military career.[41] A document dated October 1896 shows that eventually forty-six students were enrolled in these two schools, and they continued to be paid the monthly stipend of 30 kuruş.[42] In August 1897, thirty-three of the students at the Harbiye completed their military training, and twelve graduated from the Mülkiye programme – one student must have left for some reason.

In November 1896, the Ministry of Education requested the expropriation of two buildings adjacent to the school to accommodate its expansion. The Ministry of Interior prepared a memorandum with the details of the transaction, and the municipality was instructed to prepare the necessary paperwork.[43] In January 1897, the resolution for the expropriation was signed by twenty officials of the Interior Ministry.[44] This was forwarded to the grand vizier, who passed it on to the palace. Tahsin Paşa, chief scribe, delivered the approval of the sultan in writing on 16 January 1897. The expropriation was finally completed in March.

On 16 September 1897, the school director Abdulmuhsin Bey convened the students before they left for their holidays. Ahmed Cemil, who had graduated one year earlier and had just completed his training at the Mülkiye, was invited to address the students. The message of his speech was progressive and thoughtful and clearly reflects some of what had been instilled in him at the school:

> My dear brothers, sons of noble tribes,
>
> You know by now that the road to wealth and happiness of a nation depends solely on education. It is through science and technology that all these works of beauty and excellence are created. In the past every nation sought glory and power through the annihilation of others, and many wars were waged in this fashion. Today the rules of economics show us that the wealth and prosperity of nations are interdependent and that wars are destructive for both sides as well as for all participants.
>
> Today the whole world has become a playground for humanity where comradeship is the leading virtue. Those that came before us could not have imagined these developments, and similarly, we cannot envision how science and knowledge will transform the world in the future.
>
> We should remember that the hopes and watchful eyes of thousands of loyal tribesmen are now turned upon us. This is the first year that some of us received our diplomas, which indicates that we have started to climb the ladder to civilization. You are now going to your homes and should explain to your families and peers about this grand project towards prosperity. You should encourage them to be educated and increase their knowledge. You should remind them that life is more than just eating and drinking. May God keep our blessed Caliph in good health and let us pray for him together. *Padişahım Çok Yaşa!*[45]

On 12 December 1897, Ahmed Midhat, the editor of the *Tercüman-ı Hakikat* published an article about his interview with Aage Meyer Benedictsen, a Danish scholar who had visited the School for Tribes.[46] The scholar had already travelled in and around the Ottoman Empire and encountered many nomads, and stated that 'millions of Muslims are passing their lives in a state of ignorance.'[47] Benedictsen stated that he was trying to understand 'why we (Westerners) believed in the right to rule other peoples'.[48] He believed that this school would help overcome the conflicts between the tribes and the settled population. Mr. Benedictsen found the premises of the school in excellent condition and 'the students proved to me their advanced skills in mathematics and other areas.' According to Mr. Benedictsen: 'There is no question that modern civilization will enter and transform the lives of these tribes when the students return to their homes.' The editor Ahmad Midhat, pleased with the encouraging words of the foreigner, concluded his article in the following fashion:

> Naturally the success of such an endeavor would require a rather long time, but given the huge benefit, it is worth the investment. None of the countries who harbor such nomadic populations have attempted a similar project. The USA has cruelly eliminated most of the Indians on their lands, and the rest were forced into a Southwestern corner to continue their ignorant existence. If we observe the progress achieved by the urban and sedentary population in the last 20 years, we can deduce that the nomads can be transformed in a much shorter time to become useful to the cause of Islam and the Ottoman State.

On 7 June 1898, *Tercüman-ı Hakikat* published a striking photograph of a group of fresh graduates who had arrived in Erzurum on their way to their new assignments. The picture shows the proud faces of twelve graduates from the military academy and one from the civil service academy, with all their names and their tribal affiliations indicated in the caption.

By the end of 1899, the number of students had increased to 192. Given that the original enrolment was expected to be 210, at this time the school had more or less reached its target in numbers. However, the school reported that due to this increase and to unexpected repairs, the budget of 279.668 kuruş was exceeded by 120.291 kuruş, a major addition; 23.793 kuruş would be

Figure 1.8 Fresh graduates in Erzurum, *Tercüman-ı Hakikat*, 7 June 1898.

covered by the balance remaining from the previous year, and the remainder of 97.498 kuruş would be transferred from the provincial budgets to the Ministry of Education. The expenses of the school were slowly becoming a burden.

The number of archival documents and newspaper articles related to the school diminishes with the turn of the century. Most of the available correspondence concerns the requests for promotion by the graduates as they pursued their careers. On 22 October 1905, we find the last reference to a graduation ceremony of the school in the *Tercüman-ı Hakikat* newspaper. Zeki Paşa apparently distributed the diplomas and awards himself, and then the congregation prayed for the well-being of the sultan.[49] On 13 December 1905, the question regarding the career paths of civil service academy graduates was once again on the table. An array of officials including the grand vizier, the sheikh-ul-Islam, the minister of military schools and seven other ministers presented a memorandum to the palace. Apparently, the graduates were not pleased with the salaries paid to them during their initial assignments and wanted to be promoted to *kaymakam* (district administrator) positions more quickly.

> In the provinces of Yemen, Tripoli, Benghazi and Mosul, it has been difficult to identify suitable candidates to serve as kaymakam, and in many locations local staff has been acting as care-taker administrators. This has not always resulted in good management and complaints were received due to personal differences. It has therefore been resolved that the graduates of the School for Tribes who have spent some time in the provincial administration and have proven to be adept can be assigned as kaymakam to the districts where there are no other suitable candidates.[50]

The matter seems to have taken a more radical turn as can be seen from the letter sent by Hacı Recai Efendi (the first director of the school, who was still in charge of the civil service academy), to the minister of military schools, Zeki Paşa, on 25 January 1906. Recai Efendi proposed to abolish the civil service training of the tribal students altogether:

> As your Excellency is aware, a special class for the School for Tribes was organized in the civil service academy and every year fifteen to twenty students were enrolled as boarding students. However, the number of students gradually fell to around seven or eight and this year we were informed that only one student would arrive. As you also know, our institution has been transformed into a day school and therefore the maintenance of these few boarding students has become almost impossible. We request your approval to direct the tribal students from now on to Darulhayr-ı Ali or Darüşşafaka for their training.[51]

Despite the negative feedback of Recai Efendi, the documents from 1907 indicate that the school continued to function normally. In May 1907, the Ministry of Military Schools wrote a note stating that while all the other schools in Istanbul were using municipal gas supply, the school was lit with petrol, which cost much more. It was proposed to convert the lighting of the school to gas, which would also reduce the danger of fires.[52] Throughout that summer petitions arrived from various provinces to enrol students. On July 26 and 27, *Tercüman-ı Hakikat* advertised a vacant position for superintendent at the school. On 9 August 1907, the School for Tribes was included in a list of schools in which communal prayers would be held. However, there was a special piece of news in *Tercüman-ı Hakikat* on August 30. The Ministry of Education had demanded a detailed breakdown of the costs of the school pertaining to the previous two years.[53] This was the only indication that the future of the school was under discussion.

In November 1907 two articles about the closure of the school appeared in European newspapers, which were translated and reported by the Ottoman bureaucrats. The first article stated that there had been an uprising in the school, because the students were unhappy with the ranks and salaries assigned to them upon graduation and concluded thus:

> The school has been closed due to lack of new applicants. Here is another Pan-Islamic creation of the regime operating since 1892, which has led to expenditure of immense sums and which is disappearing because it was an erroneous undertaking from the beginning.[54]

The second article stated that the school was closed because the graduates attending the military academy rebelled and demanded to be given the rank of captain upon graduation. They were given a gift of 10 lira each and sent to their homelands.[55]

Scholars have advanced several theories about why the School for Tribes was shut down. Eugene Rogan's assessment is as follows:

> It could be argued that the school was closed because the authorities found that its results no longer justified the expense. Alternately, the need for the tribal school may have been obviated by the extension of the state educational system in the Hamidian period.[56]

Nevertheless, applications to the school continued. On 21 December 1907, the Jerusalem Administration sent a letter to the Ministry of Interior to enrol the son of a sheikh, which was forwarded to the Ministry of Education on 13 January 1908.[57] Finally, on 17 February 1908, the palace issued a decree officially closing the school and converting its premises into a regular high school.[58] The need of the Muslim residents of the European side of Istanbul for a state high school close to their homes was emphasized in the following letter from the grand vizier:

At present there are three high schools in the old city with over seven hundred students. It is rather difficult for students who live in Beşiktaş and the Bosphorus region to attend these schools, which are quite far from their homes. The students of the School for Tribes have been sent to their provinces, and the sultan has decreed that the budget of 632,545 kuruş reserved for the school in Kabataş should be spent to convert the premises into a regular high school.[59]

An unsigned document from 19 February 1908 confirmed that the school was abolished and that the funds would be utilized to turn it into a high school.[60] The school continues its existence today as Kabataş Erkek Lisesi. The website of the school announces that their institution was inaugurated on 18 May 1908 in the Esma Sultan palace, in place of the School for Tribes.[61]

The chronology of the school displays the complex state apparatus of the Ottoman Empire at the end of the nineteenth century. The tribes of the empire were presented with an unusual opportunity for their sons, who would be educated at the state's expense in the capital. The administration reviewed the results of the first years and devised a complementary training programme in the military and administrative apparatus to create a new breed of officers and bureaucrats. The press was utilized to disseminate information on the foundation, recruitment and placement processes of the school and entice tribal leaders to send their sons to the School for Tribes. In short, in contrast to the general assumption made in Western historiography, the Ottoman Empire at the turn of the twentieth century exercised significant initiatives for its subjects within its vast and 'Well Protected Domains'.

2

Recruitment and placement

As a first step to educate and train the sons of tribal leaders, a special school called the Aşiret Mektebi will be inaugurated in the Abode of Felicity on the holy birthday of the Prophet, namely 4 October 1892. The following quotas have been determined for the first fifty students of the school: Syria-Aleppo-Baghdad-Basra-Mosul-Tripoli-Diyarbakır provinces and Benghazi-Jerusalem-Deir ez-Zor districts will send four students each, Yemen and Hijaz provinces will send five students each. The students should be selected from the physically and intellectually gifted sons of prominent tribal leaders, who are between 12 and 16 years of age. Transportation will be provided by the government and those who wish will be sent home during the summer holidays. Clothing and upkeep will be provided by the school; additionally, the students will receive a monthly stipend of 30 kuruş. Appropriate officers should be dispatched to the respectable tribal sheikhs reporting this joyous news, and the students should be selected speedily. The students must travel in the company of a civil servant and arrive in Istanbul on time. You are expected to report on your progress on the matter.[1]

The rather lengthy text quoted above was delivered to the relevant provinces by a telegram signed by the grand vizier himself in the first days of July 1892, indicating the high level of attention given to this new school. The minister of interior was charged with closely following up on the recruitment process. As this passage shows, the provinces of Hijaz and Yemen were given the highest quotas, reflecting Sultan Abdülhamid's general policy of ranking his territories. Unfortunately, Hijaz was to consistently disappoint the sultan, starting from the first year.

Encouraging news arrived in a telegram from Baghdad on 9 August 1892. The governor, Hasan Refik Paşa, informed the palace that he had sent emissaries to each of the four prominent tribes of the region, namely the Shammar, Rabi'a, Zubayr and Dulaim. According to the governor, the sheikhs realized the importance of this missive, 'expressed their deep gratitude and rushed to Baghdad in competition to enrol their children in the school'.[2] Finally, the following four sons of sheikhs were selected: Hamid (Shammar), Suleiman (Rabi'a), Ajeel (Zubayr) and Ali (Dulaim). They arrived with their parents and relatives in Baghdad and were received by the governor. Baghdad's *Zawra'* newspaper reported that:

> Several notables and the chief secretary accompanied the group to the other shore of the river, where a feast was organized by the third governor of Baghdad and speeches were delivered. All participants prayed for the longevity of the beneficent Sultan, the Shadow of God. Finally, the students were dispatched, accompanied by police officer Zeynel Efendi.[3]

Upon their arrival in Istanbul, probably in the first days of September, the school proudly gave them the first identification numbers of 1 through 4. Ali failed at the end of the first year and was dismissed, but more importantly, the other three students from Baghdad also did not return to Istanbul for the second year. For several years thereafter, no students from Baghdad could be recruited, indicating, as in the case of Hijaz, that it was not that simple to lure the sons of 'prestigious' tribal chiefs to the capital.

The second response to the recruitment process came from Yemen. On 3 August 1892, the *Sana'a* newspaper published a copy of the full announcement regarding the School for Tribes and announced proudly that Yemen had the highest quota of five students. Praises were sung for 'Our venerable Caliph and Sultan Abdülhamid II, who never ceases to invest in awe-inspiring feats to elevate the world of Islam to the highest levels of civilization.'[4] Indeed, the five Yemeni students were soon sent to Istanbul. It is noteworthy that the departure and arrival of almost all the students of the first years were promptly reported in the newspapers of the capital and the provinces.

Four students were selected from Jerusalem, and the governor of Jerusalem decided to use this opportunity to ask for a promotion for one of his police officers, Refet Bey, who was charged with accompanying the students to the school. On 29 August 1892, the governor wrote the following:

Four students have been recruited for the School for Tribes founded under the auspices of the sultan from the tribes living in tents around Jerusalem and sent to Istanbul accompanied by Refet Bey, Chief Constable of our police force. Since the beginning of his appointment to Jerusalem, Refet Bey has been acting with great diligence and has been very useful during the Easter season when 15-20,000 people from all over the world arrive in our town. He was able to calm down several disputes among people of different sects and has proven to be reliable and sensible. As a reward, we request that he be promoted to become an officer of the second rank like many of his peers.[5]

However, around this time, there was a slight furore in the Ministry of Interior as they realized that the sultan's original quota of fifty students for the school would not be fulfilled. The minister sent the following note to the grand vizier:

The provinces of Hijaz, Mosul and Diyarbakır will not be sending the thirteen students allocated to them. Therefore, we propose to increase the quotas of Syria and Aleppo from four to six each. We also suggest instructing the provinces of Bitlis, Van, Erzurum and Mamuretulaziz to select and send sons of the Kurdish tribal leaders to fill the remaining quota of nine students.[6]

This recommendation deviated from the founding principles of the school, which clearly stated that it was intended for the sons of Arab tribes. Indeed, the Ministry of Education opposed this proposal, stating that the Arab and Kurdish students would not be compatible. Still, the sultan approved the change, and on 9 September 1892, the grand vizier ordered the minister of interior to increase the quotas of Syria and Aleppo to six each and to recruit nine Kurdish students to fill the quota of fifty.[7]

It appears that the leaders of the important Hamidiye regiments in the Kurdish region had pressured the palace to enrol their sons in the school. Specifically, Eyüp Paşa, head of the Zilan tribe, and the commanders of the fifth and sixth Hamidiye regiments had sent telegrams demanding that two students from each of the fourteen regiments be enrolled in the school. Zühdü Paşa, the minister of education, opposed this proposal stating that the school was founded for the Arab tribes and that it had neither the capacity nor the funding to accommodate so many additional students. He added that the differences in the morals and manners of the Arabs and Kurds[8] would create a degree of instability in the school. The grand vizier proposed that the Hamidiye commanders' sons be sent to the military schools of the empire.[9] However, the sultan's preference for fulfilling the quotas forced the ministers to begin the enrolment process for Kurdish students in the first year.

The Ministry of Interior promptly sent telegrams to the relevant provinces. Three sons of the leaders of the Cibranlı tribe constituted the first group of Kurdish students at the schools. A fourth Kurdish student, Mehmed Hamza from the Mekri tribe of Hakkari was also enrolled and later became a member of the Ottoman Parliament, as will be seen in Chapter 6. The governor of Mamuretelaziz wrote to the ministry on October 2 that although they were given a quota of three, the leaders of the Dersim tribes had sent six students to the provincial centre and pleaded that they all be sent to the school, a request that was accepted. Clearly, the Kurdish chiefs were intent on sending their sons to the School for Tribes.

On September 13, four students from Jerusalem arrived.[10] In order to promote the positive reception of the school, the Ministry of Interior sent the following update about Deir ez-Zor to the palace on 18 September 1892:

> We have been instructed to recruit fifty students from the leading Arab tribes of the empire for the new beneficent school founded by our exalted sultan. Twenty students have already arrived and have been handed over to the Ministry of Education. The others are on the way and are expected to arrive soon. Tribal leaders who do not even allow their sons to go out of their tents have comprehended the value of this new venture, which will enlighten the ignorant and educate their youngsters. Therefore, they are sending their children with great enthusiasm and gratitude. As an example, although the four students from Deir ez-Zor sanjak were selected and were about to be sent, Sheikh Ali al Nijris from the Uqaydat tribe brought his son Turki to the local administration and insisted on his acceptance. The sheikh stated that if his son were not enrolled in the School for Tribes, his standing among the tribes would be tainted and he would be very sad. He would be ready to cover all travel expenses of his son. Finally, it was agreed to include Turki along with the other four students.[11]

The enthusiasm and competition among some tribal chiefs to send their sons to this special school were such that they considered their prestige to be at stake.

On September 20, Tercüman-ı Hakikat reported that fourteen new students had arrived, four from Aleppo, five from Yemen and five from Deir ez-Zor.[12] On September 24, a group of students was taken on a tour of the royal printing house, where each received a 'beautiful geography atlas'.[13]

The inauguration

The school was inaugurated on 4 October 1892, as the sultan had stipulated in July, but with twenty-five students: five from Deir ez-Zor and four each from Baghdad, Jerusalem, Tripoli, Aleppo and Yemen. On the very day of the inauguration, another four students arrived from Hama and Damascus.[14] Meanwhile the struggle to fill the quota from Hijaz continued unabated. On September 23, the Emir of Mecca, Awn al-Rafiq himself (elder brother of Sharif Husayn, who was to lead the Arab revolt), sent a telegram to the grand vizier stating that although the order to recruit students had been given to the provincial authorities long before, they had only belatedly sent envoys to the regions, but confirmed they would be sending the required students soon. Grand vizier Cevad Paşa forwarded this telegram to the palace only on 9 October 1892, perhaps to gain some time.[15]

Finally, on November 7, the governor of Hijaz informed the grand vizier that two students would be sent on the first vessel. This good news was promptly relayed to the palace on November 9. The efforts of the administration finally bore fruit, and chief scribe Süreyya Paşa informed the sultan that another four students from Hijaz would arrive in Istanbul on December 10.[16] The quota of five for Hijaz was eventually exceeded, albeit with a significant delay.

On October 18, three students, including Abdulmuhsin Saadun – later to become the prime minister of Iraq – arrived from Basra.[17] The *Tercüman-ı Hakikat* reported that the Ministry of Education sent telegrams to the parents of all the students informing them of the students' well-being.[18] Two days later an interesting event was described in the newspaper:

> A tribal sheikh from Syria has arrived in Istanbul with eight family members, hoping to place one of them in the School for Tribes. They were discharged from their vessel with a twelve-oar caique (rowing boat). He has brought with him six fine horses which he would like to present to the royal stables.[19]

Shaalan ibn Shaman (student identification number 38) from the Aneze tribe of Syria, was probably the son of this sheikh. Two students from Tripoli of the Beirut province applied to the school during this period, but were not accepted since there was no quota for this province yet.[20] In December, four students from Benghazi, four students from Van and the above-mentioned six Kurdish students from Mamuretelaziz arrived.[21] Although there is no document about their exact arrival date, it is reasonable to assume that the last students enrolled in the first year's class were three Turkomans from the Karapapak tribe in Erzurum, who were given student ID numbers 59 to 61, and Sayyid Muhammad, who belonged to the Şemzina Kurdish tribe from Şemdinli (Hakkari/Van). He was assigned ID number 62, bringing the Kurdish contingent up to fourteen students.

Thus, the School for Tribes, which was established exclusively for the Arabs, completed its first year of recruitment with forty-five of the intended fifty Arab students from only eight of the ten designated provinces. The original quotas for each province had not been met, and no students were recruited from Mosul or Diyarbakır. With the arrival of fourteen Kurds and three Turkomans, the school's total population exceeded the original quota of fifty, as it began to take on the character of an 'Imperial School for Tribes'.

Recruitment for the second year

In the spring, preparations began for the second year, but with an official warning. On 16 May 1893, the minister of education issued a memorandum notifying the members of his administration that many students who had arrived in the first year did not conform to the criteria stipulated for the school. He mentioned that there were students below the age of twelve and above sixteen, some of whom were married. He continued that many students brought along some relatives and servants, which caused unnecessary costs and such practice must be avoided.

Attached to this memorandum was a list of the provincial quotas for the second year. All forty students were to be selected from the Arab tribes as follows: five each from Syria, Aleppo and Baghdad, four each from Hijaz, Yemen and Tripoli, three each from Basra, Benghazi and Jerusalem, and two each from Mosul and Deir ez-Zor. The quotas were adjusted according to the past year's performance of the regions, and Diyarbakır was deleted from the list. However, it is interesting that the administration still hoped to recruit at least two students from Mosul. It would take two more years for the first student from this province to arrive. On 15 June 1893, the following article appeared in the *Tercüman-ı Hakikat*, indicating the continued official interest in the school:

> Our mighty sultan, who like a sun of wisdom and a speedy lightening, continues to enlighten his domains, has established a school for the tribes, to free them from the valleys of ignorance and bring them the fruits of knowledge and civilization. The sixty students who were recruited in the first year have displayed their great progress and improvement. It has been reported that another sixty students will be recruited for the second year to this center of excellence.[22]

Thus, the second year of the school commenced. The student identification numbers indicate that the first recruits of the second class were from Syria and Basra and the next contingent came from Libya.[23] On 29 October 1893, the governor of Yemen sent a note to the Ministry of Education stating that two students from Sana'a and one from Asir were sent on a vessel which would make a stop in Hudayda to collect the fourth student.[24] In October 1893, a telegram was sent from Basra via Diyarbakır to the ministry of education informing them that three new students for the second year of the school as well as the current students on home leave had been sent to Istanbul.[25] The last student to be enrolled in the School for Tribes in the first months of 1894 was Izzat Abdullah, a Kurd from Şemseki (today Şemdinli) of Hakkari, part of the Van province, who was given ID number 79. An internal memorandum from the Ministry of Education reflects the continued resistance to enrolling Kurds:

> A telegraph has been received from Ali Hanzade Mehmed, Chief of the Kurdish Şikak tribe located in Başkale, Van. The chief states that the sultan has allowed his tribe to migrate from Iran to Anatolia, and he is hoping to send his two sons to the School for Tribes. Although some Kurdish students have been enrolled, it is clear that the temperament and the disposition of the Kurds and Arabs are incompatible, and therefore, it is not recommended to accept these students.[26]

Two conclusions can be drawn regarding the recruitment process for the second academic year. First, although the students were supposed to arrive in August, the process was significantly delayed, part of the reason being the late departure of the first group for their holidays. The administration probably decided that it would be more economical to bring the new students with their peers from the first year. The second conclusion is that instead of accommodating forty students from the Arab provinces, the administration resigned itself to continue with twenty Arabs and one Kurd. There was no turnout for the second year from Hijaz, Baghdad, Aleppo, Mosul or Deir ez-Zor. These missing provinces accounted for a total of eighteen of the original forty slots open for year two. For the remaining twenty-two openings, Basra sent five students (although the quota was three), while Yemen, Tripoli and Benghazi dispatched four students each. The final three recruits came from Syria and Jerusalem. Although there was no quota assigned for Kurds, a student from Van was enrolled as the twenty-first recruit.

On 28 May 1894, towards the end of the academic year, another special group of students arrived at the school. These were three Druze's from Suwayda. The first two of these students, Fahd bin Farhan and Ali bin Faris, were descendants of the deceased administrator of Jabal Druze Ibrahim Paşa al-Atrash. The third was Yusuf, son of the administrator of the Sala district of Jabal Druze. Around the same time, one student from Jerusalem and another from Basra were admitted. These students were allocated ID numbers 13 (Fahd al-Atrash), 15, 20, 57 and 58 to fill the slots vacated by failing students. The inclusion of the Druze, who were considered to be a branch of Shiites, into the school in 1894 indicates the aspiration of the administration to unify all Muslims within the empire. Together with the twenty-one who had arrived earlier, the number of students enrolled in the second year reached twenty-six.

The third year – Recruiting the fourth class

During the second year of the school, the administration decided to divide the existing student population of seventy-five students into three classes, according to their achievement. Therefore, the recruitment process of the third year aimed to bring in younger students to fill a fourth class of the school, and the candidates were to be between twelve and fourteen years old. In consideration of the low intake of the second year, the administration decided to call on eleven Arab provinces to send five students each. This was the highest annual quota ever announced for the school.[27]

On 11 June 1894, the minister of education wrote to the eleven Arab provinces (Hijaz, Yemen, Syria, Baghdad, Basra, Mosul, Aleppo, Tripoli, Benghazi, Jerusalem and Deir ez-Zor), notifying them of additional conditions for recruitment.[28] These fifty-five students were to have both the propensity to be educated and be physically fit to acclimatize to their new environment.[29] This phrase was to be frequently repeated in the correspondence for many years thereafter. The ministry also indicated that in case the sons of first-ranking tribal chiefs could not be recruited, the students from families one level lower could be selected. The younger class was expected to be present in Istanbul at the beginning of August. This moment can be defined as the completion of the establishment period for the School for Tribes and the beginning of its regular academic cycle, which would continue up to 1907. It is also worth underlining the fact that there was no allocation for the Kurds.

On 13 August 1894, the *Tercüman-ı Hakikat* published the following article:

The final examination of the School for Tribes students was completed yesterday, and thereafter preparations for the fourth class of the school has commenced. The school has flourished under the guidance of the director, Ali Nazima, and the expected results are realized one by one. This year fifty-five new students will be recruited to the school. As there are seventy-five students at present, the population of the school will reach 130 in the coming year. The grades of the existing students have been presented to the Ministry of Education.[30]

A letter dated 22 August 1894, from the governor of Aleppo stated that: 'According to the order of the exalted grand vizier on June 2, which adorns and honors us above our heads, two students from Aleppo and three students from Deir ez-Zor have been sent to the school, and the recruitment of the other five is underway.'[31] Two other youngsters from Syria joined the students mentioned above in Iskenderun, boarding the vessel *Canik* headed to Istanbul, and the next two students arrived from Syria somewhat later. The letter sent from the ministry to the governor of Syria on October 23 informs us that these students had applied to the school the previous year, but had been kept waiting.³² Since the new students who were expected from Hawran were not sent, Fayez from the Laja tribe and Sharif from Hama could now be accepted. A letter confirmed their safe arrival at the school.³³

The next arrivals were four students from Jerusalem, one from Hawran, one from Mosul (first recruit from this province) and five from Benghazi.³⁴ The interrelated life stories of Omar Mansour (ID number 99) and Sadullah Koloğlu (ID number 100) from Benghazi are examined in Chapter 5. Five students from Yemen and another from Asir arrived at the school on 1 January 1895.³⁵ The final recruits for the third year were two students from Mecca and another two from Homs/Syria (ID numbers 112–15), although there is no clear date of their arrival.

Although only thirty-six students were actually recruited instead of the projected fifty-five, the school was close to its original plan of forty per year. All the students came from the Arab provinces and, except for Baghdad, the other ten provinces sent at least one recruit each. Syria led with eight students, and Yemen followed with a contingent of six, both above the established quota of five. As usual, the Libyans loyally sent their youngsters according to the regulations, five from Tripoli and five from Benghazi; Jerusalem and Deir ez-Zor sent three students each, and Hijaz and Aleppo two each. Only one student came from Mosul, and another one came from Basra.

Quotas vs. actual enrolment

As recounted above the quotas for the first three years of the School for Tribes were announced as fifty, forty and fifty-five, respectively (total 145). Beginning with the fourth year (1895), the annual quota for the new recruits to the school remained fixed at forty until 1907. This is verified by seven records from different years in this period.³⁶ On 15 August 1907, the grand vizier himself wrote that forty students were to be enrolled in the school for the coming year. Therefore, it can be concluded that the number of students expected to be recruited amounted to a total of 625 (145 for the first three years and 480 for the remaining twelve years – 1907 excluded since the school was closed).

The actual number of students enrolled in the first three years was sixty-two, twenty-six and thirty-six, respectively (totalling 124). I have been able to certify the acceptance of 250 additional student names to the school in later years, which brings the total to 373. As data for some periods are lacking, we can safely conclude that a total of at least 450 students were enrolled in the school during its years of operation.[37] Although this is a sizeable figure, it should be noted that it is only around 70 per cent of the projected enrolment.[38] In other words, despite the generous offer of a free high calibre education in the capital, the tribal leaders were reluctant to send their sons to such a school in the capital.

A breakdown of the records for 333 students by region (some without names) reveals that the highest enrolment originated from Greater Syria (a total of ninety-two from Syria, Aleppo, Deir ez-Zor, Jerusalem, Beirut and Jabal Druze). Yemen was next with fifty-eight students and then came the Libyans with fifty-five. The Balkan recruits from the last years which could be traced amounted to fifty-three students. There were thirty-nine from Anatolia (Kurds and Turcomans), and twenty-one from Iraq (Baghdad, Basra, Mosul). Below is a brief analysis of the recruitment process of the various provinces.

Greater Syria

By virtue of its proximity to the capital, Greater Syria was the most integrated Arab region of the empire, and as a consequence, the highest number of students of the school came from this area. In the first three years, for which we have exact figures, 34 per cent of the enrolment came from Greater Syria (42 students of 123). Although this percentage is reduced to one quarter of the total in the following years, nevertheless, the greatest number of students were from this region.

The first arrivals from this Syria were four students from Aleppo. In September 1892, the governor of Aleppo proudly informed the minister of interior that the prominent chiefs of the Aneze and Hadidi tribes had realized the value of this generous offer of the Shadow of God and were willing to send their sons to the capital.[39] They received ID numbers 5 to 8. They were followed by four students from Jerusalem, five from Deir ez-Zor (including Ramadan Shallash), two from Hama and another four from Damascus in the first year. In the second year, in addition to two from Syria and two from Jerusalem, three Druze students were enrolled in the school. In the third year, this region dominated the class with seventeen students out of a total of thirty-six (47 per cent).

In 1896, the first student from the Merhebi family from Akkar in northern Lebanon arrived at the school. In the next years he was followed by eight cousins (whose story will be told in Chapter 4). In July 1897, the governor of Syria informed the Ministry of Education that they were sending four students from Hama.[40] In January 1898, Naum Paşa, governor of Mount Lebanon sent a letter to the minister of education, requesting the enrolment of Mir Muhammad Idrisi from the village of Dedeh in the Koura district, who had graduated from the Beirut high school and belonged to the Ayyubi family. Naum Paşa subsequently sent another letter on behalf of four students from the Hasan family from Mount Lebanon.[41] These students followed up their request with a letter sent directly to the grand vizier, claiming that due to the higher status of the Christians in their region, they remained in the 'realm of backwardness without an adequate education'. Reaction was delayed, however; on June 3, there was an internal correspondence in the ministry about Idrisi, emphasizing the regulation that students from urban areas would not be accepted. The minister sent a note to the governor, rejecting his request to enrol Idrisi, but the other four students were eventually admitted.[42] In the following years, the Beirut province was also regularly assigned an annual quota.

A rather flowery petition was received by the governor of Çorum in August 1898, sent by Muhammad Nassar from Jabal Hawran. The latter had moved to Çorum in central Anatolia with his family and requested that, like his son Yusuf, previously enrolled in the School for Tribes, his other sons, Suleiman (age thirteen) and Abdullatif (age eleven) also be admitted. The letter begins with a long section of praises to the sultan, who has 'expanded and reorganized the institutions of learning and started to provide education to all the sons of the country'. The letter was then forwarded to the governor of Ankara, who sent it to the minister of interior; subsequently, the matter was transferred to the Ministry of Military Schools and finally to the Ministry of Education. The Ministry of Education replied on November 14 that the quota for Syria for that year was four students, yet five had already been admitted; therefore, the Nassar brothers were advised to reapply in the following year.[43]

In October 1899, the Nablus administration forwarded a petition to the minister of interior, regarding the acceptance of three descendants of Sheikh

Zamin al-Barakat of the Masaid tribe, but only one was accepted.[44] In October 1900, a letter arrived at the Ministry of Education from Syria requesting permission for a Druze student to attend the school, which was signed by the regent to the governor of Syria, the mufti of Damascus, the Nakib-ul-Ashraf, Defterdar and the private secretary. Both this student and another Druze were enrolled.[45]

The attendance of students from Greater Syria continued regularly until the closure of the school. On 14 June 1907, Muzaffer Paşa, governor of Mount Lebanon, sent a letter on behalf of three students from the Hasan tribe, whose relatives had been enrolled previously.[46] The very last record of recruitment for the School for Tribes originated from Urfa in 1907. The governor of Aleppo requested that the two sons of Captain Abdülkadir Efendi of the Urfa 53rd Hamidiye Regiment be admitted to the School for Tribes. He added that they were from 'first class nomadic tented tribes, ages between 12 and 16 and been physically examined to be fit to adapt to a change of location'.[47] These words indicate that the requirements for new students which were defined in 1892 were preserved until the school's end. Unlike other regions, the interest of the tribal leaders in Greater Syria in having their sons attend the school was quite high.

Hijaz and Yemen

At the time of foundation of the school, Hijaz and Yemen were given the highest quotas, in accordance with the policies of Sultan Abdülhamid. However, as mentioned above, from the beginning it proved difficult to recruit students from the Hijaz. At the insistence of the palace, six students arrived from the province after the school's inauguration, but one of them dropped out after a month. Two students from Mecca arrived in the third year. No other records exist regarding the attendance of Hijazi students. This indicates the tension between Istanbul and Mecca, which escalated in later years.

On the other hand, Yemen recruited the largest number of students (a total of fifty-eight) from a single province to the School for Tribes over the course of fifteen years. After sending five in the first year, the Yemenis continued to dispatch students regularly, four in 1893 and six in 1894. On 12 September 1899, on the orders of the palace, sixteen descendants of tribal sheikhs were sent from

Yemen to attend the school, the highest number sent at a single time from any province.[48] On 15 August 1907, the grand vizier wrote to the minister of interior and attached a note from the minister of education. In this letter, the grand vizier stated that fifteen students from Yemen had been enrolled in the school; therefore, for the following year, only twenty-five students with the standard qualifications should be recruited from the provinces.[49] However, the fifteen Yemeni students would soon be sent home and the next twenty-five would never be recruited because the school was closed in the last months of 1907.

Libya

Tripoli and Benghazi were the most loyal suppliers of students to the School for Tribes. In the first twelve years, records show that they fulfilled their quotas almost every year and sent at least fifty-five students (Tripoli thirty-four and Benghazi twenty-one, it is not clear if more students were enrolled in the last three years). On 12 September 1892, the first three students from Tripoli arrived in Istanbul and settled in their temporary premises in the civil service academy like their peers, but the fourth student fell ill during the boat trip and was hospitalized in Hanya, Crete.[50] The Benghazi contingent was slightly delayed but arrived at the beginning of December. In the second year, to minimize expenses, four students from Tripoli and three from Benghazi travelled to Istanbul on the same vessel.[51] In 1894, the first five students to arrive at the school at the end of August were from Tripoli. Subsequently, the Benghazi contingent arrived, including Sadullah Koloğlu and Omar Mansour, who will be discussed in Chapter 5.

On 21 August 1898, a new group of seven young students from Libya arrived in Istanbul.[52] Two days later, Tahsin Paşa chief scribe of Sultan Abdülhamid instructed the Sublime Porte that the four sons of Sheikh Zafir were to be enrolled in the School for Tribes.[53] Sheikh Zafir, who was from Tripoli, became a trusted religious mentor of the sultan himself and settled in Istanbul as the head of the Shadhiliya order. The Zafir family will be examined in Chapter 5. However, it suffices for now to point out that this example once again underlines the close links of the sultan to the school. The last record about recruits from Libya dates from 1903, when one student from Benghazi and three from Tripoli were enrolled.[54]

Iraq

Like Hijaz, Baghdad and Mosul were disappointing provinces for the school. Already in September 1892, the ministry announced that Mosul would not be sending students and decided to recruit Kurds from Anatolia instead. Although the ministry continued to set quotas for Mosul, the only record of a student from this province appears in November 1894. Similarly, as discussed at the beginning of this chapter, Baghdad did not send any students after the first year. Basra, on the other hand, consistently dispatched students to the school. Abdulmuhsin Saadun, son of Fahd Paşa from Muntafiq, who will be discussed in Chapter 6, was among the first three students from Basra who arrived in 1892. In the second year of the school, Basra was represented with six students, one of them the brother of Abdulmuhsin. On 6 September 1894, the governor of Basra, Mahmud Hamdi Paşa, sent a telegram to the grand vizier informing him that they had communicated with various parties but were only able to recruit Hashim bin Jabir from the Es-Suud tribe of Amarah, who arrived in Istanbul on November 17.[55] There are three more records about enrolment from Basra: two new students in 1895, two in 1897 and one in 1903. Towards the end of the school's existence, we encounter another interesting recruitment story. Ohannes Paşa, one of the ministers sent the following letter to the Sublime Porte in March 1907:

> Arabi Paşa, Sheikh of the Albu Muhammad tribe of Amarah, has paid all his debts to the Government. As a reward and as per his petition, the Amarah royal lands commission has requested that his son Muhammad Izzat, who is currently residing in Istanbul, be accepted and enrolled at the School for Tribes for his training and education.[56]

The minister's wish was granted, however, the new recruit could not attend the school because it was closed down.

Kurds and Turcomans

As discussed above, fourteen Kurds and three Turcomans were enrolled in the school in the first year. Although the quota announced for the second year did not include any Kurds, one Kurdish student from Van was nevertheless accepted to the school. In July 1895, the official quota included for the first time an allocation for four students from Bitlis and four from Mamuretelaziz, provinces in Anatolia. Two Kurds from Dersim (Mamuretelaziz) and one Turcoman from Erzurum arrived at the school that year. The Anatolian quota was increased in 1896 to ten out of forty: two students each from Bitlis, Erzurum, Van, Diyarbakır and Mamuretelaziz.

Three Kurdish students were enrolled in the school in 1897. On 2 March 1898, the governor of Erzurum wrote the minister of education a lengthy note. Two sons of the Turcoman Karapapak tribe had already arrived in Istanbul, hoping to enrol in the school. The governor was informed that there was only one place left according to the quota for Erzurum. The governor then asked that at least Şükrü Abdülkadir be admitted. Another application arrived from Aleppo asking approval for the acceptance of a student from the Chechen tribe in Kilis in Southern Anatolia. On the first day of 1899, two sons of Kurdish chieftains were enrolled in the school.[57] In July 1899, Mustafa, son of Nebi Aga, commander of the 37th Hamidiye regiment, applied for acceptance and was enrolled in the school at the end of November. His application contained numerous stamps testifying to his tribal origins.[58] Aleppo also requested the enrolment of another new student, this one from a Turcoman tribe, which was approved by the ministry, and he arrived in Istanbul on 11 December 1899.[59]

In July 1900, the Van province sent letters of recommendation for two Kurdish students from the Haydaranlı tribe to be enrolled. Interestingly, while one letter on behalf of the students was signed by the kaymakam and eight military officers, there was also another letter signed by the governor, the Catholic Church representative, the Armenian Church representative, the finance officer and the chief scribe.[60] The 1901 quota included eleven students from Anatolia. Two more students from the Kurdish Haydaranlı tribe were admitted in November 1901.[61]

On 8 August 1903, Şehabettin from Erzurum wrote the following dramatic petition to the ministry:

> Your slave is the son of Osman Bey Chieftain of the Karapapak tribe, which is proud to have formed the 6th light cavalry Hamidiye brigade in the Kara Kilise district of the Erzurum province. Last year my brother Husayn and I arrived at your just and shining door with letters from the district administration and the army, but since another student named Zamanhan from Erzurum was already enrolled, the Ministry of Interior notified us on

11 January 1903 that only my brother can be enrolled. I was promised that I would be accepted for the next year and have been waiting in a wretched and miserable state in hotel rooms. In the name of the justice of the sultan, I plead to be accepted to the school.⁶²

Fortunately, Şehabettin was given a letter of endorsement from Erzurum and was enrolled. An extensive correspondence between the centre and the province took place from August 1904 to October 1905, regarding two descendants of Mehmed Paşa from Eleşkirt, Erzurum. Mehmed Paşa and his son Kamil were part of the 62nd Hamidiye Regiment and gathered references from all local civil and military notables. However, since one of the sons was discovered to be around twenty years old, only the younger son was eventually enrolled.⁶³

The Balkans

On 28 June 1902, a striking instruction was sent from the palace to the ministry of education. The sultan had decided that twenty sons of Albanian chieftains should be enrolled in the School for Tribes.⁶⁴ Previously many Albanians had attended the civil service academy,⁶⁵ but the opening of the doors of the School for Tribes to the younger sons of rural leaders created quite a furore in the Balkan provinces. The governor of Kosovo requested that the quota of ten students for his province be increased to at least twelve.⁶⁶ In August, the minister of interior informed the grand vizier that a quota of four students was allocated to Manastır province, two for Debre and another two for Elbasan. The Debre governor replied that fifteen tribal chiefs had requested that their sons be given the privilege of attending the school.⁶⁷

On September 23, a special budget of 64,650 kuruş was transferred from the construction allowances of the ministry to the school to finance this Balkan project.⁶⁸ On the next day, *Tercüman-ı Hakikat* confirmed that Sultan Abdülhamid had decreed that the sons of Muslim tribes living in his 'Well-Protected European Domains' should also benefit from the education provided by the School for Tribes: 'The students from Kosovo and Manastir already arrived some days ago. Yesterday twenty specially selected students from Bulgaria and Eastern Rumelia came to Istanbul accompanied by Ali Aga Kavasbaşı of the Bulgarian commissariat.'⁶⁹ Four students from Işkodra

(Albania) were enrolled the next month. The addition of around thirty students from the European provinces in one year constituted another major change to the original concept of the school.

I found no records about any students from the Balkans for the next three years. In February 1905, the governor of Kosovo applied to the ministry of interior on behalf of Ali Zubeyr from Yakovo and Hacı Ali Aga from Mitrovice, who wanted to enrol their sons in the school. Later in the year, the governor of İşkodro requested that two other students be accepted. However, the ministry of education rejected all of these applications since twenty students from Albania had already been enrolled in the school.[70] It appears that a second group of Albanians had arrived in 1904. On 17 December 1906, the grand vizier Ferid Paşa, who was himself Albanian, wrote to the sultan requesting that the son of one of the notables of the Janina region be allowed to attend the school, which was approved by the palace on 9 April 1907.[71] There is no clue about how these students interacted with their Arab or other cohorts.

Egypt, Kuwait and Java

In February 1893, Gazi Ahmed Muhtar Paşa – Ottoman High Commissioner of Egypt – sent a plea to the palace, stating that the tribal sheikhs of Egypt would also like to send their sons to the School for Tribes; however, the quotas remained restricted to the Ottoman lands for the time being.[72] In March 1895, Ahmed Muhtar Paşa sent another letter to the grand vizier explaining that the Muslims on the island of Java were oppressed by the Dutch and that a sheikh from Hadramut, domiciled in Java, had sent his two sons with four other boys to Egypt to be educated. In his letter, he requested that these students be enrolled at the School for Tribes. Although they were not found suitable for the School for Tribes, the two older ones were placed in the civil service academy, and the others were enrolled in *Mekteb-i Sultani* and *Darüşşafaka*.

On 26 October 1896, the minister of education informed the grand vizier that the Sabah family, kaymakams of Kuwait, had applied to the governor of Basra to send three of their sons to the School for Tribes. The minister added that because the previous recruits from Basra had travelled by the land route the cost was exorbitant, future students from Basra should travel by sea. However, since the sea voyage could take up to two months and classes had already started, the Sabah family were advised to send their students to Istanbul the following summer, to be present at the beginning of that academic year. Even though the grand vizier approved their enrolment, the Kuwaitis never arrived.[73]

For the School for Tribes, the year 1903 stands out for the final expansion of its horizons. After several previous attempts, seven students from Java were enrolled in the fourth class of the school at the sultan's orders. However, it appears that they were not able to adapt and got sick. On 28 July 1903, the Ministry of Education informed the Ministry of Military Schools that the students should be sent to Aleppo for four months to recover, and detailed calculations were made regarding the expense which amounted to 1,557.5 kuruş (including the expenses of the officer who would accompany them). However, Zeki Paşa, the minister, replied that there was a plague epidemic in Aleppo and that the island of Midilli would be a better choice, also bringing down the expenses significantly to 400 kuruş. The Ministry of Education sent a letter to the Midilli administration, and the students boarded their ship on August 8. They seem to have recovered quickly and sent a telegram on August 26 requesting to return to Istanbul. The Javanese arrived in the school on 20 October 1903 and it is certain that at least three of them graduated.[74] In 1905, one of them is reported to have made a donation of 4.804 kuruş towards the Hijaz railway.[75]

Logistics, holidays and the purge of city-dwellers

Transporting the students to and from the School for Tribes was a costly and time-consuming affair. Perhaps the luckiest students were the Libyans, who enjoyed a seven-to-ten-day boat ride to the capital. In contrast, students from Basra faced a journey that took up to eight weeks. Although the school's original plan was to send the students home every year, after 1894, the holidays were granted every two years. To reduce expenses and simplify the process, the students returning from holidays would be joined with the newly enrolled candidates from their provinces.

On 10 July 1893, the director wrote to the Ministry of Education that the exams were almost over and the first group of thirty-three students were eager to go home for their holidays. The Ministry of Education was asked to notify the Ministry of the Navy to give passage to the students to and from the school free of charge.

> The majority will be travelling to Iskenderun, Beirut and Jaffa. We propose that one of the staff of the school accompany the students on the boat to Iskenderun and then continue the land journey with those destined to Baghdad and Basra. He would also be charged with bringing them back to Istanbul. The students need to be paid three months salary in advance. For those who will disembark at Beirut and Jaffa, it is important to assign local government employees to accompany them to their homes and later collect them to return to school.

This letter is the only example in the archival documents where the official stamp of the school is clearly displayed.[76]

Two years later, on 15 July 1895, the palace sent instructions to the Ministries of Interior, Navy, and Finance, informing them that ninety-one students from the school were given permission to go home for the holidays. The sultan demanded that they travel in comfort and allocated a special budget as follows:

> Their good treatment will naturally lead them to transmit their satisfaction to their families, which will be beneficial. In this case, expenses will not be in vain. Exclusively for this year, a budget of 50,000 kuruş has been allocated for this purpose. 37,000 will be spent for their land travel costs according to the budget. Students will be sent on government vessels to appropriate ports without charge. The balance of the budget will be distributed to the students as a gift from the sultan. Required measures should be taken by all the related Ministries.[77]

The students were to travel under close supervision. The first group of seventeen students were sent off on 27 August 1895. Since the Iskenderun port was under quarantine due to a cholera pandemic, the students travelled to Latakia and then continued their journeys to various locations, some all the way to Basra. In November, nine Yemeni students were sent home for a three-month holiday, while five of the seven Syrians who had gone home returned to the school.[78] Also in November, the province of Erzurum notified Istanbul that they had paid the travel expenses of the students who had spent their holiday with their families and were now travelling back to school.[79]

Twenty-five students from Libya were sent for a three-month holiday on 7 December 1897.⁸⁰ Meanwhile, twenty-three other students were sent to Samsun and Trabzon for their summer holidays, while thirty-two were put on board vessels bound for Syria and Libya.⁸¹ As is clear from the above, the logistics of the school were a very complicated affair.

In May 1901, the administration decided to issue standard allocations for travel expenses of the students per region as follows:

Yemen and Basra	1,800 kuruş
Baghdad and Mosul	1,500 "
Diyarbekir, Van and Mamuretelaziz	1,000 "
Erzurum and Bitlis	800 "
Deir ez Zor	700 "
The other six provinces	600 "

An important milestone in the history of the school occurred in the spring of 1899. The sultan ordered an investigation into the backgrounds of the students enrolled in the School for Tribes, and a large number were found to have settled in towns rather than the countryside at the time of their application and therefore should not have been enrolled in the school in the first place. Thirty such students were transferred to the civil service academy and an unknown number to the military academy, and, thus, were allowed to continue their studies in the capital. Most of the transfers were from the towns of Homs and Nablus; however, there were also students from Damascus, Yemen and Baghdad, among others. Some were identified as sons of government officials; others were sons of artisans of various types. There were even two whose fathers were employed in the capital by the state. One of the students carried the identification number 247, which indicates that the total number of students enrolled until 1899 had surpassed 250 (several numbers had been recycled).⁸² Below is the decree on the subject of the purges of students from the towns:

> The School for Tribes, which was founded by our sultan, who has taken the light of knowledge to the farthest corners of his realm, is undoubtedly a very significant achievement which brings the fruits of civilization to the tribes. The main purpose of this school is to educate and train the young nomadic

leaders and allow them to appreciate the progress in the world. They will, thus, be able to explain the difference between wandering in the wild and the advanced urban life to their families and cohorts in their own words. They would also be able to convince the nomads to settle. However, it appears that some of the students who were recruited had been living in towns and cities. This diminishes the value of the school, which is specifically designed to train the sons of nomadic tribes. The other youngsters can go to the already existing schools in their towns. Our exalted Caliph has underlined the importance of sending sons of the leaders and sheikhs who are living in the deserts and rural areas to the school.[83]

A new breed of soldiers and bureaucrats

As outlined in Chapter 1, in October 1896, twenty-six graduates of the School for Tribes and twenty-five students enrolled in the fifth class were transferred to the professional academies to attend a special one-year training programme. It was envisaged that such training would better prepare the students for their future careers. From this first group fifty-one students, forty-five were able to graduate on 23 July 1897.[84] However, their assignments took a rather long time, and they were later referred to as the class of 1898. Since two classes were jointly enrolled in the first year, the next intake occurred two years later. The number of graduates of these two institutions clearly indicates the preference of the students for a military career. Although the civil service academy records indicate that the programme was implemented every two years, the data obtained from the archives and newspapers proves that both institutions produced graduates annually after 1900. These figures also indicate that around half of the students who were enrolled in the School for Tribes Mektebi were able to receive diplomas from the military or civil service academy.

The placement of these students became a complicated affair for the army and the bureaucracy, especially in the first year. A note sent to the sultan on 6 October 1897, by his chief scribe Süreyya Paşa, verified the existence of problems in the situation of the military academy graduates. Although they were assigned to military posts and given the prestigious appellation of honorary aide-de-camp to the sultan, some of the graduates asked to be relieved of their duties, citing the illness of their parents or unique personal situations. Zeki Paşa, in charge of these students, confirmed the unhappiness of some of the graduates.[85] Sayyid Muhammad Khalid, a member of the military High Inspectorate, sent a note to the palace explaining that the dissatisfied ones were mainly the Arab graduates assigned to the Kurdish Hamidiye regiments who wished to be sent to their hometowns.[86]

On the other hand, one of the students of the first graduating class of the military academy was Nawwaf al-Salih from the Hadidi tribe of the Aleppo province. He served in the army loyally and retained his rank until 1918 and later remained a powerful and respected figure in his homeland. Similarly, his classmate Barjis al-Farhan from the Aneze tribe served in the Ottoman army until the death of his father in 1906. He became a wealthy and respected landlord in his later years.[87] Halid Cibran, one of the first Kurdish students to enrol in the school and graduate from this same class of the military academy, rose to the rank of colonel during the First World War. He then joined the forces of Ataturk; however, he gradually began to defend the establishment of an independent Kurdistan and was hanged during the heyday of the Sheikh Said rebellion in 1925.

The assignment of the first twelve graduates of the civil service academy to their posts was not a quick affair either. It was only on 10 April 1898, that these graduates were each paid 10 liras as a gesture from the sultan and assigned a salary of 500 kuruş.[88] In April 1898, these graduates were finally dispatched to their provinces.[89] Below is the announcement in the newspaper about the first Ottoman bureaucrats from the school:

> Five of the twelve students who completed their training at the civil service academy have boarded the Abbas paşa vessel of the Khidival Lines yesterday to begin their new assignments. Muhammad Abdullah and Abdullah Najib have been appointed as clerks to the Yemen Administration; Mukhtar and Husayn to the Tripoli Administration; and Ali Nureddin to the Benghazi Administration.[90]

The careers of two of these Yemeni graduates are detailed in the academy records. Sayyid Abdullah (mentioned above as Muhammad Abdullah) taught in several schools and then became a treasurer in the education administration of Yemen. Hafiz Ahmad, his classmate, also began his career as a teacher and later served as principal in several institutions. In 1912, he became the Kaymakam of Yarim in Yemen.[91]

On 16 March 1899, another group of students completed their studies at the School for Tribes, eight of whom were admitted to the civil service academy, and nineteen were enrolled in the military academy.[92] Four of them failed or left, and the remaining twenty-three students from this group graduated on 8 April 1900.[93] Omar Mansour and three others who graduated with high honours were given third rank positions in the administration, while Fahd al-Atrash and another student who graduated with honours received fourth rank positions.

In the summer of 1901, eight students graduated from the civil service academy (perhaps including some students from the previous class) and another fifteen from the military academy.[94] One of the students who graduated with high honours from the civil service academy was Sadullah Koloğlu, future prime minister of Libya.[95] On 3 December 1901, the sultan decided to promote the sixteen graduates of the military academy to the rank of captain and bestow on each of them 10 liras before they left for their new assignments.

In February 1902, two officers from Syria wrote a petition to the sultan. The first four lines were probably composed by a professional writer who sang incredibly flowery praises to the caliph. The letter continued as follows:

> Our illustrious sultan founded the School for Tribes to enlighten his subjects living in tents in a state of savagery with knowledge and science. His nomadic subjects have flocked to the school to be trained and educated and later employed with pride in his service. We, the undersigned, are among the blessed who benefited from this revered institution. After continuing our education at the military school, we have been assigned to the 5th army stationed close to our tribes.
>
> Although our peers before and after us were given the rank of lieutenant, our position has been questioned by our families. We are very honored to serve our sultan, but we would also like to benefit from his exalted justice. We humbly plead to be promoted to the rank of lieutenant like our peers.

Ahmad bin Salim, son of the Chief of the Albu Khash (?) tribe and Second Lieutenant of the 29th cavalry regiment stationed in Damascus.

Shaalan bin Shaman, son of Sattam Paşa, Chief of the Aneze tribe and Second Lieutenant of the 29th cavalry regiment stationed in Damascus.[96]

Although the reply is not available in the archives, we can safely assume that these officers were promoted, because it had already been decided to give all the graduates the rank of captain.

In January 1904, ten graduates of the military academy were given cavalry positions in the army, and another four were assigned to the infantry. Three new graduates of the school were admitted to the civil service academy, while another nine were enrolled in the military.[97] In May 1905, Mukhtar Fahmi, one of the graduates of the civil service academy, sent a letter to the grand vizier. He stated that he had been working in the Jabal Garbi administration of Tripoli for seven years and requested a promotion to the position of kaymakam; it is not clear whether his wish was granted.[98] On 21 September 1906, we can find the final record for nineteen military academy graduates.[99] These one-year special programmes were still in operation in August 1907, as can be seen in the letter below from the minister of military schools to the Sublime Porte, which also reflects the choice of the majority of the graduates for a military career:

> This year half of the graduates of the School for Tribes were placed in the military academy and the other half in the civil service academy. Those assigned to civil service have complained and claimed that their parents would be unhappy with this career. They would like to transfer to the military, and if this would not be possible to be given permission to pursue their own careers. Therefore it will be reasonable to allow any of these students who so desire to enroll in the military academy. We trust this will meet with your approval.[100]

As this chapter has illustrated, the recruitment and placement of students of the School for Tribes was a complicated process. Nevertheless, the administration continued to make utmost efforts to recruit up to forty students every year and to provide them with additional training in the military and civil service academies, to produce a new breed of special soldiers and bureaucrats. However, the enrolment figures were quite erratic and from the very first year until the closure of the school it was not possible to achieve the targeted numbers. Some provinces like Hijaz, Baghdad, Mosul and Diyarbekir were abandoned after the initial years. In the other locations, the number of students recruited deviated from the assigned quotas almost every year. The best performers were undoubtedly Greater Syria, Libya and Yemen.

It is surprising that the central administration did not make any effort to target specific tribes, although they had detailed knowledge about the more powerful groups. There are many records and reports about the number of tents of the tribes in different regions, which could have been utilized to prepare a strategic plan for recruitment. The archival documents indicate that the initiative to fill the quotas was left to the governors, whose performance varied significantly by region.

The deviation from the original mission of training and cultivating the loyalty of exclusively Arab students affected the nature of the school significantly. There are numerous records throughout the years about fights between Kurdish and Arab students. The decision to bring in Albanians in 1902 proves that any visions of an Arab-Turkish integration had waned by this time. The lack of participation from the Hijazi tribes was obviously a disappointment for the sultan. Nevertheless, the students who completed this rigorous programme in the capital benefited greatly from their education and experience and served their communities as leaders in the following turbulent years.

Four tables presented below summarize the student data retrieved from the archives and newspapers. Table 1 shows the quotas and actual enrolment figures for the School for Tribes between 1892 and 1907. Table 2 displays the breakdown of 333 students by region. Table 3 has a summary of the numbers of the military and civil service academy graduates. A list of the names of the 373 students culled from the archives and newspaper articles is presented in Table 4.

Table 1 Quotas and actual recruitment figures

	Quota	Minimum actual
1892	50	62 (Batch 1–33, Batch 2–29)
1893	40	26
1894	55	36
Total first 3 years	145	124 (85% realized)
1895 (Year 4)	40	24
1896 (5)	40	1
1897 (6)	40	21
1898 (7)	40	20
1899 (8)	40	25
1900 (9)	40	11
1901 (10)	40	2
1902 (11)	40	40
1903 (12)	40	15
1904 (13)	40	4
1905 (14)	40	22
1906 (15)	40	6
1907 (16)	40	18
Total 13 years	520	209 (48% excluding 1896 and 1907)
Grand Totals	665	333 (57% excluding 1896 and 1907) 450 (72% excluding 1907 and compensating for missing records)

Table 2 Breakdown of 333 students by region and year

YEAR	1892	93	94	95	96	97	98	99	1900	01	02	03	04	05	06	1907	Total
	1	2	3	4	5	6	7	8	9	10	11	12	13	14	15	16	333
Greater Syria	19	6	17	4	1	16	11	2	2	-	4	-	3	-	5	2	92
Syria	6	2	8	1	-	4	5	-	-	-	-	-	-	-	-	-	26
Jerusalem	4	2	3	3	-	1	-	1	-	-	4	-	3	-	1	-	22
Aleppo	4	-	2	-	-	3	2	1	-	-	-	-	-	-	-	2	14
Deir ez-Zor	5	-	3	-	-	-	-	-	-	-	-	-	-	-	4	-	12
Trablusşam	-	-	-	-	1	8	-	-	-	-	-	-	-	-	-	-	9
Druze	-	2	1	-	-	-	-	-	2	-	-	-	-	-	-	-	5
Beirut	-	-	-	-	-	-	4	-	-	-	-	-	-	-	-	-	4
Yemen	5	4	6	7	-	-	-	18	-	-	-	3	-	-	-	15	58

(*continued*)

YEAR	1892	93	94	95	96	97	98	99	1900	01	02	03	04	05	06	1907	Total
	1	2	3	4	5	6	7	8	9	10	11	12	13	14	15	16	333
Hijaz	6	-	2	-	-	-	-	-	-	-	-	-	-	-	-	-	8
Tripoli	4	4	5	5	-	-	5	3	2	-	3	3	-	-	-	-	34
Benghazi	4	4	5	3	-	-	2	-	2	-	-	1	-	-	-	-	21
Iraq	7	6	2	2	-	2	-	-	-	-	-	1	-	-	-	1	21
Anatolia	17	1	-	3	-	3	2	2	5	2	1	-	1	2	-	-	39
Balkans	-	-	-	-	-	-	-	-	-	-	-	32	-	-	20	1	53
Java	-	-	-	-	-	-	-	-	-	-	-	7	-	-	-	-	7
Total	62	25	37	24	1	21	20	25	11	2	40	15	4	22	6	18	333

Table 3 Number of students who graduated from the military and civil service academies

	#Military	#Civil service	Total
1898	33	12	45
1900	17	6	23
1901	15	8	23
1902	40	7	47
1903	14	-	14
1904	9	3	12
1906	19	-	19
Total	147	36	183

Table 4 List of names of 363 students

First batch of thirty-three students				
ID-name	Father	Province	Tribe	NOTE
1-Hamid	Farhan	Baghdad	Shammar	(Did not return)
2-Suleiman	Habib	"	Rabia	(Did not return)
3-Ajeel	Ali	"	Zubayr	(Did not return)
4-Ali	Suleiman	"	Dulaim	(Failed-not to return)
5-Muhammad Nawwaf	Salih al Jarrah	Aleppo	Hadidi	

(*continued*)

Recruitment and Placement

	First batch of thirty-three students			
ID-name	Father	Province	Tribe	NOTE
6-Ahmad Fuad	Hamud	Aleppo	Hadidi	
7-Muhammad Barjis	Farhan	"	Aneze-Seba	
8-Fadel	Sultan bin Hudayb	"	"	(Did not return)
9-Khalil	Muftah	Trablusgarb	Zintan	
10-Muhammad	Abdullah	Dersaadet/Taiz	Yemen/Hijaz/Amarah	
11-Husayn Husnu	Jabir	Trablusgarb	Farshafana/Aziziyah	
12-Hafith Ali	Abdulqadir	"	Tawalib/Khums	
13-Darwish	-	Jerusalem	-	(Failed-not to return)
14-Jabir Jawdat	Hammud	"	Wahidat	
15-Husayn	-	"	-	(Failed-not to return)
16-Suleiman	Abu Eid	"	Hanajira	
17-Sayyid Abdallah	Muhammad	Yemen-Yarim	Amarah/Saadat	
18-Hafiz Ahmad	Muhammad	Yemen	Anas	
19-Abdullah	Ahmad	Yemen	Hajji	
20-Shatheli	-	Yemen	-	(Failed-not to return)
21-Muhammad	Sultan	Deir ez-Zor/Syria	Jabbur	
22-Isa Ali	Hajj Fahd	"	Sabka	
23-Ramadan Shallash	Abdullah	"	Uqaydat/Busaraya	
24-Ahmad Shallash	"	"	"	
25-Zaki Turki	Ali Al Nijris	"	Uqaydat/Azar	
26-Suud	-	Hama/Syria	-	(Did not return)
27-Muhammad	Juma	"	Beni Khalid	
28-Muhammad	Sattam	Damascus/Syria	Wuld Ali	

(*continued*)

First batch of thirty-three students

ID-name	Father	Province	Tribe	NOTE
29-Muhammad	Shibli	Damascus/Syria	Fawairi	
30-Abdulmuhsin	Fahd	Basra/Muntafiq	Saadun	
31-Shayya	-	Basra	-	
32-Fandi	-	Basra	Bani Lam	
33-Zafir	Muhammad	Yemen/Asir	Qahtan	

Second batch who arrived in the first year

Id-name	Father	Province	Tribe
34-Muhammad Sharif	-	Bitlis	Cibranlı (Kurdish)
35-Qasim	Ahmad	"	"
36-Khalid	Mahmud	"	"
37-Mustafa Nadir	Mufti Mustafa	Dersaadet	
	Hijaz/Medina		
38-Samhan	"	Damascus/Syria	Aneze
39-Mustafa Faris	-	Hijaz/Medina	Dersaadet
40-Ali Nureddin	Hamid	Benghazi/Derna	Ubeidat
41-Husayn Nuri	Muhammad	Benghazi	Baragith
42-Abdulcalil	Osman	"	"
43-Mahmud	Abdulhadi	"	Arafa
44-Hashim	Jabir	Basra	Amarah
45-Mehmed Hamza	Husayn	Van (Şemdinli)	Mekri (Kurdish)
46-Muhanna	Omar bin Saad	Hijaz	Hamidat
47-Tahir	-	Van	Haydaranlı (Kurdish)
48-Ziya	Abdullah	"	Şemseki "
49-Muhammad Sıddık	Ömer	"	Merzeki "

(continued)

Second batch who arrived in the first year

ID-name	Father	Province	Tribe	NOTE
50-Suleiman Nuri	İbrahim	Mamuretalaziz	İzollu (Kurdish)	
51-Yusuf Jamil	Murtaza	"	Karaballı (Kurdish)	
52-Hasan Hayri	Omar	"	"	/Siverek
53-Ali Haydar	Sayyid Qasım	"	"	
54-Muhammad Şükrü	Kadir	"	"	
55-Ahmad Ramiz	İsmail	"	"	
56-Ali	Hasan	Hijaz	Zahran	
57-Unknown	-	-	-	(Left)
58-Abdullah	-	Hijaz	Bani Sufyan	(Left)
59-Salim Zaki	Abdullah	Erzurum	Karapapak (Turcoman)	
60-Anis	Osman	"	"	
61-Veli	Ali	"	"	
62-Sayyid Muhammad	-	Dersaadet	Şemzina/ Şemdinli (Kurdish)	

Second year students

Id-name	Father	Province	Tribe	
63-Muhammad Hattab	Bro. Sheikh Rahil Syria/ Hawran	Turki		
64-Muhammad Taleb	-	Nefsi Basra/ Dersaadet		
65-Muhammad Salih	Hajj Taleb	"		
66-Haidar	Said el Nacaf	Trablusgarb	Huwawata/ Khums	
67-Muhammad	Mustafa		"	Zemamete
68-Suleiman	Izzat	"	Usca	
69-Muhammad	Hamza		"	"
70-Madi	-	Benghazi	Nefsi Benghazi	

(continued)

Second year students				
ID-name	Father	Province	Tribe	NOTE
71-Salih	-	Benghazi	Nefsi Benghazi	
72-Garaybil (?)	-	"	"	
73-Hamid	Ali	Yemen/Sana	Nefsi Sana	
74-Ihsan Muhammad Jundari	"	"		
75-Abdullah	Muhammad Yemen	Al Kathiri		
76-Abdulkarim	Fahd Pasha	Basra/Muntafiq	Saadun	
77-Ubaid	Yasin	Basra	Miyah	
78-Thubian	Musa Muhammad "	Al Sawaid		
79-Izzat	Abdullah	Van	Şemseki	

ID's reallocated - 1894			
1-Rashid	-	Syria/Homs	
3-Abdulwahid	-	Yemen	
4-Ahmad	Salim	Jerusalem	Abu Keshk
8-Abdulqadir	-	Benghazi	
13-Fahd	Farhan alAtrash Syria	Suwayda/Druze	
15-Yusuf Kenan	Muhammad Nasarek Syria	Sale/Druze	
20-Muhammad	Tuqan	Jerusalem	-
57-Ali	Faris al-Atrash	Syria	Suwayda/Druze
58-Fazlullah	-	-	-

Third year students			
Id-name	Father	Province	Tribe
80-Mukhtar	Abubakr Sidqi	Trablusgarb	-
81-Ahmad	-	"	-

(*continued*)

Third year students				
ID-name	Father	Province	Tribe	NOTE
82-Ali	-	Trablusgarb		-
83-Mahmud Tahir	-	"	-	
84-Amir	-	"	-	
85-Mahmud Zahir	Mustafa	Aleppo	Bani Said	
86-Muhammad	Darwish	"	Ibriz	
87-Jadan	Deir ez-Zor			
88-Abdulmuhsin	-	Deir ez-Zor	-	
89-Mahmud Salim	-	"	-	
90-Mahmud Fayez	Al-Fasih	Syria	Bani Khalid	
91-Mahmud Sharif	Hamid Shibli Syria/ Hama	Fuwara		
92-Raghib	-	Jerusalem	-	
93-Mahmud	"		-	
94-Muhammad Abdulqadir Hashim	Jerusalem/ Basra (reallocated)			
95-Suud	-	Jerusalem	-	
96-Mahmud	Sheikh Khalil Hawran/ Syria	-		
97-Abdulmajid	Sheikh Judi	Mosul	Jabur	
98-Milad	-	Benghazi	Nefs-i Benghazi	
99-Omer Mansour	-	"	"	
100-Sadullah	Mabruk	"	Derna/Kuloglu	
101-Omar Qadi	-	"	"	
102-Abdulqadir	-	"	-	
103-Ali	-	Syria	-	
104-Mahmud Hakim	-	Syria/Homs	-	
105-Bashir	-	"		
106-Abdurrahman Abdullah Al-Shihri Yemen		Asir		

(*continued*)

ID-name	Father	Province	Tribe	NOTE
Third year students				
107-Sayyid Muhammad Ahmad al Hayfi	Bir al-Azab	-	-	
108-Sayyid Muhammad Yahya Zabare	"	Salahaddin		
109-Sayyid Ali	Galib	"	Tawashi	
110-Sayyid Muhammad Abdurrahman Fayez "	"			
111-Sayyid Ahmad	Ismail al-Ashifi "	Dawud		
112-Sharif Nasır	-	Mecca/Hijaz	-	
113-Sharif Mansour	-	"	-	
114-Mahmud	-	Syria/Homs	-	
115-Ahmad	-	"	-	
Fourth year students				
Id-name	Father	Province	Tribe	
116-Suleiman	-	Syria/Homs or Jerusalem	-	
117-Mansour	-	Hawran	/Syria	-
118-Mahmud	-	Jerusalem	-	
119-Suleiman	-	"	-	
120-Salim	-	"	-	
121-Ahmad	Miftah	Trablugarb	-	
122-Emin Khalifa	-	"	-	
123-Mahmud Khalifa	Ahmad	Benghazi	Badr	
124-Mahmud Habib	-	"		-
125-Mustafa	-	Benghazi	-	
126-Unknown				
127-Abdulqadir	-	"	-	
128-Kamil	-	Basra	-	

(continued)

Fourth year students

ID-name	Father	Province	Tribe	NOTE
129-Ibrahim	-	Basra	-	
130-Veli	-	Bayazıd/Erzurum	Karapapak	
131-Mirali	-	Dersim / Mamuretalaziz		-
132-Mahmud Hızır	-	"	-	
133-Ismail	-	Yemen/Sana	-	
134-Ahmad Nasir	-	Yemen/Asir	-	
135-Mahmud al Hadhari -	Yemen	-		
136-Unknown				
137-Ali Abdi	-	Yemen/Sana	-	
138-Mahmud	-	"	-	
139-Yahya	-	"	-	

130 other students with identification numbers (up to 1900)

140-Resul	Bayezid		
141-Abdullah Avni	"		
143-Husayn Hayri	Diyarbekir		
145-Mehmed Milad			
146-Rustam Bahaeddin	Celalzade Yusuf	Mamuretelaziz	Umran
147-Mustafa			
148-Ibrahim			
149-Haidar			
150-Muhiyiddin			
151-Khalifa	Benghazi		
152-Abdusselam			
155-Omar			
157-Muhammad Mouin Ferab/Merhebi	Mustafa Abdülqadir	Trablusşam/Akkar	Bani
158-Khalid			
159-Mahmud			
161-Ahmad			
162-Farah			
163-Muhammad			
164-Anis			
165-Ahmad			
166-Mustafa			
167-Muhammad			

(*continued*)

130 other students with identification numbers (up to 1900)

168-Suleiman
169-Ahmad
170-Abbas   Muhlis Aga   Hamidiye 47 regiment   Cevale/Diyarbakır
171-Arif
172-Muhammad Hasan
173-Abdulfattah   Abdulmajid al-Sharif   Akkar/Trablusşam   Merhebi
174-Muhammad Salim
175-Muhammad Arif
176-Muhammad Beri
177-Sayyid Saleh
178-Muhammad
181-Abdullah
183-Rushdi   Nablus
184-Abdurrahman
186-Khalid
188-Osman
189-Cemşid
190-Arif   Istanbul
191-Akif   Nablus
192-Afif   "
193-Muhammad Said
194-Abdünnafi   Selim   Mamuretaziz   Melli
195-Muhammad Tawfiq   Trablusgarb
197-Hamid Muhammad   Mosul/Sulaymaniya   -
198-Salih
199-Nusret   Saida
200-Ahmad   "
202-Salahaddin   Damascus
205-Kamil   "
206-Shukri   "
207-Abdulqadir   Homs
208-Abdülaziz   "
209-Muhammad Yasin   "
210-Rashid Faisal   "
212-Ahmad   "
213-Muhammad   "
214-Muhammad Kurdi   "
215-Ahmad Mouin   Muhammad al-Hasan   Akkar
216-Muhammad Arif Khalid Hasan   Jabal Lubnan
217-Qasim Anwari   Hajj Zekariya al-Hasan Jabal Lubnan
218-Yusuf Bahaeddin   "
219-Numan   "
222-Abu al Khayr   "
223-Zulfiqar   -
224-Ali Rıza   Mamuretelaziz/Arapkir
225-Muhammad Mukhtar Muhammad Kanan   Trablusgarb   Gharzan
226-Ahmad
227-Mustafa Faik
228-Husayn Kamil

(continued)

130 other students with identification numbers (up to 1900)

229-Ali
230-Hasan
231-Sayfunnasr   Sheikh Fadil   Benghazi
233-Sayyid Ahmad   Syria/Hama
238-Hamid   Baghdad
239-Feyzi   Mosul/Kerkuk
240-Hakki
241-Bashir
242-Muslim
243-Muhammad Siddiq Hajj Jabri   Benghazi   Beragit
244-Yusuf
245-Bahri
246-İsmail
247-Najib   Damascus
248-Muhammad Adib
249-Suleiman Nuri
250-Abdullatif
256-Husayn
257-Muhammad Abdullah
258-Ahmad Misri   Java
259-Said Bajanid   Java
260-Ahmad Bajanid   Java
261-Davud Senker   Java
262-Abdullah Senker   Java
263-Suleiman Senker   Java
264-Muhammad Senker   Java
265-Muhammad   -
266-Qasim   -
267-Saleh   -
268-Mustafa
269-Haidar
270-Ali Niyazi
271-Husayn
272-Muhammad
273-Abdelqadir
274-Ali
275-Suleiman
276-Mahmoud
277-Mirza
278-Shukri
279-Namik
280-Abdusselam
281-Ali
282-Muhammad
283-Ahmad
284-Muhammad
285-Miskal Daher
286-Muhammad Ali
287-Muhammad Rashid

(continued)

81 additional names found in the archives/newspapers/other sources

1.	Ahmad	Molla Abdurrahman	Diyarbakır	Tay 1897
2.	Abdulkarim	Shadi	Basra	
3.	Osman	Zahir	"	
4.	Mahmud	Khalid al Jasim	Syria/Hama	Turki
5.	Khalid	Suleiman	"	"
6.	Khalil	Khalid Salih	"	"
7.	Ahmad	Hasan	"	Nuaym (?)
8.	Kamil	Abdulkerim	Erzurum/KaraKilise	Karapapak 1898
9.	Yakub	Rasul	Aleppo/Kilis	Çeçen
10.	Muhammad Arif	Khalid Hasan	Jabal Lubnan	Betoraric
11.	Yusuf Bahaeddin	Muhammad al-Hasan	"	"
12.	Muhammad	Kurdi	Aleppo/Maare	Bani Khalid
13.	Sami Haraki	Nuri	"	-
14.	Najmeddin Haraki	"	"	-
15.	Abdussalam	Zafir	Trablusgarb	
16.	Omar	"	"	
17.	Mahmud	"	"	
18.	Abu Bakr	"	"	
19.	Ali Nureddin	-	"	
20.	Hasan Sabri	Sheikh Said Najm	"	Botin
21.	Husayn Husni	Lutf ul-Huda	Yemen/Sana'	1899
22.	Muhammad	Abdullah	Yemen/Hudayda	
23.	Muhammad	Sheikh Zamin al Barakat	Nablus	Masaid
24.	Namık	Mustafa Basho	Syria/Bab	Bekmishli 1900
25.	Khalil Rıfaat	Bahij Isa	Syria/Hawran	Al Mikdad
26.	Faris Fayyad	Sheikh Qais	Syria	-
27.	Nezir Cihangir	Muhammad ibn Ali	Van	Liyoli
28.	Hasan	Muhammad Sıddık	"	Haydaranlı
29.	Mabruk	Abdullah	Benghazi/Derna	Kubbe
30.	Ramadan	Huyuni	Benghazi/Bumba	Bucaziye
31.	Muhammad	Sheikh Khalil Halabi	Hawran/Druze	Um al Harisiya/Ahira
32.	Muhammad	Sheikh Khalil Kiwan	Hawran/Druze	Salkhad
33.	Suleiman	Ali	Kiğı/ Erzurum	Şadili/Kerasor
34.	Ahmad	Huseyin	Kiğı/Erzurum	Sevkar
35.	Ahmad	Mehmed/Qasim Pasha	Trablusgarb/Jabal	Mahamid
36.	Ali	-	Trablusgarb/Aziziya	Suud
37.	Abdurrahman	-	Asir/Yemen	
38.	Salih	Huseyin Pasha	Van	Haydaranlı 1901
39.	Abdullah	Huseyin Pasa's bro Van	Haydaranlı 1902	
40.	Shaalan	Sattam Paşa	Syria	Aneze
41.	Fahd	Sheikh Jabir	Jerusalem/Gaza	-
42.	Ahmad	-	"	Beersheba Jabarat
43.	Salim	Yunus al Amir	"	"
44.	Muhammad		Trablusgarb	
45.	Ammar		"	
46.	Suud Sheikh Suleiman		Beirut	Sahur al Ghur

(continued)

81 additional names found in the archives/newspapers/other sources

47.	Şehabettin	Osman Bey	Erzurum/KaraKilise	Karapapak 1903
48.	Hüseyin	"	"	"
49.	Zamanhan	-	Erzurum	-
50.	Ibrahim Hakki	Abdurrahman	Diyarbakir	Miran/Sinikan
51.	Ali		Tripoli	
52.	Qasim	"		
53.	Muhammad	"		
54.	Muhammad Zaim	Barak	Basra	Al Jassham
55.	Sayyid Ahmad	Ahmad Ishak	Asir/Yemen	
56.	Muhammad	Abdulaziz	Rida/Yemen	
57.	Muhammad	Sayyid Muhammad	Ayiz/Yemen	
58.	Şahin Yusuf		Berat/Albania	1904
59.	Fazıl	Kamil/Mehmed Paşa	Erzurum/Eleşkirt	Badilli/Hamidiye
60.	Hamza	Sultan Bey	Van	Hamidiye 1905
61.	Bahri	"	"	"
62.	Mukhtar	Fahmi	Trablusgarb	Jabal Gharbi
63.	Ahmad	Salih Ali al Nijris	Syria/Deir ez-Zor	-
64.	Ali	Qamar	"	
65.	Jasim	-	"	Jenha 1906
66.	Hasan	-	"	Al Busaraya
67.	Suleiman	Salman	Beersheba/Jerusalem	Tayih
68.	Hashim	Muhammad Salim	Hijaz/Mekke	
69.	Hamza	"	Hijaz/Mekke	
70.	Muhammad Izzat	Arabi Paşa	Basra/Amarah	AbuMuhammad 1907
71.	Muhammad Şükrü	Abdülkadir	Diyarbakir/Urfa	Hamidiye
72.	Muhammad Sabri	"	"	"
73.	Suleiman	Sheikh Rida	Nablus	
74.	Ibrahim	Sheikh Muhammad		Bani Aqaba
75.	Majdi	Suleiman al Bakr		-
76.	Khudayr	Abbas		Dulaim
77.	Şevket	Hacı Ali Ağa	Mitrovice	
78.	Ahmed	"	"	
79.	Salih	Mehmed	Akova	Goşmir
80.	Eyüb	Mehmed	Skopje	
81.	Younus	Hafez	Trablusgarb	

5 additional names from Civil Service Academy (Mekteb-i Mülkiye) records

1.	Mehmed Cemil	Hacı Ismail Neşet	Diyarbakir	-
2.	Muhammad Nadir	Muhammad Salim	Hijaz/ Mekke	-
3.	Salih	Ibrahim Salim	Hijaz/ Mekke	-
4.	Mustafa Adib	Osman Paşazade	Trablusşam/Akkar	Merhebi
5.	Muhammad Akram	Hasan bey al-Sharif	"	"

3

Educators and curriculum

In the nineteenth century, the Ottomans created a state-sponsored educational curriculum, designed in part to create loyal citizens, as their Western counterparts had done. The system was intended to transform the way Ottoman subjects perceived themselves, their relationship with the state and the position of the Ottoman Empire in the world. On 29 January 1887, Sultan Abdülhamid authorized his Sheikh al-Islam, Üryanizade Ahmad Esad Efendi, to chair a commission designed to review and revise the content of education at all levels. Recai Efendi, the assistant director of the civil service academy, was appointed the coordinator of the commission. Recai Efendi was to become an important figure in the Ottoman educational system and would serve as the first director of the School for Tribes.

Recai was born in Istanbul in 1852; his father, Hacı Ahmed Rasih, was a captain in the army.[1] After completing his education at the Eyüb high school (second in his class), he was sent to Mekteb-i Aklam, a school specialized in training bureaucrats.[2] Ranked first in his class at graduation at the age of nineteen, he was assigned to work as a clerk in the same school. In 1873, he was appointed to a post in the library of the Ministry of Education and his salary was doubled to 400 kuruş. The following year, he was given the additional responsibility of teaching the Ottoman language in the prestigious Galatasaray Sultani school. In 1878, following other teaching jobs in the capital, he gained a position at the civil service academy as a French language tutor. His diligence earned him a promotion to the position of assistant director of the civil service academy in 1883,[3] with his salary in this position reaching 2.750 kuruş. He was awarded several medals and ranks during his tenure.

Recai Efendi acted as one of the leaders of a movement which came to be known as *Takviye-i Akaid* (bolstering religious instruction). When he joined the education commission in 1887 as the right hand of the Sheikh al-Islam, one of his first acts was to modify the highly Western curriculum of the prestigious Galatasaray Sultani.[4] He proposed to abolish Latin and philosophy classes and to appoint a qualified member of the ulema to train the students in Islamic principles twice a week.[5] The students at this school, located in the heart of the Western district, were warned to abstain from any immoral behaviour.[6]

The commission of 1887 also decreed that French would be abolished from the junior high-school programme and replaced with additional religious training.[7] While French was retained in the high schools, Arabic was added to the curriculum. New courses were prepared on the biographies of the prophets, the companions of Muhammad and other important Muslim authorities. Morality and Islamic jurisprudence were the other additions to the high-school programme.[8] Another important decision of the commission was to conduct compulsory daily communal prayers in all state schools in the empire.[9] The authorities also deliberated on the success of foreign schools within the empire, discovering that even Muslims had begun to send their children to these schools. State schools numbered as only one-third of the missionary and minority schools, highlighting the urgent call for action.[10] It is interesting to read the comments of an Englishman written in 1888 regarding the state of the education system in the Ottoman world: 'Let us imagine a Mahometan Potentate sending missionaries to England and opening schools denouncing Christianity in London. I doubt if we should bear it silently.'[11]

Recai Efendi was known as a rather strict and authoritarian figure. According to the memoirs of one of the graduates of the civil service academy, some students petitioned Recai Efendi to lower the twenty-five-year minimum age requirement for government postings. In response, he dismissed them, stating that it was none of their business. The petitioning students contacted their elderly relatives who were close to the grand vizier, Said Paşa, and asked them to raise the matter with him. Said Paşa found the request reasonable and sent the petition to the minister. When Recai Efendi heard of this development, he became furious and wanted to expel the students. One of his colleagues, Zihni Efendi, who had travelled to Mecca with Recai Efendi for their pilgrimage, intervened on behalf of the students. The students thereupon spread a rumour that during their pilgrimage, it was Zihni and Recai Efendi's camel that became *Hacıs* (those who earn the title of pilgrim).[12]

On 17 September 1892, just before the inauguration of the School for Tribes, Recai was appointed as the school's director, while also retaining his position in the civil service academy. Hüseynizade Abdulmuhsin Efendi from Beirut became the assistant director.¹³ On 29 September, Recai's salary was increased from 4,000 to 6,000 kuruş, and he received an additional payment of 1,000 kuruş for his transportation expenses to the school.¹⁴

However, the tenure of Hacı Recai Efendi as director of the School for Tribes was extremely short; it appears that he preferred to place one of his protégés from the civil service academy in the position of director of this novel institution. The sultan's decree dated 3 October 1892, stated that Recai Efendi had stepped down from the directorship of the School for Tribes, forsaking his increased salary, but would continue in his post as the assistant director of the academy.¹⁵ Recai Efendi was replaced by Ali Nazima, and the first mention of the new director in the newspapers appeared shortly thereafter, on 17 October 1892, when he distributed the first stipends of 30 kuruş to the students.¹⁶

According to his official biography, Mehmed Ali Nazima Bey was born in Istanbul in 1861.¹⁷ His grandfather, Arif, was one of the first graduates of the medical school and was sent to Vienna to complete his studies.¹⁸ His father, Ahmed Servet, also became a doctor, but he combined his medical career with governmental positions and became a district administrator. Ahmed Servet was also one of the founders of the Ottoman Red Crescent organization. Like Recai Efendi, Ali Nazima was sent to the prestigious Mekteb-i Aklam to be trained for government service. Subsequently, he studied for five years at the Galatasaray Mekteb-i Sultani and for one more year at the civil service academy. He was fluent in French and familiar with Arabic and Persian. In 1882, he was appointed as an Ottoman language instructor in the Mekteb-i Sultani with a salary of 400 kuruş. One year later, he received an additional posting (and salary) as an assistant in the translation bureau of the Sublime Porte. In 1884, he moved to the Ministry of Foreign Affairs. In the following year, he found an additional job at the academy as a tutor. In 1888, he received an official permit to establish his own private school, named Mekteb-i Edeb.¹⁹

As mentioned above, Ali Nazima left his other positions and was appointed as the director of the School for Tribes in 1892. His passionate speeches at the royal picnics in 1893 and 1894 were presented in Chapter 1. The efforts of Ali Nazima and his colleagues to develop and apply the curriculum, as well as the good performance of the students, was recognized by the minister of education, who wrote a memorandum to the palace in September 1894 requesting to reward them as follows:

> The School for Tribes has completed the second-year final examinations and the results are presented in the attached booklet (below) prepared by the administration of the school. The grades achieved in the examinations and my personal visit to the school have shown me that the level of knowledge of the students is increasing every day. I would like to propose to present to the attached list of staff and teachers who have worked tirelessly for the last two years the specified medals as a reward.
>
> | Ali Nazima bey | Director | 4th Osmani medal |
> |---|---|---|
> | Abdulmuhsin bey | Assistant Director | 4th Mecidi medal |
> | Nureddin | Tutor | 4th Mecidi medal |
> | Reşid-Accountant,Tutors-Ahmed, Musa, Kaşif, Zeki 5th Mecidi medal | | |
> | Asım | Scribe | Promotion to Level 5[20] |

In 1895, Hacı Recai Efendi was promoted to the coveted position of director of the civil service academy. He requested that his protégé, Ali Nazima, be appointed in his place as assistant director in the academy, which was accepted.[21] On 14 March 1895, Ali Nazima's assistant director, Abdulmuhsin Efendi, replaced him as the third director of the School for Tribes.

Recai Efendi and Ali Nazima worked closely at the academy, and when Sultan Abdülhamid inaugurated the university, Darülfünun, both educators were rewarded with additional positions. While keeping directorship of the academy, Recai Efendi was also appointed as the director of the university in September 1900. Nazima was given the role of assistant director of some departments of the new institution. Both men kept all these posts until Sultan Abdülhamid was deposed in 1909. Recai Efendi then retired, but Ali Nazima continued an active career into the republican period. Two significant differences between these educators were that unlike Recai Efendi, Ali Nazima began writing and publishing educational books early in his career, and he was well-liked and respected by his cohorts.

It is worth examining briefly Ali Nazima's oeuvre, which consists of over seventy-five books, including textbooks, dictionaries and works written for

Figure 3.1 Decorative booklet (front-back cover, 3 pages report card) sent to the palace containing exam results, Ottoman Archives, Y-EE.-D 962, 14 August 1894.

children. He followed the trend of publications in the West and emphasized the importance of producing works which would be enjoyed and easily read by students. This was in contrast with most written material in the Ottoman Empire at the time, which used a flowery style including complicated Arabic and Persian phrases. Ali Nazima's second book was dedicated to physical exercise and workouts,[22] in which he stated that although many new textbooks had been published during the reign of Sultan Abdülhamid, nothing was available on the subject of sports, crucial for the healthy development of the young generation. However, this book was banned by the palace in 1896 because some of the pictures on the cover were deemed to conflict with Islamic tenets.[23] In another book, *A Garden for Children*,[24] he emphasized the significance of spacious and well-lit classrooms, with maps and pictures on the walls. He encouraged the tutors and students to use blackboards and suggested the allocation of a plot in the gardens for the youngsters to learn how to grow plants. A later book titled *Look and Learn*[25] is a collection of 650 pictures that aim to teach pupils basic sciences.

In 1909, Ali Nazima continued his career as a Turkish language tutor at the university. In 1910, he published a book dedicated to the Young Turk revolution with the title: *10 July Learning about Civilization*.[26] In this text, he elaborated on the concepts of liberty, equality and fraternity as well as the definition of civic terms like the parliament, municipality and ministry of education.[27] His last book was a Turkish-French mini-dictionary published in 1912. In 1916, he was appointed as the director of the newly opened University for Women.[28] Ali Nazima continued working in various governmental posts but had to retire because of his age in 1925. However, he kept on teaching students at the American and French schools in Istanbul until his death in 1935.

In 1899, Ahmed Midhat, a leading columnist and opinion maker wrote the following description of Ali Nazima in the Tarik newspaper:

> Our lives are full of debates and discussions. Poets, writers, philosophers write pages and pages adamantly defending their views. Do you ever come across the name Ali Nazima in this crowd? No. This is not because he is not present. On the contrary, Ali Nazima is well-known and famous. However, he never stoops to engage in such fiery battles. His name shines on serious books prepared to educate and train our young ones. Have you met him or seen him? No, because he is not eager to promote himself.[29]

One of his long-time colleagues, Şahap Nazmi Coşkunlar, wrote that his good friend Ali Nazima educated thousands of students and during his fifty-four years of teaching was only late to his class three times due to extenuating circumstances.[30]

Hüseynizade Abdulmuhsin Efendi, who had been the assistant director of the School for Tribes since its foundation, replaced Ali Nazima as the school's next director in March 1895. Abdulmuhsin Efendi represented a different profile than the previous two directors. He was born in 1851 in Jerusalem, the son of Muhammad Amin Efendi.[31] According to his official biography, he began his education in Jerusalem and then was sent to Istanbul to study at the civil service academy.[32] He became proficient in Turkish and Arabic and was assigned to his hometown as a tutor in the Kudüs-i Şerif high school with a salary of 315 kuruş in 1872. Within a couple of years, he was able to increase his salary to 1,000 kuruş. In 1884, he was given an additional post in the education administration of Jerusalem. In September 1885, Abdulmuhsin Efendi was transferred to Benghazi, Libya, as assistant prosecutor at the Court of First Instance. He was given letters of commendation from the vali of Benghazi, Musa Kazım Paşa, as well as from the minister of justice, Cevdet Paşa. Abdulmuhsin Efendi's next assignment was to the finance administration of Beirut in 1888, where he was promoted to fifth rank.

On 17 September 1892, Abdulmuhsin Efendi, probably due to his language skills and good connections, was appointed as the assistant director of the newly formed School for Tribes in the capital. After working with Ali Nazima, Abdulmuhsin Efendi became the third director of the school in 1895, and his salary was increased to 2,000 kuruş. A few months later, he also took on the tutorship of the Arabic and Ottoman law classes, for which he received an additional 400 kuruş. On 15 June 1896, Zeki Paşa, the minister of military schools, wrote to the minister of education praising Abdulmuhsin as a devoted and diligent servant[33] and suggesting that he be promoted to second rank. This prompted an investigation into his past services, and it was reported that since he had reached third level only three years earlier, he must wait for one more year to receive the next rank.[34]

In September 1897, the newspapers announced that Abdulmuhsin Efendi had attended the farewell ceremony of the departing students. During this ceremony the student who earned first place in the graduating class, Ahmed

Cemil, gave a long speech about the new world as noted previously. At the end of the ceremony, in accordance with Hacı Recai Efendi's tenets, the Persian instructor of the school, Zeki Efendi, recited prayers in Arabic and all the students chanted *Padişahım Çok Yaşa* and reiterated their allegiance to the sultan. The director of the school accompanied the students to their ship.[35]

On 14 December 1900, the grand vizier wrote to the ministers of interior, education and military schools informing them that the sultan had issued instructions to dismiss Abdulmuhsin Efendi from his position as director of the School for Tribes, and to reassign him to a post in the provinces. The reason cited was Abdulmuhsin's display of dissident attitudes and actions.[36] It appears that someone had filed a complaint about him to the palace. The minister of interior promptly replied to the grand vizier that Abdulmuhsin would be transferred to Diyarbakir and asked permission to adjust his directorship salary of 2,300 kuruş to 2,000 in consideration of his new position.[37] The grand vizierate did not reply. Abdulmuhsin travelled to Diyarbakır, but when he arrived discovered that there was no job waiting for him. In a state of desperation, he sent the following telegram to Zeki Paşa, minister of military schools:

> As instructed by the ministry of gendarmerie, I arrived in Diyarbakır with my children and dependents after a rather dangerous journey. However, the governor had no knowledge about my new position. As I ran out of funds, I am now in dire straits. In the name of the sultan, I beg you to extricate me from this state.[38]

Zeki Paşa wrote to the grand vizier regarding Abdulmuhsin's predicament and three days later, the grand vizier received written confirmation from the palace that Abdulmuhsin's salary in his new post in Diyarbakır would be 2,000 kuruş. This was confirmed in writing to the minister of interior.[39] The extensive centralization of decision-making and the sluggishness of the bureaucracy in the Ottoman Empire are evident in this episode. It also never became clear who reported on Abdulmuhsin's supposed deviant behaviour.

After Abdulmuhsin's tenure, Nadir Efendi, a tutor who had been working at the school for several years, became its new director. The only information about Nadir Efendi found in the archives is that he was not given the 500 kuruş salary raise to match his predecessor, but only received a raise of 150 kuruş. The balance was distributed to some other personnel.[40] Four and a half years later, on 26 October 1905, Nadir was replaced by Major Kamil Efendi, who had been serving as his assistant since 30 March 1904.[41] The director of the Damascus military school, Major Mustafa Aziz Efendi, was appointed as the new assistant director.[42] The *Tercüman-ı Hakikat* reported on 14 September 1906, that several staff members at the school, including Kamil Efendi, had contributed donations for the Hijaz railway.[43] On 17 January 1907, Kamil Efendi was demoted to become a school inspector, and Major Mustafa Aziz Efendi replaced him as the last director of the School for Tribes.[44] It appears that once the curriculum and the system of the school were established, the role of the director became that of an overseer to maintain the status quo.

Curriculum of the school for tribes

Classes at the School for Tribes began on 5 October 1892. Hacı Recai Efendi was the architect of the school's first curriculum. It was jointly decided that, because the backgrounds of the students were unknown, it would be best to design with a two-year programme, which would be eventually expanded to five. The two-year curriculum presented to the grand vizier on 11 July 1892, and adopted at the inauguration of the school, can be seen below. For these initial years, the emphasis was on teaching the Turkish language and introducing the students to basic Islamic religious training. They would also begin to learn mathematics and acquire elementary calligraphy skills.

FIRST-YEAR COURSE PROGRAMME

Elif-ba	The alphabet will be taught by using a blackboard. Other courses will not begin until the students are comfortable with the alphabet.
Ecza-ı Şerife	All thirty chapters of the Quran will be read by all the students.
Kıraat	Basic texts on moral instruction and on the names of God will be read in Ottoman Turkish and written on the board for memorization.
Hesab	After learning numbers, the four arithmetic operations will be practiced.
Hatt-ı Rika	Introduction to standard calligraphy.

SECOND-YEAR COURSE PROGRAMME

Quran	After the recitations for daily prayers are memorized, the students will practice the Quran.
Ilmihal	Concise manual of Islamic faith, worship and ethics will be mastered.
Kıraat ve Imla	Reading skills will be improved; basic writing will be practiced on the board.
Hesab	Students will proceed with arithmetic skills, including fractions.
Hatt-ı Rika	To be instructed according to the established method used in high schools.

It was added in a footnote that priority was to be given to Turkish instruction.

The curriculum for the last three years was later prepared by Ali Nazima and his colleagues and presented to the ministry on 9 June 1894.[45] This curriculum clearly reflected the educational philosophy of Recai Efendi. Memorizing the Quran, recitation and religious instruction classes were given priority in every year. The other courses for the third year were as follows: The life stories of the prophets, Turkish grammar, vocabulary, reading and writing skills, mathematics, geography and French. The fourth year curriculum included Arabic and Persian language instruction, with the history of Islam listed as a separate course. In the final year, the students were to continue to improve their language and writing skills. In addition, they were introduced to the standard textbook on the history of the Ottoman Empire. The fifth-year programme also included classes in Turkish discourse and in geometry. It was explicitly stated in the curriculum that loyalty to the exalted office of the caliphate should be instilled in the students.

The strenuous curriculum presented difficulties for many students. From the first year onwards, many students failed and were either dismissed or left of their own accord. Five students from the first group of thirty-three were asked not to return at the end of the first year. At least three others did not show up the following September of their own volition. The detailed report card issued at the end of the second year on 18 August 1894, which lists a total of seventy-one students, shows the following grades:[46]

Outstanding (*Fevkalade*)	1
Excellent (*Ala ül Ala*)	20

Fair (*Ala*) 25
Pass (*Karib-i Ala*) 19
Fail (*Zayıf*) 6

The document also notes that seven students needed to retake an exam in orthography, three had to repeat the exam in arithmetic, and one student was sick during the exam period.

At some point in the following years, the school switched to a numeric grading system (from 1 to 10, ten being the highest). The 1896 report card shows a breakdown for the five classes, with a grade for each course and a total score for each student. The first class of twenty-three students had seven subjects, and no one was able to get a full score of seventy (the lowest score was thirty-three). They were instructed in calligraphy, Turkish writing, orthography, vocabulary, arithmetic, introduction to religion and the Quran.

The second class with thirty-one students had eight courses, and four students received the full mark of eighty (the lowest was thirty-eight). Their subjects were religion, Turkish writing, the Quran, orthography, arithmetic, calligraphy, recitation and vocabulary. The third class with twenty-eight students had ten courses, with six students reaching the total score of 100 (the lowest score was sixty-two). The courses they attended included calligraphy, arithmetic, Turkish writing, the Quran, Islamic history, orthography, Ottoman grammar, recitation, Ottoman geography and religion.

The fourth class had eleven courses, and two students out of twenty got the full grade of 110 (the lowest score was seventy-nine). The subjects were Ottoman history, geography, calligraphy, Ottoman grammar, general knowledge, Turkish writing, arithmetic, recitation, religion, Arabic and Persian. The fifth class of the most advanced twenty-six students (they had arrived in the first and second year of the school's operation) had to take fifteen courses, and two students were able to get the full score of 150 (the lowest score was 110). Their courses in the order listed were as follows: geography, Ottoman history, calligraphy, general knowledge, recitation, Algebra, religion, Turkish writing, health, law, Arabic, art, geometry, accounting, Persian.[47]

As mentioned earlier, Benedictsen, the Danish scholar who visited the school in December 1897 reported that he tested the students in mathematics and found them very advanced.[48] The curriculum was modified slightly during the school's remaining years of operation. A new course was introduced in 1896 for the fourth and fifth years, titled General Knowledge.[49] The fifth-year students also began to be instructed in health and hygiene. In 1899, two new courses were added, calligraphy in the French language (Latin script) and painting, which were taught by Hamdi Efendi, the Ottoman calligraphy tutor.[50] However, in 1901, French instruction was removed from the fourth and fifth years, and in 1903 it was eliminated completely.

The *Tercüman-ı Hakikat* reported on 16 May 1902: 'The Caliph has found it appropriate that like other high schools, the School for Tribes should include gymnastics in its curriculum. Kolağası Tevfik bey, one of the gymnastics tutors at the military academy, has been accordingly assigned to the school.'[51] The five-year curriculum published in the 1903 yearbook of the ministry of education is summarized below and shows that gymnastics classes were added at all levels.

First Year: Quran, Elif-Ba, Religion, Turkish, Gymnastics.
Second Year: Quran, Recitation, Religion, Turkish Reading and Writing, Arithmetics, Calligraphy, Gymnastics.
Third Year: Quran, Recitation, Religion, History of Islam, Turkish, Arithmetic, Calligraphy, Geography, Gymnastics.
Fourth Year: Quran, Recitation, Religion, Arabic, Turkish, Persian, Ottoman History, Geography, Arithmetics, Geometry, Ottoman Law, Gymnastics.
Fifth Year: Quran, Recitation, Religion, Arabic, Persian, Ottoman History, Ottoman language, Geography, Algebra, Geometry, Health and Sanitation, Ethics, Turkish Writing, Gymnastics.[52]

One of the school's prominent graduates, Omar Mansour from Libya (discussed in Chapter 5), included a detailed account of the curriculum and the tutors in his memoirs:

> The curriculum included Turkish, Arabic, Persian, French, Mathematics, Geography, History, and Calligraphy. Some of the teachers were religious, while others were secular, such as Nadir Beik, the French language teacher, and Ali Nureddin, the history and ethics teacher, who was later appointed as a judge in Benghazi and then in Beirut. Kaşif Efendi was the religious science, Quran and exegesis teacher. Tawfiq Efendi was the geography teacher. Ibrahim Beik Adham taught geometry and drawing. Abdulmuhsin

Beik al-Hüseyni, the former public prosecutor of Benghazi, was the teacher of morphology and grammar for Arabic. Ali Nazima Beik was the teacher of morphology and grammar for Turkish and the school director. Hamdi Beik was the calligraphy teacher. He was one of the most prominent calligraphers of the palace.[53]

Curriculum of the military and civil service academies

As described earlier, a special one-year training programme to prepare the graduates of the School for Tribes for their future careers was initiated in the military and civil service academies in 1896. Both of these schools normally admitted students who had completed their seven-year high school education. Both academies offered their students a three-year programme. An exceptional training of one year was designed for the sons of the tribal chiefs.

The weekly curriculum of the special class for the graduates who attended the military academy consisted of a total of twenty-three hours as follows:[54]

> War Tactics and Mobilization, Writing – 3 hours each per week (six hours)
>
> Religion, Drill – Theory and Practice, Fortification, Military Geography, Map Drawing – 2 hours each per week (ten hours)
>
> Military Training, Army Organization, Military Regulations, Sword Training, Hygiene and Health, Topography, Chemistry – 1 hour each per week (seven hours)

The integration of the students into the military academy programme was swift; students began classes on the day of their arrival. There are several records of the students being taken out to the well-known Silahtarağa grounds for training.[55]

In contrast to this disciplined approach of the military school, the civil service academy was reprimanded for keeping the new students waiting. The minister of military schools wrote on 15 October 1896 that the graduates sent from the School for Tribes to the civil service academy were treated as visitors and not given any instruction.[56] Three days after this letter, the academy issued a special one-year curriculum prepared for the graduates and started their classes.⁵⁷ As would be expected, the curriculum included a heavy emphasis on religious studies (*Ilm-i Kelam, Tefsir, Hadis*). Turkish grammar and writing, calligraphy, Arabic and Persian courses were continued. In addition, there were special courses on the civil code, law and administration methods.⁵⁸

The curriculum administered to the students reflects two important themes of the Hamidian period. First, the School for Tribes presents a good example of the concept of the 'Ottomanization of the Sharia'. The codification of Hanefi law into a modern format to be utilized in all the courts of the empire was completed in the first years of Sultan Abdülhamid's reign. The *Mecelle*, as this corpus of sixteen volumes was called, remained in force in numerous Arab countries for many decades after the demise of the Ottoman Empire. Ahmed Cevdet Paşa, the primary author of this work, states that it was imperative to organize the loose practices of religion and public conduct into a written form to join the civilized and advanced countries. Deringil compares the School for Tribes with the Russian efforts to integrate their non-Russian subjects and the struggle of the British to 'create an indigenous elite who would be Indian in blood and colour, but English in taste, in opinion, in morals and intellect'.⁵⁹ The curriculum clearly incorporated all the features of the *Takviye-i Akaid* movement to train the students as proper Muslims, as defined by the state.

Second, the curriculum of the school signified the critical issue of language for the centralizing of the state. The virtues of Ottoman tolerance for language and religion in the Balkan territories have been a frequent source of discussion. Even before the Ottomans conquered the Arab lands, learning the language of the Quran was imperative for the elites of the empire. However, in the nineteenth century, when the Ottoman state attempted to extend its authority to all corners of its vast lands, the lack of a common language presented a significant barrier. After the *Mecelle* was codified, all courts in the empire were expected to conduct their business and file reports in Turkish, which was not practical in the Arab provinces, as the citizens frequently could not speak the language. In the School for Tribes, the Ottoman state had begun the curriculum with an intensive programme in Turkish.

There is no doubt that the students received a rigorous education, which left an imprint on their future careers. The sons of nomadic tribesmen were transformed into an elite corps of Ottomans. As Omar Mansour from Libya stated simply in his memoirs: 'We returned to our hometowns proficient in

Turkish, Persian and Arabic, and familiar with French and the situation in Istanbul, the most important city of the empire.'[60] Travelling back and forth from the provinces to the capital was also part of the education of these youngsters. The following chapters will outline the life stories of some of the prominent graduates. The outstanding careers of these students clearly reflect the high calibre training they received.

4

Life stories – Greater Syria

In 1802, the Wahhabis occupied Mecca and their leader, Saud, personally led the pilgrims during the annual *Hajj* (pilgrimage) ceremonies, dealing a significant blow to Ottoman claims to the Caliphate. In 1804, the Wahhabis also captured Medina, where the Prophet and his companions are buried. The sultan asked the governor of Egypt, Mehmed Ali, to cleanse the holy cities of the invaders. In 1812 after a great deal of fighting, Mehmed Ali was able to reclaim Mecca and Medina. In 1821, Mehmed Ali helped the sultan put down the Greek rebellion and then demanded Syria for himself, but Istanbul ignored his request. In retaliation, Mehmed Ali sent his son Ibrahim at the head of a modern army and defeated the Ottomans badly. As a result, the sultan was forced to hand over Syria, the Hijaz and Crete to the Egyptians in 1833. It was only through the intervention of Britain in 1840 that Mehmed Ali was obliged to withdraw to Egypt, and the Ottomans were able to restore their claims to Syria and the Holy Lands.

The Ottomans attempted to re-establish and maintain control in the region with their modernized army, as well as steam vessels, railroads and telegraph lines, and by modifying the relationship between the centre and the periphery. Settling the nomads and expanding the agricultural base became a constant goal during this period. A sustainable peace and order was critical to enable the trade volume to expand in the region. An important milestone was the land reform of 1858, which gradually changed traditional rural relationships. Regulation to reorganize the provinces in 1864 brought about significant changes in the structure of the empire. Mehmed Raşid Paşa served as governor of the newly created province of Syria for five years (1866–71). He established a local council, composed of elected representatives from all the *sanjaks* (districts), which prioritized road construction and investments in education.[1]

The first years of Sultan Abdülhamid's rule were marred by the disastrous Balkan wars.² However, Abdülhamid was determined to strengthen the links between Istanbul and the Arab provinces. In 1892, he initiated a project to link Damascus with Medina via telegraph lines, a precursor of the Hijaz railroad. The first telegram from Medina was sent to the sultan on 6 January 1901.³ The Ottomans came to believe that the region presented an enormous opportunity to multiply agricultural production and generate significant revenues for the empire, and the sultan personally acquired vast tracts of land for himself.

The no-man's-land of Deir Ez-Zor

In 2014, the region of Deir ez-Zor, located in eastern Syria on both sides of the Euphrates river and possessing lucrative oil fields, was occupied by ISIS. The December 2017 Chatham House report states that: 'Damascus aims to recruit men from each area and charge them with protecting that area. The regime will assign the task of protecting the Western Deir ez-Zor countryside to men from the local al-Busaraya tribe.'⁴ This was actually a continuation of the involvement of the regime with the al-Busaraya; already in 2007, Bashar al-Assad had visited Deir ez-Zor, where he gave a speech about the importance of local tribes and their role in having resisted the French mandate after the First World War.⁵

It is perhaps not that surprising that in August 1892, Sultan Abdülhamid sent his emissaries to recruit the son of the al-Busaraya chieftain, Shallash al-Abdallah, to the School for Tribes. Like the current Syrian regime, the hope at that time was to utilize the tribes to protect the interests of the Ottoman Empire in the region.

Deir ez-Zor, part of the Aleppo province, was elevated to the status of *sanjak* in 1870. The *sanjak* of Deir ez-Zor consisted of the following subdistricts: Mayadin (Işare), Al Bukamal, Al Busaraya, Al Sabkha (Sence) and Raqqa. In 1871, the governor Arslan Paşa petitioned the sultan to make Deir ez-Zor an autonomous region, a request which was granted.⁶ Arslan Paşa succeeded in convincing many of the nomadic tribes to settle and begin to pay taxes.⁷ The next governor Ömer Şevki Paşa employed an architect and engineer named Ch. S. Aloe to plan and begin the expansion of the city of Deir ez-Zor.

Another notable figure of the period was Muhammad Hilal Efendi, who was born in Aleppo and assigned as deputy *qadi* of Deir ez-Zor in 1870. During his tenure, he wrote a long treatise about the city, which was presented to Sultan Abdülhamid in 1881. Muhammad Hilal began his treatise with a comparison of Deir ez-Zor with Egypt, claiming that the agricultural potential of the region was vast. He suggested building several irrigation canals around the Euphrates, Habur and Balikh rivers and populating this fertile area. Insuring safety of the roads would result in trade caravans travelling between Aleppo and Baghdad, to abandon the longer route via Diyarbakır and revert to Deir ez-Zor. According to Hilal, the al-Busaraya was one of the five clans which composed the Uqaydat tribe of Deir ez-Zor.[8]

Another treatise was presented to Sultan Abdülhamid in 1892 by Kürd Ismail Hakkı Paşa, who visited Deir ez-Zor during his tenure as the governor of Diyarbakır between 1874 and 1876. In his treatise, Ismail Hakkı repeated some of Muhammad Hilal's statements, especially the comparison of Deir ez-Zor to Egypt. Ismail Hakkı recounted his experience of reforming and settling the Aneze and Shammar tribes and explained how the state could benefit from the agricultural income generated as a result. He advocated that state lands should be distributed free of charge to settlers, concluding his plea to the sultan as follows:

> The reform and construction of Deir ez-Zor, will allow the tribes, who are living in a state of nomadism and savagery, to enjoy the taste of good governance and the blessings of civilization. When they settle and begin agricultural production, they will benefit from your charitable investments in education, roads and buildings which are flourishing all around our realm.[9]

This treatise was presented at the time of the foundation of the School for Tribes. Sultan Abdülhamid was hoping to educate and settle the tribes, and a son of the al-Busaraya chieftain from Deir ez-Zor was one of the targets for the School for Tribes in 1892. In fact, the chieftain, Shallash al-Abdallah requested to send not one but two of his sons, Ramadan and Ahmad, to the school, which was accepted. The quota assigned to Deir ez-Zor for that year was four students, so, Muhammad, son of Sultan from the Jabur tribe, and Isa, son of Haj Fahd from the Sabkha tribe, were also recruited. As mentioned in Chapter 2, a fifth student, Turki, was also enrolled from Deir ez-Zor that year.[10] The *Tercüman-ı Hakikat* reported on 20 September 1892 that fourteen students from Deir ez-Zor, Aleppo and Basra arrived in Istanbul, including Ramadan and Ahmad Shallash.

Probably due to the additional student recruited in 1892, the quota for Deir ez-Zor in the second year was reduced to two students.[11] It appears that even this low quota was not fulfilled. Nevertheless, in June 1894, the quota for the third year was raised to five. The fluctuation in the number of students can be further observed in the telegram sent by the governor of Deir ez-Zor to the grand vizierate on 10 August 1894, in which he stated that it was only possible to recruit three students for the coming year instead of five.[12]

The first students from Deir ez-Zor were given the following student identification numbers: Muhammad 21, Isa 22, Ramadan Shallash 23, his brother Ahmad 24 and Turki 25. The school published a report card on 14 August 1894 with the grades of all the students, who were divided into three classes.[13] It appears that Muhammad and Isa were older and put in the third class at this time. Ramadan, Ahmad and Turki were in the second class. The report card indicated that Turki needed to take a second exam in orthography.

The *Tercüman-ı Hakikat* informed its readers on 7 February 1895 that there was a fight between the Arab and Kurdish students in the School for Tribes. According to Omar Mansour, the chief culprit in this commotion was Ramadan Shallash from Deir ez-Zor, who got into a 'fierce fight with the guard'.[14] Ramadan's temperamental nature did not prevent him from graduating with honours in 1897, whereupon he chose to attend the special training at the military academy. He then served in the Upper Euphrates region, either in the regular army or in the special Hamidiye Cavalry brigade.[15] After some years, Shallash was transferred to the Balkan front where he commanded a unit of Palestinians.[16] In 1909, he joined the Literary Society in Istanbul.[17] The society organized lectures given by Arab members of parliament. Many members of this organization would later form the Arab Club of Damascus.[18]

In 1911, Shallash volunteered to go to Libya. During the difficult struggle against the Italian colonizers, Shallash met several Arab officers serving in the Ottoman army as well as Mustafa Kemal (Ataturk). The Ottomans in Libya joined forces with the tribes to counter the invaders by waging a guerrilla war. It was in Libya that Ramadan Shallash was first exposed to the training and organizing of local fighters into regular units.

After the defeat in Libya in 1912, Shallash was assigned to serve in Medina. Dr. Talal Chalch (youngest son of Ramadan Shallash) recounted that his father 'enjoyed close and intimate relations' with Sharif Husayn, the famous Amir of Hijaz.[19] On 4 March 1916, the leaders of the Committee of Union and Progress, Enver and Cemal Paşa, arrived in Medina on the Hijaz railroad and decorated Sharif Husayn with medals. However, only months later, Sharif Husayn came to terms with the British and began the Arab revolt, ejecting the Ottomans from Mecca. It was during these months that Ramadan Shallash voluntarily left the Medina garrison for Mecca and joined the army of Sharif Husayn. However, he was suspected of being an Ottoman spy and was sentenced to death, only to be pardoned through the personal intervention of Sharif Husayn, who then appointed him his adjutant.[20] It is worth noting that unlike Shallash, who joined the revolt of his own accord, most other well-known Arab officers were recruited from the British prisoner of war camps.[21]

Ramadan Shallash remained with Husayn in Hijaz until the armistice on 30 October 1918 at the end of the war, when he joined Sharif Husayn's son, Abdallah, in Aqaba. However, he had a 'dispute with a British officer, whom he struck with a riding whip'.[22] Abdallah had to dismiss his volatile aide, and Shallash went to Damascus to meet Yusuf al-Azma and Yasin al-Hashimi, who were commanding the army of Sharif Husayn's elder son, Faisal.

On 6 November 1918, in accordance with the terms of the armistice, the remainder of the Ottoman army left Deir ez-Zor and the region became, in the words of Arnold Wilson, British Commissioner in Iraq, 'now as in the past, a no-man's-land between Syria and Mesopotamia'.[23] While the British had effectively taken control in Iraq, Faisal had declared his Arab constitutional government in Damascus. As the borders between Iraq and Syria were unclear, the population of Deir ez-Zor appealed to the Arab government to include them in Syria. A camel corps led by Ali Riza al-Askari was sent from Aleppo to occupy Deir ez-Zor, and Mar'i al-Mallah was appointed the Arab governor. Askari had served in the Ottoman army, and al-Mallah had previously represented Aleppo in the Ottoman Parliament. The locals were unhappy with the Aleppine troops dressed in Ottoman uniforms, and at the end of November 1918, secretly sent a note to the British asking them to annex Deir ez-Zor.[24]

As a result, the British sent Captain Carver to Albu Kamal, situated 120 kilometres south of Deir ez-Zor. Carver was surprised to be greeted there by an Arab administrator, who claimed he had been appointed by the new governor of Deir ez-Zor. When Carver reported the situation to Baghdad, Commissioner Wilson sent a telegram to the India Office. The Foreign Office there replied that although the status of Deir ez-Zor was 'hazy', Albu Kamal definitely belonged to British Iraq. Reinforcements were sent from Baghdad and the British entered Deir ez-Zor on 14 January 1919.

In February, Ramadan Shallash returned to his homeland on behalf of the secret society al-Ahd based in Damascus. He toured the lands of the Shammar, Aneze and other tribes, encouraging them to reject the rule of the British imperialists and collected letters from local notables declaring their loyalty to the Arab government of Damascus. In September 1919, the al-Ahd society decided to launch the Iraqi revolt against the British and chose the no-man's-land of Deir ez-Zor as their new base. The Arab high command in Damascus appointed Ramadan Shallash as the military governor of the Raqqa region and instructed him to occupy Deir ez-Zor. Amir Zeyd, the brother of Faisal, gave Shallash over thirty signed letters addressed to the tribal chiefs, requesting that they support the new military governor.[25] On December 10, the British contingent in Deir ez-Zor got news of the approaching attack by Shallash and telegraphed Baghdad for help.

The next day, the tribal forces captured Deir ez-Zor and surrounded the small group of British officers and soldiers in the military barracks.[26] Around noon of the same day, two military planes from Mosul arrived and began aerial bombardment. The atmosphere quickly changed, and both sides agreed to a twenty-four-hour truce, but in the afternoon, Ramadan Shallash entered the town with his men and raised the Arab flag from the government building. Before releasing the besieged British squadron, he wanted assurances that the British would not attack Deir ez-Zor. On December 12, Shallash sent letters to the regional tribal sheikhs demanding that they join the Arab government and fight the British invaders. Shallash wrote: 'It is your duty to do this according to the requirements of the Muslim religion, patriotism and Arab sagacity. This is your only chance to liberate yourselves from the infidels.'[27]

Shallash continued his attacks on the British and captured Mayadin on December 13 and Albu Kamal the next day. However, on December 21, the British retaliated and reoccupied Albu Kamal. Interestingly, when Faisal, in Paris at this time, was informed about the developments, he refused to acknowledge Shallash's ventures and wrote: 'Those responsible for this action are rebels and will be punished as outlaws.'[28] Faisal then sent a telegram to his brother Zeyd in Damascus, telling him to immediately dismiss Shallash and release the British soldiers. It was reported that Faisal wrote that 'people like Ramadan Shallash were revolutionaries who deserved the stick.'[29] An Arab contingent from Aleppo arrived in Deir ez-Zor on 21 December 1919.

To the astonishment of the Arabs, the British Commissioner Wilson informed them that according to a new agreement with France, Britain would no longer be involved in Deir ez-Zor. On the same day, a British plane dropped leaflets over Deir ez-Zor, stating that if the hostages were released in forty-eight hours, there would be no punitive action. On December 25, Christmas day, the British hostages departed from Deir ez-Zor and joined their comrades in Albu Kamal. However, Shallash would not stop. He incited the tribes to rebel against the British and attacked Albu Kamal on 11 January 1920, looting the town with his men. The British hastily sent a squadron and aircraft to defend Albu Kamal, and the Arabs retreated to Mayadin once again.

At the same time, the Damascus government sent a brigade from Aleppo to Deir ez-Zor to oust Shallash. Mawlud Mukhlis was appointed as the new governor, and Shallash was forced to report to Aleppo.[30] In May, the Arabs and the British agreed that the Khabur river border should be revised so that Albu Kamal remained within the Deir ez-Zor province of Syria, almost identical with what the Ottoman borders of the province had been. This remains the border between Syria and Iraq today.

In June 1920, Faisal convinced Shallash to go to Najd in central Arabia as his emissary to Ibn Saud. On July 24, the French army defeated the Arabs in Maysalun and entered Damascus, ending Faisal's rule, and by October 1920, the French had also completely subdued Deir ez-Zor.[31] In 1921, Ramadan Shallash returned to his village al-Shumatiyya in Deir ez-Zor to lead a peaceful life with his family for a couple of years.

Ramadan Shallash, national hero or collaborator?

By 1925, the French believed that they finally had their mandate over Syria under control, but the flames that rose from Jabal Druze were to spread like wildfire all around the country and continued for two years. The Great Syrian Revolt, like the Turkish war of independence, started in the provinces.[32] The participation of different segments of the population in the struggle against the colonizers boosted the establishment of a Syrian national identity. On 19 July 1925, the Druze in Jabal Hawran shot down a French plane, and the next day Sultan al-Atrash, the leader of the Druze fighters, attacked the French troops and occupied Salkhad. On August 23, in collaboration with nationalists, al-Atrash distributed a letter in the capital, which he signed as commander of the Syrian Revolutionary Army, urging all Damascenes to rise against 'the usurper'. He demanded the complete independence of Arab Syria and wrote 'Let us wipe out this insult in blood. Our war is a holy war.' But the uprisings in Damascus were quelled by the French, who also bombarded Jabal Druze.[33]

However, the fight against the colonizers was not over. On October 4, hundreds of rebels led by former Ottoman officer Fawzi al-Qawuqji and supported by the Mawali tribesmen occupied the city of Hama. The French retaliated viciously by severely bombing all parts of the town. Urged by the notables of the city, who wished to protect themselves and the city, the rebels eventually withdrew. On the outskirts of Hama, Qawuqji joined forces with Ramadan Shallash, who had arrived to help the insurgents, and in the following weeks, different groups began guerrilla attacks in and around Damascus. Shallash wrote letters to villagers demanding that they join the struggle. Below is one of these letters:

> To the mukhtars and shaykhs of the village of Qutayfa,
>
> Greetings and blessings of God.
>
> We need you to gather your *mujahidin* (fighters) and leave one part to guard your village from the [French] troops and bring the other part to Yabrud tomorrow for the greater glory of the religion of Islam. If you bring them late, you will be responsible before God and before the partisans. If you do not respond to this appeal, and assemble [the mujahidin] today, we will come and take them tomorrow.
>
> 14 October 1925, General Ramadan Shallash[34]

Qawuqji and Shallash quickly moved to the capital and supported Nasib al-Bakri's forces in the attack on the Azm Palace, the residence of the French high commissioner, on October 18.[35] That night, the French began the forty-eight-hour bombardment of Damascus, leaving entire quarters flattened. Shallash criticized the French as follows:

> With cannons and aeroplanes you bombed a large city like Damascus without any warning: this has turned all of Syria against you and irritated the whole Muslim world and made you a laughing stock of nations, because you forgot the simplest of international laws.[36]

Once again, the notables of the city, including the Azm family, interceded and agreed to pay a hefty fine to the French authorities as a penalty. Nevertheless, the bombing of Damascus resulted in the dismissal of the French commander, who was replaced by Henry de Jouvenel, a journalist by profession and the first civil High Commissioner.

The revolution, however, could not be quelled. All around Damascus, the local population protested the mandate regime in various ways. The southern part of Damascus was cut off from any outside contact, with the rebels blocking roads, trains and telephone lines. Al-Atrash arrived with his troops from Jabal Druze to support the insurgents. In November, Ramadan Shallash organized attacks on the French barracks, and the rebel leaders began to call themselves joint commanders of the National Army.[37] They began pillaging government buildings in the northern parts of the capital, and Shallash delivered fiery speeches in the squares, comparing their venture to Mustafa Kemal's in Anatolia. The Palestine newspaper reported on November 6:

> Ramadan Paşa Shallash sent 100 people to blow up the bridges on the Damascus-Homs road, all of which were destroyed according to *al-Muqtabas* (newspaper). The rebels were divided into two parts: one group intended to cut off the railway line, and the second was sent to the city of Homs to attack it.[38]

Shallash made strenuous efforts to support the insurgency. He wrote numerous letters to administrators and notables of these villages asking them to send their 'mujahidin' to support the 'holy' cause. He delivered two pleas to the Shishakli family in Duma, north of Damascus, asking them to send 2,000 gold pounds to support the fighters. Another letter was sent to the village of Ma'alula, ordering them to supply him with weapons because he knew that the French had armed the Christians in this village. At the same time, some locals accused Shallash of pillaging their villages for money and ammunition.

Jouvenel, the new high commissioner who had arrived in December, issued press statements confirming his willingness to come to a peaceful agreement with the 'nationalists' and offer amnesty to the 'rebels', but the fighting raged on. French aerial bombardment continued unabated in many parts of the country. Shallash and his comrades were based in Ghouta at this time and organized raids in different locations, cutting communication lines and attacking trains. The French built a ring road around Damascus in two months to serve as a protective shield for the city.

Shallash, in the meantime, had acquired the reputation of a local Robin Hood. However, many other rebel leaders were critical of his unruly behaviour, and he was considered to be a loose cannon. On December 5, the leaders met in the house of the mukhtar of Saqba in Ghouta. According to the minutes of the meeting published later, the complaints of the residents of the villages of Meda, Al-Qassa and Saran al-Awamid concerning the 'acts of vandalism

Figure 4.1 Photo of Shallash in Ghouta.

of Ramadan Shallash' were reported. Shallash was accused of collecting heavy fines for his own pocket from these villages.[39] After a heated debate, it was decided that Shallash was 'transgressing the objectives of the nationalist revolt'.[40] The majority ruled that he should be expelled from their ranks. Two weeks later, Hasan al-Kharrat, entrusted to enforce this decision and one of the main accusers of Shallash, was killed by the French.

Shallash, cut off from his comrades, tried to organize a revolt in his hometown, Deir ez-Zor, but he was unsuccessful. He then attempted to join forces with another rebel leader, Hananu, in Aleppo, which also did not work out. In January 1926, in the outskirts of Hama, Shallash declared to his friends that he would surrender to the French. The Palestine newspaper reported on 2 February 1926:

> The authority officially announced that Ramadan Shallash has submitted to the French and that he had travelled to Beirut with Amir Tamer (his son). According to a bulletin of the Syrian Information Office, the court of Suwayda tried Ramadan Shallash on charges of violating the orders of the high commanders, delinquencies in the villages of Ghouta and the area of al-Nabak and committing some acts that contradict the purposes and principles on which the revolution was founded. The court ruling has stripped him of his titles and obliged him to return to the people what he has taken unlawfully. He was expelled from the Arena of the National Jihad.

Photographs of Shallash with Jouvenel were then released.

Shallash claimed that he would act as a go-between to find an honourable settlement between the French and the nationalists. His rather contradictory position about his relationship with the French was reported in the Palestine newspaper on February 5:

> Ramadan Shallash told the owner of the *al-Ma'rad* (newspaper) in Beirut that he had great hope of reaching an understanding with M. De Jouvenel to obtain Syrian national demands, and that he believes in the necessity of the French mandate, which will preserve Syria's independence and national sovereignty. He also declared that what was reported by the Syrian Information office was sheer lies. Beirut newspapers say that Ramadan Shallash briefed the High Commissioner on important secrets related to the revolution. It was also understood that he would send leaflets to be distributed by French planes inviting the rebels to negotiate with the High Commissioner, who is inclined to meet national demands.[41]

Figure 4.2 *Filistin* newspaper, 2 February 1926.

On 14 February 1926, the *Yarmouk* newspaper published a very long interview with Shallash. The journalist claimed that Shallash was 'frank and sincere and on many occasions took an oath on his integrity, patriotism and loyalty to the Syrian-Arab cause'. Below is the narrative of Shallash from that interview:

I went to Jabal Druze shortly after the revolution where I met Sultan Paşa al-Atrash for the first time. We had a lengthy discussion and I suggested

Figure 4.3 Ramadan Shallash and the French High Commissioner Jouvenel.

the expansion of the front to other parts of Syria. He agreed and I moved to al-Marj with a group of soldiers where Nasib al-Bakri joined me. I took it upon myself to spread the revolution and was performing the task as I saw fit. I had no commander or supervisor. Then they accused me of looting, but in reality, I was the protector of the villages from looters. I am a man of no honor if I took a penny from the beginning of the revolution until the time I surrendered.

Shallash explained that he met with the Ismaili and the Uqaydat sheikhs, who urged him to go to Beirut to broker an agreement between the rebels and the French to stop the bloodshed. Shallash insisted that Jouvenel had given him confirmation that he was ready to reach an understanding with the rebels. Such an agreement did not come to pass, but the French gave Shallash a house and scholarships for his sons. He continued to send letters to his former comrades proposing that they end the insurrection.

Figure 4.4 *Al-Yarmouk* newspaper, 14 February 1926.

On 23 November 1926, Shallash once again went to see Jouvenel. The Palestine newspaper reported that he proposed to the high commissioner that Sharif Ali Haidar be appointed king of Syria. Apparently, Shallash presented three letters to the French at this time, emphasizing that the republican system they had tried during the previous seven years had not worked and that the Syrians could only be united under a member of the Hashemite family. He described himself as an 'Arab military leader who expelled the British in 1919 from Deir ez-Zor and forced them to abandon it for the benefit of Syria'. In this document, Shallash rationalized his surrender as follows: 'I surrendered myself to his Excellency, M. De Jouvenel, in exchange for one condition, namely that France guarantee the rights and interests of the Arab nation in Syria.'[42]

The French eventually crushed the revolt, and most of its leaders spent around ten years in exile. Shallash was held under house arrest in Beirut by the authorities until 1937, and only then he was allowed to return to his village in Deir ez-Zor. His son, Muhammad Amir, attended the Damascus Military Academy and eventually became a major general and chief-of-staff to President Shishakli in Syria. After Shishakli's ouster, Muhammad Amir served as an advisor to the Kuwaiti government. As for Ramadan Shallash, he once again got involved in a skirmish with the French authorities in his village in 1939. He was captured and returned to house arrest in Beirut until 1944, when he was finally released by the British general Edward Spears. He went to Damascus for medical treatment in 1961, where he died on August 21.

The Hawran Druze

Although there are more than one million Druze living in different countries today, many people have never heard about this unique offshoot of the Shiite sect of Islam which originated in the eleventh century. The Fatimid ruler of Egypt, al-Hakim, embraced the Druze doctrine; however, after his mysterious disappearance, the sect was severely persecuted. The Druze escaped eastwards and settled mainly in parts of today's Lebanon. One of the most famous Druze leaders was Fakhr al-Din, who made alliances with the Maronite Christians and the State of Tuscany against the Ottoman Empire and controlled vast holdings in the seventeenth century.[43] In 1711, the new Druze leaders of the region, the Shihab family, ousted the Alam al-Din faction, who migrated to Hawran, Syria, eventually establishing their own Druze mountain there. However, the real expansion of Jabal Druze in Hawran took place after the calamitous wars in Lebanon in the nineteenth century. In 1832, the invading Egyptians dispersed the recalcitrant Druze, many of whom escaped to Hawran. In 1860, the Druze in Mount Lebanon ignited a widespread civil war and attacked the Christians. The harsh response of the Ottomans resulted in the largest exodus of the Druze to their second mountain in Hawran. In fact, when Fuad Paşa arrived in Beirut in July 1860 and summoned the forty-seven Druze rebel leaders, thirty-three of them fled to Jabal Druze.[44]

In 1918, Rustum Haydar, a minister under Faisal in Damascus and Baghdad, described the Druze of Hawran as follows: 'They only differ from the nomadic bedouin in having agriculture and houses of stone; otherwise, there is only a slight difference between them and the roaming tribes in their way of life, the food they eat and their dress. Even their speech is closer to that of the Bedouins than to that of the sedentary Arabs.'[45] The inhabitants of the Jabal 'denominate their clans either with the word *ashira* or with *aila*'.[46]

I have been able to identify the names of five Druze students who were selected to attend the School for Tribes, all of whom came from Jabal Druze in Hawran. Clearly, the Ottoman administration identified the Druze as members of the Muslim Arab tribes whose loyalty they wished to cultivate. Of these five students, Yusuf Kenan, son of Muhammad, arrived from the district of Sala; Muhammad, son of Sheikh Khalil Halabi, came from Ahira; and Muhammad, son of Sheikh Khalil Kiwan, came from Salkhad. The last two students, Fahd and Ali, both belonged to the famous al-Atrash family, and are the focus of this section.

Atrash means deaf in Arabic. According to family legend, one of the ancestors of the Atrash clan was deaf and the epithet stuck. Ismail al-Atrash emerged as a strong man of the region both during the Druze revolt against the Ottomans in 1852 and during the Lebanese civil war in 1860 against the Maronites.[47] Ismail gradually took over leadership of the Jabal Druze from the Hamdan tribe, forging alliances with or fighting the Ottomans as the occasion demanded.[48] Ismail al-Atrash was invited in 1866 to Damascus by the Ottoman Governor Mehmed Reşit Paşa, who recognized him as the new leader of the Jabal.[49] However, he was officially chosen as the *Sheikh al-Mashayik* (Leader) by the Hawran Druze only in 1869, a position the family maintains until today.[50] Ismail died soon thereafter.

Ismail had eight sons, among whom Yahya, Shibli and Ibrahim became Druze leaders in their own right. Although Shibli attempted to take over the leadership after his father, both the Ottomans and most of the Druze elders supported Ibrahim as the next Sheikh al-Mashayik. Ibrahim moved his headquarters to Suwayda in 1882 and was officially appointed as the governor of Jabal Druze and given the rank of paşa.[51]

In 1889, the efforts of Ibrahim to increase tax revenues and establish a dedicated gendarme force made the people of the Jabal rebel against their al-Atrash overlords, in a movement called the *Ammiya* (popular revolt).[52] Ibrahim had to retreat to Damascus, and the Ottomans supported him by sending an army to quell the uprising, reasserting the traditional Ottoman system. However, at the end of the strife, the peasants were given the right to own property and were thus mollified by their transformation into small landholders. When calm had returned to Jabal Druze in 1892, Ibrahim, his brother Yahya, his son Farhan and five other Druze notables were invited to Istanbul. Many documents in the archives refer to this trip. The sultan gave Ibrahim a precious belt worth 150 liras and to each of his companions a purse of 50 liras.[53] In addition, Yahya was promoted to become a senior captain in the Fifth Army cavalry division; and Farhan, became a captain in the same division in March 1893.[54] It should be noted that 1892 was the year Sultan Abdülhamid II inaugurated the School for Tribes in Istanbul, so Ibrahim Paşa and Farhan must have learned about the school during their visit and considered sending their descendants to the capital for their education. Upon the group's return to their hometown, Ibrahim Paşa al-Atrash passed away.

Fahd Al-Atrash and his family

Ibrahim Paşa al-Atrash had four sons: Hamud, Faris, Farhan and Abd al-Ghaffar. Faris and Farhan sent their sons Ali and Fahd al-Atrash together to the School for Tribes in 1894. In the same year, Shibli al-Atrash was appointed governor in place of his brother Ibrahim.[55] The news article below, published in the *Tercüman-ı Hakikat* newspaper, announced the arrival of three young Druze boys in the capital in May 1894:

> The tribal leaders have observed the progress made by the students who have attended the School for Tribes last year and now are very willing to send their sons to the school. The deceased Kaymakam of Jabal Druze Ibrahim Paşa al-Atrash's descendants, Fahd bin Farhan and Ali bin Faris, as well as Yusuf efendi, son of Muhammad Nassar, administrator of the Sala district, submitted petitions which were accepted by the province of Syria. These three students have now arrived in Istanbul accompanied by the gendarme Muhammad Aga.[56]

These students seem to have arrived much later than the typical enrolment calendar, because the semester began in the fall. Still, in August 1894, all the students of the school completed their final examinations and the results were reported officially.[57] Fahd, given a student identification number of 13 (a number

Figure 4.5 Photo of Fahd al-Atrash, Sharifa Zuhur, *Asmahan's Secrets, Woman, War and Song,* University of Texas at Austin, 2000, p. 166.

reassigned to Fahd after an earlier student failed his courses and left the school), managed to pass with an average score.[58] His cousin Ali, whose ID was 57, failed and was required to take another examination in Ottoman orthography. It is most likely that Ali did not return to the school for the second year.

Fahd continued his studies at the school for five years. He is reported to have had 'strong aristocratic features and a bone-crushing handshake'.

In March 1899, *Tercüman-ı Hakikat* published the names of the eight graduates, including Fahd al-Atrash and Omar Mansour, who were admitted to the civil service academy, and nineteen graduates, who were admitted to the military academy.[59] Of the eight graduates to attend the civil academy, six were able to complete the programme and receive their diplomas the following year. The minister of military schools, Zeki Paşa, sent a memorandum to grand vizier Halil Rıfat Paşa in April 1900, requesting the appointments of four graduates to positions of third rank and two graduates to positions of fourth rank; the latter were Fahd and Yusuf Kanaan from Jabal Druze.[60] On 14 May 1900, a news article published in *Tercüman-ı Hakikat* confirmed the appointments, as cited below:

> Six Graduates of the Mülkiye
>
> The students of the School for Tribes who have completed their additional training at the civil service academy have been given ranks in the bureaucracy: Muhammad Fayez, Omer Mansour, Halil Rıfaat and Faris Fayez – third rank as they graduated with high honors, Fahd and Yusuf Kenan – fourth rank as they graduated with honors.[61]

The memorandum below, which was sent from the Ministry of Interior to the Syria province in April 1901, shows that Fahd's actual date of employment was in August 1900:

> Four graduates of the School for Tribes were sent to your province for employment in the civil administration. Their salaries for last year, which accrued from their date of employment on 8 August 1900 until the end of the year, amounts to 14,387 kuruş. This amount is hereby transmitted to your province as a supplement to the 1900 budgetary allocation.[62]

Thus began the bureaucratic career of Fahd as a fourth rank officer in the Ottoman administration in his hometown Suwayda in 1900. Fahd married Alia al-Mundhir from Hasbaya and they had a son named Fuad. Following seven years of service, he was transferred to the Hawran region, and in 1909 he was appointed as an accountant in the provincial administration of Damascus. In 1910, the couple had another son, Farid, and in the same year, Fahd was appointed as the district administrator of Ara.

Dhuqan, the son of Mustafa (another brother of Ibrahim al-Atrash), led the Al-Quraya branch of the family, who were known to be much more rebellious than their cousins in Suwayda. In 1909, Dhuqan al-Atrash was imprisoned for organizing an armed attack against the Busra district, his son Sultan was conscripted into the Ottoman army and sent to the Balkans. Eventually the minister of war, the grand vizier and the sultan all approved Dhuqan's execution.[63] The hanging of Dhuqan al-Atrash was frequently cited by the Druze as a prelude to later executions by Cemal Paşa in Damascus and

Beirut, and also caused his son Sultan al-Atrash to view the Ottoman state as his father's murderer.[64]

During this turbulent period, the CUP decided to award medals to the loyal Atrash family members, namely Fahd, Hamud and Salim al-Atrash.[65] When the First World War started, Salim al-Atrash became leader of Jabal Druze and marched to meet Cemal Paşa in Damascus with 500 of his men, thereby demonstrating his allegiance to the Ottoman state.[66] His cousin Fahd al-Atrash was promoted to become the governor of Hasbaya in December 1914.[67]

Three years later, Fahd was assigned to central Anatolia as administrator of Vezirköprü in Sivas.[68] While it is not clear whether he was the one requesting this appointment due to the intense fighting in the Middle East, what is recorded is that eventually Fahd did not go to Sivas but requested a special permit to travel by train to Damascus in March 1918.[69] Presumably, he asked to be transferred to a more desirable location, because in April, a ciphered edict was dispatched appointing him as the administrator of Demirci in Izmir, confirmed by a longer letter which explained that the former officer of Köprü (read Vezirköprü) had been transferred to Demirci, Izmir.[70] An unusual correspondence followed, when a telegram was sent from the ministry of interior to the vilayet of Aydın stating that the new administrator's name should be corrected as Fahd, not Ferid (they probably never had an Arab kaymakam in Izmir before).[71]

Thus, Fahd al-Atrash moved to Izmir. But soon thereafter, the Greeks invaded the city, and he and his family, fearing for their lives, boarded a ship for Beirut sometime in the early summer of 1919. (In a document dated 1 August 1919, Fahd is already referred to as the previous Kaymakam of Demirci.)[72] When they fled, Fahd's wife Alia was heavily pregnant and their daughter was born during this boat trip on the Mediterranean. She was named Amal, meaning hope.[73] After the family returned to Jabal Druze, Fahd was appointed as a *qadi* in Suwayda during the rule of Faisal in Damascus.

Unfortunately, these were troubled times marked with conflict between the Syrians and the French. In June 1921, a group of revolutionaries, including one Adham Khanjar, attacked a French convoy aiming to assassinate the French high commissioner, General Henri Gouraud, in his automobile.[74] Although the general survived, several high-level members of the French administration were killed or wounded. Khanjar and his companions escaped south, where Khanjar sought refuge in Sultan al-Atrash's village of al-Quraya. In July 1922,

French soldiers arrested Khanjar. Sultan suggested a prisoner exchange: the release of some French soldiers, held captive by the Druze, in return for Khanjar, whom he considered his guest. The French appeared to agree, but after their cohorts were released, they opened fire on Sultan's men and took Khanjar to Damascus, where he was executed. Sultan retaliated by attacking the French, and the troubles in Jabal Druze continued for over a year.

When the French began aerial attacks on Jabal Druze in 1923, Alia al-Atrash, against the wishes of her husband Fahd, decided to flee to Cairo with her three children.[75] It was in Cairo that the family learned about the Great Syrian Revolt, which was ignited by their relative, Sultan al-Atrash. Things came to a boiling point on 3 July 1925 in the town of Suwayda when the Druze protest was met with gunfire by the French.[76] Sultan set out to mobilize the young men in all the surrounding villages to prepare for an organized attack. He argued that there were only 7,000 French soldiers in all of Syria and that a collaborative effort would expel them from the homeland.

The French subsequently dispatched a larger army only to be routed by the now popular rebels on August 3. On August 23, a letter signed by Sultan was distributed in Damascus, calling for the people to revolt against the foreign oppressor, and the next day a coalition force of around one thousand men attacked the capital. However, the French responded with heavy aerial bombardment and dispersed the revolutionaries. This was followed by the arrest of prominent leaders in Damascus who had supported the uprising.

Sultan responded to this attack by sending propaganda letters in the name of 'liberty, fraternity and equality' to all corners of Syria. On October 3, there was an uprising in the city of Hama, led by Fawzi al-Qawuqji, who was in close contact with Sultan. The French responded again with fierce aerial bombardment of the city on the next day. Qawuqji left the town and on his way to Damascus met another graduate of the School for Tribes, Ramadan Shallash, who had come from Transjordan to join the rebels.

Ramadan Shallash from Deir ez-Zor and Ali al-Atrash, son of Faris, had become friends at school in Istanbul, and were to meet again in 1925 when the attacks of the rebels in Damascus brought on a catastrophic reaction.[77] The French bombed the ancient city on October 18 and 19, leaving over 1,500 people dead. Although the Great Syrian Revolt continued for more than a year, the incessant French bombing all around the country and the difficulty in forming a consensus among the rebels finally ended the uprising. Sultan and other insurgents had to spend ten years in exile. Faisal, King of Iraq, supported Sultan throughout his years of exile in Wadi Sirhan. In 1970, Syrian President Hafez Assad honoured Sultan al-Atrash for his historic role in the Syrian Revolution. Sultan's most lasting legacy was probably his slogan: 'Religion is for God, the fatherland is for all.' He died in 1982.

As for the immediate family of Fahd al-Atrash, as stated earlier, Alia settled in Cairo with her three children in 1923. Farid and Amal learnt to play the oud at an early age. Daoud Hosni, a famous musician, was highly impressed by Amal's beauty and her voice and insisted on giving her a stage name. It was, thus, that Amal Al-Atrash became Asmahan.

Fahd remained as *qadi* in Suwayda during the French mandate, while his daughter became a popular singer in Cairo. Farid, her brother, also become well known in Egypt for his recordings and films. In 1940, the British recruited Asmahan as their messenger to Syria to ensure the cooperation of the Druze when the Allied armies moved north to defeat the Vichy/German troops.[78] Asmahan was with General de Gaulle during his triumphal entry into

Figure 4.6 Asmahan, Second photo shows her attending the speech of General De Gaulle at the American University of Cairo, wearing a brooch of the Croix de Lorraine, symbol of Free France, 1941, Zuhur, p. 167.

Damascus. Asmahan then returned to Egypt to star in her second film. As fate would have it, she was never able to complete this film. While the studio was preparing the set for the last scene, Asmahan mysteriously died in a car accident. The film ending was revised by the studio to reveal the sudden death of the beautiful heroine and it became a resounding success. She was only twenty-five years old. Farid al-Atrash was to remain on the music and cinema scene for many years. However, while most Arabs in various countries still listen to the songs of Asmahan and Farid al-Atrash, almost nobody knows that their father was educated in Istanbul in this very special school.

The Merhebis of Akkar

Akkar is a little-known region located in the north of today's Lebanon, extending from the Mediterranean to Western Syria.[79] During the Ottoman period, Akkar was part of the Trablussam administrative centre, and one of its dominant Sunni families was known as the Merhebi. Today there are around 25,000 Merhebis settled in diverse countries from Brazil to Australia. In Lebanon itself, many Merhebis have held political positions as ministers and members of parliament. It is quite interesting that nine young Merhebis attended the School for Tribes, perhaps the highest number from a single family in the school's history. The first Merhebi to be enrolled was Ahmad in 1896.

According to the chronicle of Emir Haidar Shehab, the Merhebi family trace their origins to a strongman named Nasir, who moved to the Akkar region of Northern Lebanon at the beginning of the eighteenth century.[80] His son, Shadid Nasir, known for his courage and horsemanship, gained control of a sizeable area of land and extended his control of the area. Indeed, in the middle of April 1711, instructions were sent from Istanbul to the governor which read as follows:

> Sheikh Shadid Nasir and his cousins, Khalil and Abdulmalik, are villains who live in Akkar in the muqataat of Tripoli. They have gathered forty to fifty mounted men and have started to plunder the villages, seizing tools, fodder and the food of the poor subjects. Furthermore, they hold up travellers, plunder their money and possessions and obstruct the collection of taxes.

The aforementioned villains are to be removed from these locations, exiled to the island of Cyprus and imprisoned in the citadel.[81]

It is not clear if Shadid Nasir was ever sent to Cyprus, but it is certain that he founded the Merhebi family. One of Shadid's ten sons, Osman, became an Ottoman Paşa, while one of his grandsons, Ali Bey al Asad, became the governor of Trablusşam. The family was proud to have had five more Paşa's appointed in the following centuries. The Ottoman archives indicate that five descendants of Osman Paşa, three descendants of Osman's brother Asad and another Merhebi relative attended the School for Tribes.[82]

Probably the most successful and powerful among the nine students from this family was Aboud Muhammad Merhebi.[83] On 30 October 1897, the grand vizier wrote to the Ministry of Education, that Aboud Bey was eligible to enrol in the School for Tribes along with two of his cousins, Ibrahim Bey and Asad Bey.[84] Asad was the son of Omar Paşa and Ibrahim was the son of Hanifa, both siblings of Aboud's father, Abd al-Razzaq. No other information on Asad and Ibrahim is available.

Aboud was the grandson of Muhammad Bey, who was promoted to the second rank in the administration by the palace for supplying animals (horses, camels and sheep) to the Ottoman Army in 1886.[85] Subsequently, Muhammad Bey decided to establish a school, a *Madrasa Ilmiya*, in his hometown, Massha in Akkar. The following document dated 7 June 1892, which coincides with the year of the foundation of the School for Tribes, attests that Sultan Abdülhamid gave permission for his name to be given to this school in Akkar:

> Osman Paşazade Muhammad Bey, one of the tribal leaders of the district of Massha in Akkar, who previously received the rank of distinction, has commenced the construction of a *madrasa* in his home town. He has presented a petition to the Mutasarrifate of Trablusşam requesting that the school be named after our sultan, a request which has been transmitted to Istanbul by telegram. Our exalted ruler looks favorably upon this request and has given his kind permission to name the school 'The Hamidiye Madrasa'.[86]

On 9 January 1893, Sultan Abdülhamid decided to send books and cabinets as gifts to the library of the new madrasa of Akkar. Abdullah Galib Paşa, the minister, reported to the palace on 16 March 1893 that letters of gratitude

Figure 4.7 Aboud Abd al-Razzak Merhebi in his uniform.

from the tribal leadership, the local administration and the populace had been received.[87] Muhammad Bey, once again recognized for his services by Sultan Abdülhamid in 1896, was presented with a silver and gold medal for his exceptional bravery and loyalty.[88] In May 1901, he was given the title of Mirmiran, and became Muhammad Paşa.[89]

Muhammad Paşa's son Abd al-Razzaq died when his own son Aboud was quite young. Muhammad Paşa nurtured his grandson Aboud and sent him with his two cousins, Ibrahim and Asad, to be educated in the School for Tribes in Istanbul in the fall of 1897.

Aboud returned to his hometown, Berqayel, after studying for some years at the school. He is reported to have been ruthless in land acquisition and tax collection. His property extended 'from the snow to the sea'.[90] The following document dated 8 April 1915 reflects the complaints of an absentee landowner to the sultan regarding Aboud's usurping of his produce:

> Your slave was given the right to retain nine plots of orchards in the Miniara district of Akkar, part of Trablusşam. One of the brigands of the region, named Aboud Bey, has illegally occupied these lands and confiscated the produce. When I demanded a compensation of 2,100 kuruş, he refused to pay.
>
> I urgently beg our righteous sultan to instruct the Governor of Trablusşam to apply his justice in this matter. Sayyid Muhammad Sadiq, Muftizâde, Trablusşam.[91]

During the unsettled period following the First World War, most Sunni notables of the region lobbied for Akkar to become part of Syria. Aboud, however, decided to side with the French, who wanted Akkar to be part of Greater Lebanon, and thereby consolidated his power. In 1922, the French set up a Representative Assembly for Lebanon and Aboud was chosen as the representative of Akkar. The following year, Berqayel, Aboud's hometown,

Figure 4.8 Three graduates of the School for Tribes and the French Consul in Zahle, 1928. 1-2. The French consul and his wife. 3. Louis El Fakhori, assistant of consul. 4. Ibrahim Bey Mustafa, graduate of Aşiret Mektebi. 5. Mouin Bey, graduate of Aşiret Mektebi. 6. Aboud Bey Abd al-Razzaq, graduate of Aşiret Mektebi. 7. Mohammad Bey, son of Aboud. 8. Joud Bey, son of Ibrahim.

was made the centre of the Qayta, one of the five administrative areas of the district of Akkar. Aboud was to continue his political role in the First and Second Assemblies of Deputies from 1927 until 1932. Above is a photo of Aboud with the French consul and his wife, taken in Zahle in 1928. This photo is notable because it includes the two cousins who went to the school with Aboud, namely Mouin and Ibrahim and also reflects the close relationship the Merhebis established with the French authorities.

Aboud's only son Muhammad was sent to Paris to study law, and subsequently married the daughter of a leading Hama landowning family (the Barazis). Muhammad took his father's place as deputy in the Lebanese parliament and served as minister in several governments until he lost the election in 1951.[92] This was a major blow for the family, and Aboud supported his son's attempt to win in the next election in 1953. However, Muhammad was assassinated in Beirut a couple of days before the election. Aboud, who was close to seventy by this time, married a teenage girl and had another son he also named Muhammad. In 1958, five years after the death of his first son, Aboud himself was shot while driving in Beirut, and he died some days later. Berqayel has ceased to be a centre of power ever since.[93]

Another member of the Merhebi family, Muhammad Mouin Merhebi was sent to the School for Tribes along with his cousins in 1897. In 1908, Mouin and his cousin Khaled, who had completed their studies at the school and the civil service academy, were employed in Beirut, when the Trablusşam authorities attempted to recruit them into the army. They objected, claiming exemption due to their studies at the school. The minister of war, Rıza Paşa, then sent a note to the Ministry of Education on 21 June 1908 enquiring about their status.[94] The civil service academy replied to the Ministry of Education on June 26 that both students attended the school and graduated from academy in 1903; however, the school had no information regarding their exemption from military service.[95] The Ministry of Education wrote to the Ministry of War on July 9, also claiming no competence in the matter.[96] As there had been many such previous examples, the Ministry of War must have let these two graduates be exempt from military service. Mouin was then promoted to the position of the administrator of Şiran, Gümüşhane, part of the Erzurum province and returned to Anatolia. In 1943, he supported his cousin Khaled's election as a member of parliament. Later Mouin's son Tareq and his grandson Mouin also became members of parliament, and the same grandson, Mouin Merhebi served as minister of state for refugee affairs from 2016 to 2019.

The next Merhebi student of the school was Mustafa Adib. He was posted to the Beirut governorate upon graduation and was then transferred to Trablusşam. In 1909, he was promoted to the position of administrator of Kaş, Antalya. He was then moved to Hayrabolu, Tekirdağ in the European part of the empire in 1911. In 1912, he was appointed as the administrator of Iskilip, part of the Çorum *sanjak* in the province of Ankara.[97] A photo of Mustafa Adib from this period shown below displays the proud young officer, who was able to collect funds from the local notables and thereby construct a road between Iskilib, Çorum and Konya.

During or after the war, Mustafa Adib returned to his homeland and was appointed as the kaymakam of Hasbaya.[98] Mustafa later served as administrator of Baaklin, Rashaya and Baalbek. During the French mandate, he was promoted to governor of Jounieh and later became governor of the Bekaa. While he was in the Bekaa, he made a great effort to arrest some outlaws; however, the Lebanese President Emile Edde called him and asked him to release them as

Figure 4.9 Photo of Mustafa Adib during the road construction in Konya, 1913. The caption states that the road was constructed without costing the Treasure a single penny. Mustafa is quite handsome with his stick in the centre. 1- Chief of Gendarmerie 2- Mayor 3- Mustafa Adib.

Figure 4.10 Sultan's decree for Abdel Fattah 1915 and Collage of members of the Syrian Congress 1919.

a special favour. Mustafa refused and resigned. Later, President Bechara El-Khoury wanted to appoint Mustafa to his cabinet, but the latter did not accept, stating he had enough of politics.

The sixth student from the Merhebi family was Abdel Fattah, who also graduated from the civil service academy in 1903. He was a descendant of Osman Paşa's brother, Asad. He was first appointed to Damascus and then transferred to Beirut in 1904. After several postings he became administrator of Baalbek in 1912. The sultanic decree dated 8 August 1915 certifies that he was awarded the fourth rank of distinction in recognition of his efforts and services during his term in Baalbek. After the war, Abdel Fattah was elected to the Syrian Congress (*Al-Mutamar al-Suri*) in 1919 under King Faisal's leadership, and his photo can be seen in the striking collage published in Damascus at that time. The juxtaposition of Abdel Fettah's Ottoman award with his membership in the first Arab Nationalist Congress reflects the major transition in the Middle East during this period.

The officials of the defunct Ottoman state in Syria had to find their place in the new order. Abdel Fattah became administrator of Karak in 1920, then

Figure 4.11 The Merhebı Family in Hotel Royal, Tripoli, circa 1920. Seated Omar Paşa (died 1922) 1- Aşiret Mektebi student Asad, son of Omar Paşa 2- Aşiret Mektebi student Ibrahim, son of Hanifa, sister of Omar Paşa 3- Aşiret Mektebi student Aboud, son of Abd al-Razzaq, brother of Omar Paşa 4- Adham, who went with his cousins but was too young to attend.

Table 5 Merhebi family tree – *Students highlighted*

Mirab – founder of family / Mirab's son Nasser / Nasser's son Shadid (1711)

Shadid's sons: Selheb, Nasir, İsmail, Husayn, **Asad**, Ahmad, **Osman Paşa**, Zubeyr, Abdusselam, Abdulqadir

Osman Paşa's five sons: Abd al-Razzq(Aboud), **Khidir**, **Ibrahim**, Husayn, Yusuf

Khidir's son Asad had two sons: Ahmad and Khidir.

Khidir had two sons: Asad and Khidir; Khidir's son Khidir (Bibnin) had five sons: Muhammad Said, Rashid, Mahmoud, Toufik, *Mustafa Adib*

Mustafa Edib had one son from Haldiye (Hatice-Turkish) Mirab, no offspring. Two sons from Amira Fariza (Shihabi) Amir and Zeyd. Amir had one son Nasir who works for Abdülfettah today. Zeyd who was an actor died recently and had two sons Samir and Omar.

Ibrahim had five sons: Abdullah, Mahmoud, Muhammad, Mustafa, Huseyn

Muhammad's head was chopped off by Muhammad Ali of Egypt. His son was Muhammad Paşa-Mirmiran. Muhammad Paşa had five children: Ali Paşa, Omar Paşa, Abd al-Razzaq, Hanifa, Hatice

Omar Paşa died in Trablusşam 1922, one son *Asad*.

Abd al-Razzaq's son *Aboud*. Aboud had two sons both Muhammad.

Hanifa's son *Ibrahim*.

Asad's four sons: Muhammad, Ali Paşa, **Mustafa**, **Shadid**

Mustafa (Burg) had two sons Abdelkader and Awad.

Abdelkader's son Mustafa had four sons: Abdelfettah, *Muhammad Mouin*, Abdelkader, Mahmoud

Muhammad Mouin had three sons and one daughter: Faruk, Tareq, Mustafa and Büşra

Faruk's son Abdallah, Tareq's sons Bassam and Mouin (minister in 2016), Mustafa's sons Hani, Farouk and Muhammad Fadi

Shadid had five sons: Asad, Ibrahim, Ali, Muhammad Sharif and Mahmoud.

Asad's son *Ahmad*.

Muhammad Sharif had four sons: Abdullah, Hasan, Mustafa, Abdulmecid.

Hasan had eight children one of them *Akram*, another son was *Khalid*.

Abdulmecid had five sons: Cemil, *Abdülfettah*, Mahmoud, Khidir, Abdelqadir

Abdülfettah had three sons: Suhayb (Brazil), Muhammad Faisal, Abdulmecid served in Rashaya and finally during the French mandate administration was reappointed to Baalbek. The above photo from 1928, which includes several students of the School for Tribes, testifies to the strong ties among the Merhebi family.

A compact family tree for the Merhebis highlighting the graduates of the School for Tribes is presented in Table 5 above.[99]

The life stories of the students from Greater Syria reflect the close links of the region with the capital. Damascus, Aleppo and Beirut were not only physically close to the centre, they were also economically integrated. In her comprehensive study on the Syrian graduates of the civil service academy between 1890 and 1915, Corinne Blake has demonstrated the imprint of the Ottoman education on the Arab students. 'Culturally, they continued to be Ottoman as well as Arab, and politically, they remained loyal Ottomans... until 1918.'[100] Sultan Abdülhamid's attempt to integrate the Arabs into the empire was probably most successful in Greater Syria. The examples of Ramadan Shallash, Fahd al-Atrash and the Merhebis demonstrate that the School for Tribes created well-educated and powerful leaders, who consolidated their position first within the empire and later during the French mandate.

5

Life stories – Libya

The history of Ottoman North Africa is one of the many interesting chapters in the six centuries of the empire. The Ottoman corsairs occupied Algiers in 1516 in the same year that the land armies of Sultan Selim were marching through Damascus. In 1534, Hızır Reis, who was later known as Barbaros Hayreddin Paşa, was appointed as the chief admiral based in Algiers, where the Ottomans were to remain until the French occupation of 1830. Also in 1534, the Ottomans attacked Tunis, which was fully annexed in 1574, and remained part of the empire until the French took over in 1881. Among the North African provinces, Libya was closest to the Ottoman capital and remained part of the empire for the longest period, from 1551 until 1911.

It is interesting that the word *ocak* (hearth) was used to identify both the Janissary corps (*Yeniçeri Ocakları*) and also this region, that is, North Africa (*Garp Ocakları* or Western Hearths). For centuries, while bringing new janissary recruits from the Balkans to the centre, the Ottomans settled Anatolian Turkish boys in North Africa. Many of these Turks married locally and created an elite class which became known as the *Kuloğlu* (sons of slaves of the palace – sometimes called Koloğlu or Cologhli).[1] Between 1711 and 1835, Libya was ruled by members of the Turkish Karamanlı dynasty, who were also of *Kuloğlu* stock. Displeased with the French occupation of Algiers in 1830, and taking advantage of the internal strife among the ruling elite there, the Ottomans decided to exercise stronger control in Libya. In 1835, a large fleet was dispatched and the Karamanlı dynasty was deposed, starting the era commonly known as 'The Second Ottoman Occupation', which would last until Libya was ceded to the Italians in 1911. The borders between Libya and Egypt were officially delineated in the imperial edict of 1841, after the settlement with Mehmed Ali Paşa.[2] On the western and southern fronts, however, the Ottomans had to finance heavy fighting for many years, with Fezzan finally taken in 1842, and Berber Ghadames occupied the following year.[3]

At that time, Libya was dominated by various nomadic tribes, and the urban population was very small. Tripoli had fewer than 20,000 inhabitants, while Benghazi and Derna each had around 8,000.[4] In 1864, Tripoli was reorganized as a province, while Benghazi was made into a separate *sanjak*, reporting directly to Istanbul. Municipal councils were established in all the major towns of Ottoman Libya and a new judicial system was introduced, setting up criminal and civil courts.[5] Pushing for land reform, the Ottomans encouraged tribes to settle and expand agricultural production. Tribal chiefs were recruited to serve as administrators.[6] Tripoli and Benghazi developed into export ports for the Libyan hinterland, strengthening the ties between the urban and tribal groups.

The Sanussi movement, founded by Muhammad bin Ali al-Sanussi (1787–1859), also known as the Grand Sanussi, played a very important role in the history of Libya. The Grand Sanussi studied in Algeria, at the Qarawiyyin in Morocco, at al-Azhar in Egypt and also in the Hijaz and Yemen. His first *Zawiya al-Bayda* (white lodge) was built in 1843, in the *Jabal al-Akhdar* region (green mountain) between Benghazi and Derna.[7] Sanussi formulated a liberal Islamic ideology, which found its expression in the statement, 'there are many paths to God', and appealed to the nomadic tribesmen.[8] The Grand Sanussi always maintained careful and calculated relations with the Ottomans. In 1855, he decided to move his main centre to the remote southern oasis of Jaghbub.[9] Eventually, the Sanussi established zawiyas in 146 locations, including the Arabian peninsula, Egypt, Sudan and Chad as seen below.

These religious learning centres (the Jaghbub library is reported to have contained 8,000 books), were also organized to accommodate trade caravans and their goods as well as to serve pilgrims on the way to Mecca.[10] The Sanussi network became a safe zone for men from all walks of life, allowing trade to flourish and sustaining the order itself, and by 1870, the Sahara trade became a crucial source of revenue for the order. The movement was led by the Grand Sanussi's son, Muhammad al-Mahdi, from 1859 until 1902. Very successful in negotiating tribal conflicts and in forming the core of a *de facto* state, Al-Mahdi founded schools which trained many of the future leaders of Libya, including

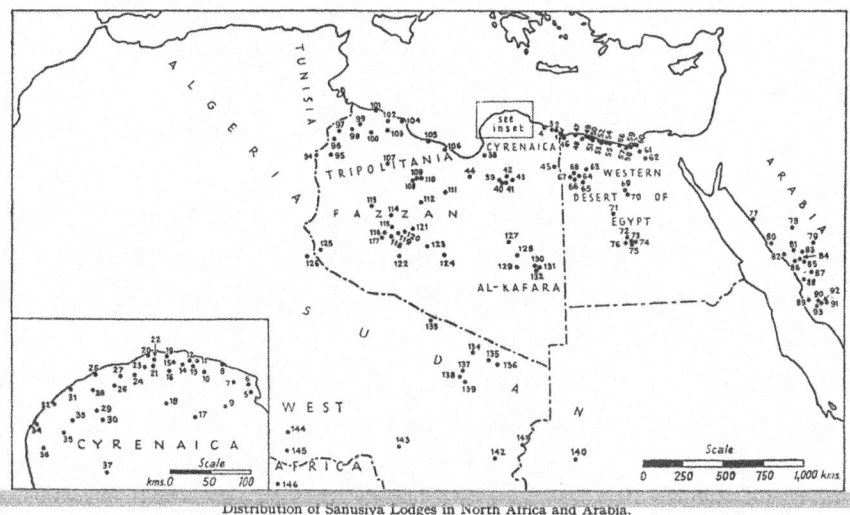

Figure 5.1 Map of 146 Sanussi lodges (Africa and Hijaz), E.E. Evans-Pritchard, *The Sanussi of Cyrenaica*, Oxford, 1949 (reprint 1973), p. 24.

Omar Mukhtar. The students received religious training and were also drilled as fighters for the Sanussi militia.

Meanwhile, the French penetrated Libya from the south, displacing the Tuareg tribes of the Sahara, who in turn requested assistance from the sultan. In 1875, the Ottomans sent forces to Ghat, Fezzan, and built new forts in the south of Libya.[11] Because the occupation of Tunis by France in 1881 and Egypt by Great Britain in 1882 alarmed the Ottomans, the number of troops in Tripoli was increased to 12,000.[12] Ahmad Rasim Paşa was sent to Libya in 1881, built a military school, constructed a system to supply drinking water to Tripoli, initiated the silk industry and significantly increased the export of agricultural products.[13] During the same period, Sheikh Zafir, one of the religious leaders of the region, was invited to Istanbul and became a close confidant to Sultan Abdülhamid II. In 1895, Muhammad al-Mahdi moved the Sanussi headquarters further south to the Kufra oasis, which was interpreted by Western sources as a worsening of the relationship between the Sanussi movement and the Ottomans. However, other sources testify to the movement's close links with the Ottoman palace and explain the reorganization as a joint attempt by the Ottomans and the Sanussi to stop the encroachment of the

French in the Southern regions.[14] Diplomatically, the Berlin Conference of 1884–5 defined the new rules for the scramble for Africa, a conference to which Ottomans were invited as participants. In the aftermath, Sultan Abdülhamid attempted to legitimize his efforts in the Libyan hinterland by referring to the rules set out in Berlin for the scramble for Africa.

It is in this historical context that the Ottoman minister of interior sent a letter to the governors of Tripoli and Benghazi in July 1892, asking them to recruit four students each for the new School for Tribes, which corresponded to 16 per cent of the total quota of fifty students for the first year. In its fifteen-year existence, the school regularly hosted Libyan students from all parts of the province. I have been able to identify twenty-two Libyan names among the graduates, two of whom, Omar Mansour and Sadullah Koloğlu, served as prime ministers under King Idris Sanussi in the middle of the twentieth century. The life stories of the two prime ministers and the four sons of Sheikh Zafir, as well as brief biographies of sixteen other Libyan students who attended the school, are presented below.

The memoirs of a graduate

On 15 March 2019, late in the evening in Beirut, I was searching the internet for names matching the student records and sent an email to a professor at the University of Texas. Approximately one hour later, I received the following reply:

> Hello and thank you for contacting me. I went to AUB, and it has a special place in my heart. Omar Paşa Mansour was my father. He was born in 1880 and died in 1962. He went to the Aşiret Mektebi and the Mülkiye and after graduation was appointed as Kaymakam in the Oasis of Jalu in Libya. Two years later, he defeated the French when they attempted to take southern Libya and he raised the Ottoman flag on the border between Libya and Chad.
>
> Abdülhamid called him to Istanbul and bestowed upon him the title of Paşa. He was later appointed as a member of the Ottoman parliament and Abdülhamid's brother Mehmet Reşad, who became Sultan Mehmet V, was one of his closest friends.
>
> Dr. Mansour Omar El-Kikhia.

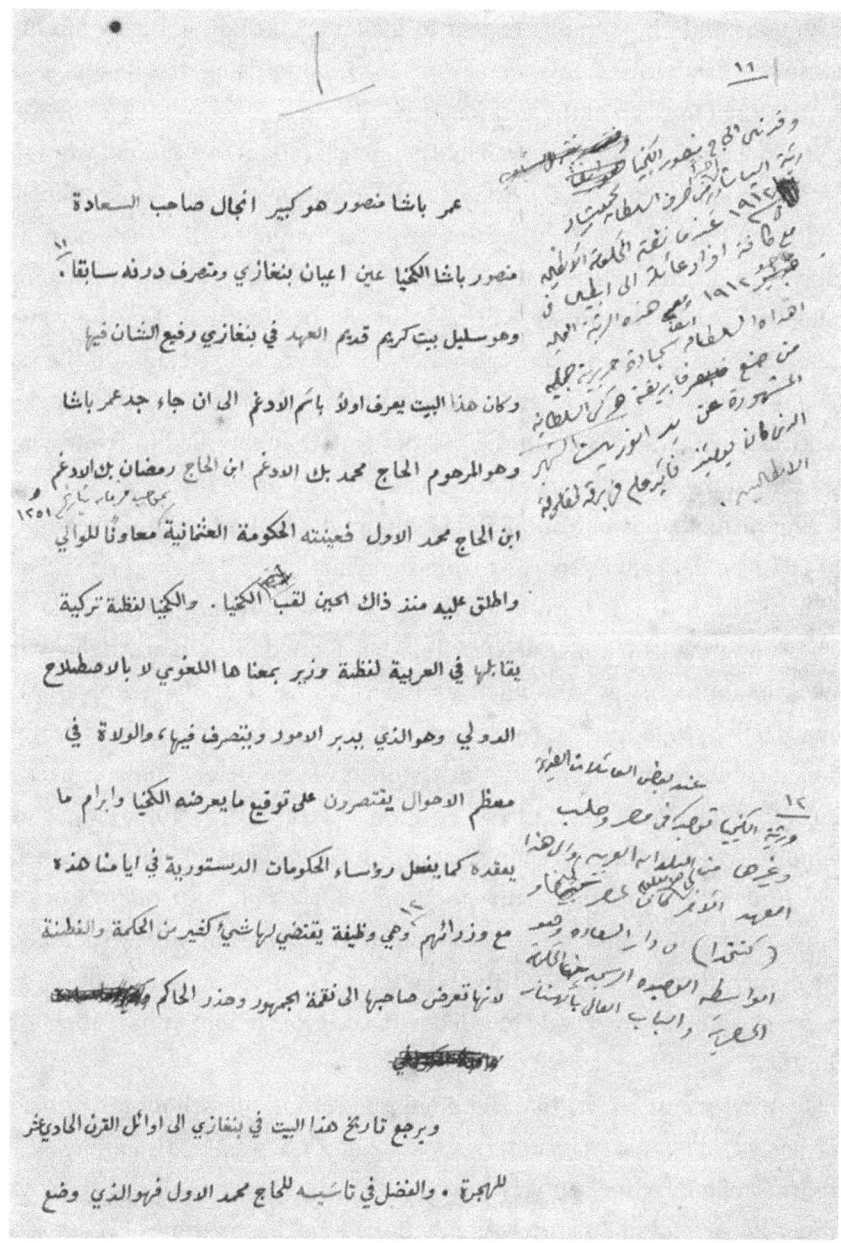

Figure 5.2 Photograph of first page of Omar Mansour's memoirs.

This correspondence led to one of the most important discoveries of my research about the School for Tribes. Professor Kikhia sent me several documents and photographs related to his father including a copy of Omar Mansour's handwritten memoirs from 1919, comprising twenty-six pages, above is a photograph of the first page.

This document is the only available personal account of a student from this special school. The memoirs begin with the fourteen-year-old Omar Mansour aboard the steamship *Inayet* on his way to the school in 1894. The boat first stopped in Derna, where they picked up three more students, including Sadullah Kologlu, whom we will meet in the next section. On the way to Crete, the ship encountered rough waters, but eventually sailed into the port of Hanya. Omar was impressed by the area's beautiful women and the delicious grape juice that was offered to the guests. Next, they travelled to Izmir where they toured the mosques and 'beautiful Arab-style baths (*hammams*)'.[15] After making further stops in Midilli and Gallipoli, the *Inayet* finally arrived in the capital seven days after departing from Benghazi.

Omar Mansour was born in 1880 to a prominent family. His grandfather, Hajj Muhammad Beik al-Adgham Ibn Hajj Ramadan Beik al-Adgham Ibn Hajj Muhammad, was appointed as the right hand of the Ottoman vali. Omar's father, Mansour Paşa al-Kikhia, also rose in the ranks of the Ottoman bureaucracy, serving as the administrator of Derna before moving back to Benghazi and taking his father's position. According to Omar Mansour's memoirs, in 1894, the governor Ahmad Tahir Paşa had difficulty convincing local leaders to send their sons to Istanbul. He put a lot of pressure on Mansour Paşa al-Kikhia to register Omar in the school and finally succeeded. Apparently, this choice added to the credibility of the new institution and afterwards 'almost everybody pleaded with the government to have their sons admitted'.[16]

Omar Mansour recalls that the building housing the School for Tribes in Kabataş was a big old mansion, renovated and expanded by two annexes. He confirms that the school provided them with all their needs and also gave them a monthly stipend of 30 kuruş. As mentioned in Chapter 1, he also describes the meticulously designed special uniforms of the school in his diary. Omar Mansour confirms that Sultan Abdülhamid was personally involved with the school: 'Whenever the sultan passed by, he would order his men to give each one the students a golden lira and each one of the teachers an amount equivalent to half of their salary.'[17]

The students were invited to many ceremonies and celebrations where they were introduced to high-ranking officials. Omar Mansour's memoirs contain a unique anecdote about the visit of Kaiser Wilhelm to Istanbul in 1898. On a much-publicized trip, the kaiser travelled to Jerusalem and Damascus after Istanbul and declared that he was 'a friend of the Muslims'. According to Omar, the sultan invited some students from the School for Tribes to the dinner hosted in honour of the emperor and the empress in Dolmabahçe Palace. The records indicate that the event took place on 22 October the last day of the kaiser's Istanbul trip, although there is no mention of students attending the dinner in any other account.[18] Omar states that grand vizier Halil Rıfat Paşa was present and the students were dazzled with the Empress Augusta Victoria, whose hat was adorned with ostrich feathers.[19]

Omar Mansour refers to two of his friends from the school who became prominent leaders: Abdulmuhsin Saadun, future prime minister of Iraq, and Ramadan Shallash, one of the propagators of the Great Syrian Revolt of 1925. Although the students were not allowed to read newspapers, they were very keen to follow the developments of the Ottoman-Greek war of 1897. They took turns among themselves sneaking out of the school and buying a paper in town. Omar writes in his memoir:

> Once it was Abdulmuhsin Saadun's turn, but going out that day was extremely difficult as the guard was very alert. Luckily the guard had a newspaper with him. Abdulmuhsin played all his tricks until he successfully got that newspaper. Ramadan Shallash, from Deir ez Zor, was also excitedly following the news. One day he had a fierce fight with the guard when he tried to confiscate the newspaper Shallash was reading. Shallash later came to Libya and participated in the war. He was known for his brave encounters with the French, which were recounted in the newspapers.

After completing his studies, Omar Mansour moved to the civil service academy, where he was greatly impressed with his tutors.[20] Omar Mansour lists some of his classmates as follows:

> Among the students who attended the school was Muhammad Fayez beik al-Ghusayn, the son of Sheikh Zaghal al-Ghusayn, one of the Laja sheikhs.

Muhammad Fayez is currently a prominent lawyer in Damascus. Other students were Khalil Efendi Rıfaat from Houran, Faris Efendi al-Fayyad from Homs, Fahd Efendi al-Atrash and his cousin Yusuf Efendi from the Jabal Druze.

Below is a photo of Omar Mansour's civil service academy diploma.

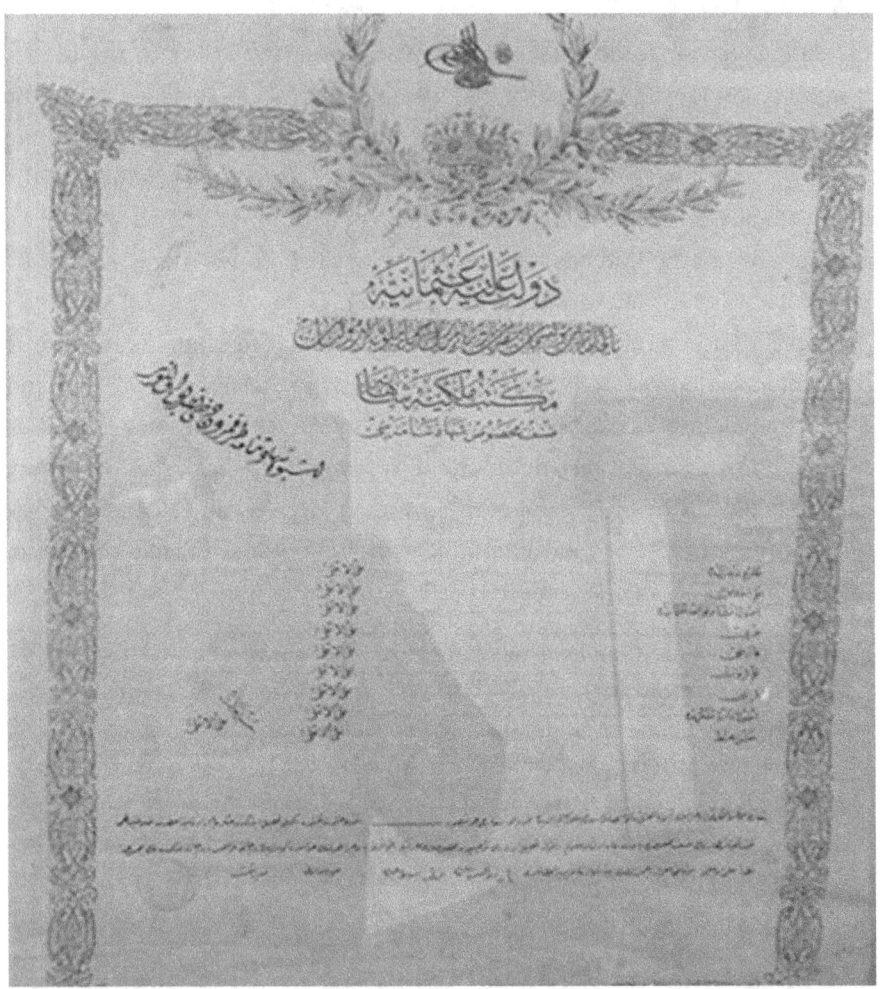

Figure 5.3 Photograph of Omar Mansour's civil service academy diploma. 'This diploma is presented to Omar Mansour, son of Mansour Kahya Efendi, leader of the Koloğlu clan of Benghazi and a member of the Administration of the District, who graduated from the Aşiret Mektebi and thereafter completed the required courses at the special class in the Mulkiye Mektebi with the grades stated above and earned high honours. 13 March 1900.'

All the students mentioned in Omar Mansour's memoirs were appointed to their posts in 1900. Omar became second clerk in the administrative council of Benghazi, of which his father was a prominent member. He commenced his employment in Benghazi on 28 August 1900, with a salary of 500 kuruş.[21]

The first occasion that helped Omar Mansour gain the attention of the governor Ahmed Tahir Paşa was partly coincidental, but it demonstrated his resourcefulness. There was an urgent document to be sent to Istanbul, but the Italian vessel in the port was ready to depart and refused to wait for the document to be delivered. Omar, witnessing the frustration of the governor, went to the Italian consul and convinced him to instruct the vessel to carry the letter. Omar rowed out to the ship and delivered the document himself. Omar's next achievement was related to the Hijaz railway. The government had started a campaign to raise funds for the project from the public, an operation Omar was put in charge of in Benghazi, and his efforts were rewarded with a promotion.

A more difficult task assigned to Omar Mansour was the maintenance of telegraph lines. The government had just built a line between Tripoli and Benghazi and then extended it to the 'Marconi wireless station in Derna'. The locals around Derna regarded the poles and the insulator caps at the top as attractive shooting targets. The Istanbul government was upset with the disruption of operation and the governor decided to send Omar Mansour to the area. Omar summoned the tribal leaders and persuaded them to protect the telegraph lines in return for a fee. In 1903, the same problem arose in the Eastern region. Once again, Omar gathered the chiefs on both sides of the telegraph line and put an end to the vandalism.[22]

During these years the French were gradually expanding their control in the Sahara, threatening several Muslim tribes. The Ottoman government decided to appoint Omar Mansour as administrator to the southern towns of Awjilah and Jalu in 1905. The government rewarded him with an Ottoman medal and the rank of distinction on 30 September 1907. As France's occupation of Wadai worried the Ottomans further, Omar Mansour was sent to Kufra to meet Ahmad al-Sharif Sanussi. According to the diary, he was accompanied by fifteen gendarmes and sixty camels carrying water, supplies and fodder:

The convoy saw no man, no jinn, no water, or greenery. The heat was so unbearable that we set up two tents on top of each other to block the sun in the daytime, and in the evening, we would build fires around the tents as a fence to keep the snakes away. Al-Tajj is the center of the Sanussi masters and the place where the tomb of Sayyid al-Mahdi al-Sanussi (may God be pleased with him) is located. Al-Tajj, where we met Sayyid Ahmad al-Sharif, is considered the capital of al-Kufra, an oasis in the south of Burqa, 900 kilometers from Benghazi. Al-Mahdi established mosques, buildings, schools, and markets in al-Kufra, and its population increased to more than ten thousand.

Omar Mansour recounts the achievements of the Sanussi and refers to the visit of Sadiq al-Mouayad al-Azm[23] to Kufra in 1895, noting the warm welcome given to Sadik Paşa by al-Mahdi and his pledge of loyalty to the sultan. In his book, Sadiq Paşa clearly states that Omar Mansour's father, Mansour Efendi, accompanied him on this journey.[24] However, Omar Mansour does not refer to his father at all, despite his account of the trip being quite extensive.

Thirteen years after his father visited al-Mahdi, Omar Mansour met al-Mahdi's nephew, Ahmad al-Sharif, who had become the leader of the Sanussi order in 1902. The Ottoman flag was prominently displayed in Kufra during his visit. Omar describes al-Sharif as a 'virtuous, pious and religious man of medium height and fair skin'. During the meeting, the Sanussi leader agreed that Kufra would be declared part of the Ottoman Empire and that Sheikh al-Kilani would be appointed as its administrator.[25] He also wrote a letter declaring his allegiance to the sultan, which Omar delivered to Benghazi four months after his departure from his hometown. Sultan Abdülhamid was very pleased to receive such a letter, and summoned the vali of Benghazi, Ömer Ali Bey, and Omar Mansour to Istanbul in 1908. Below is Mansour's account of his meeting with the sultan in the palace:

The meeting took place in the morning. We entered the palace and were instructed on the proper way of greeting the sultan. The chief chamberlain, Hacı Ali Paşa, and the First Secretary, Hasan Tahsin Paşa, were waiting in the large hall. Then a door was opened and Sultan Abdülhamid made his appearance. Everybody immediately folded their hands to their chest and bowed their heads. Hacı Ali Paşa approached the sultan and introduced both, saying: 'Your servant Ömer Ali' and 'Your servant Omar Mansour'.

'Omar Mansour!' said the sultan. 'I thought you were an old man! God willing, you will live long to serve the religion and the state.'[26] Then he asked me about the things I saw on the trip. I mentioned the great services of the Sanussi to spread knowledge and abolish decadent customs and ill behaviors that were widespread.

Then the sultan inquired about the rank of the governor and promoted him. Subsequently, he inquired about my rank, and was told that I had the rank of distinction. The sultan granted me the rank of *Mirmiran* (equivalent to Paşa). The sultan's extreme kindness encouraged me to ask his permission to kiss his hand. His hand was tender and soft, and he wore a gold ring.

Figure 5.4 Omar Mansour as a young Ottoman Paşa.

Celal Tevfik Karasapan, the first ambassador of the Turkish Republic to the new Libyan state in 1953, recounts his meeting with Omar Mansour and his account of the audience with Sultan Abdülhamid in some detail. During this meeting in 1954, Omar Mansour confirmed to Karasapan that he had hoisted the Ottoman flag in Kufra and was then invited to Istanbul to be presented to the sultan. In this version, Sultan Abdülhamid angrily asks Omar: 'Who is this Sanussi? Does he claim to be a Caliph?' whereupon Omar confirmed the allegiance of Ahmad al-Sharif to the sultan. Apparently, after he left the sultan's chambers, Omar Mansour was given a red silk purse with 500 gold coins as a token of appreciation.[27]

The sultan then offered Omar Mansour the post of governor of Jerusalem; however, his father intervened and asked that he be excused from taking up this position. After his return to Benghazi, the 1908 revolution took place and the elections were held for the second Ottoman parliament. Omar Mansour and Yusuf Shatwan were chosen as the delegates from Benghazi. Back to Istanbul, Omar became one of the most vocal members of the parliament. According to his memoirs, his pro-Arab speeches were published in many newspapers in Egypt, Syria and Iraq.[28] He also became closely associated with Arab delegates who were pressing Arab demands; these included Saeed Efendi Al-Husayni, Reza Beik al-Sulh and Rifaat Beik Barakat. They met with the grand vizier Hakkı Paşa to advance the Arab cause.

The Ottoman parliament records from 1908 through 1912 show that Omar Mansour made twenty-seven interventions during this term. He questioned the budget proposals of various ministries, but more importantly defended the interests of Benghazi. His first petition on 3 March 1909, was about the disruption in the construction of the Derna-Sellum telegraph lines, an issue he was well-versed in, as discussed earlier. Ten days later, he presented a written complaint about the problems regarding the renovations in the Benghazi port. He demanded the reduction of taxes on exports of camels and sheep to Egypt, claiming that if the taxes were cut in half, smuggling would be prevented and the total tax revenue would increase. Similarly, he pushed for lowering the tax on dates grown in Jalu, explaining that exports to Sudan were disrupted and Jalu could no longer afford to pay higher taxes than other provinces. He promoted the construction of schools and artesian wells in Benghazi. Perhaps most important was his petition regarding the monthly salary allocated to the Sanussi Sheikh in Benghazi. Omar Mansour objected vehemently to the reduction of this salary from 1,000 to 250 kurus. He explained that the Sanussis had been providing significant educational services for decades and were very loyal to the Ottoman state. However, in the ensuing discussion, other parliamentarians questioned whether this allocation was educational or political (most of the deputies were anti-Abdulhamid). Omar Mansour elaborated on the role of the Sanussis in Libya, but the matter was referred to a bureaucratic committee for reassessment.

Omar Mansour was re-elected to parliament from Benghazi with the highest number of votes in the 1912 elections, but this parliament was dissolved in August of the same year. After the Ottomans ceded Libya to the Italians in October, Omar was offered the choice of the governorship of Basra or membership in the Shura Council in Istanbul. However, he decided to move to Alexandria, because he knew the Khedive Abbas Paşa quite well and also wished to be close to his hometown. Before Omar Mansour left Istanbul, Sultan Mehmed Reşad bestowed upon him a watch with precious stones designed with the initials of the sultan, a photograph of which Professor Kikhia has kindly sent to me. Omar Mansour Paşa's memoirs end at this point.

During the Italian occupation of Libya, Omar Mansour was exiled to Italy for several years and thereafter lived in Alexandria, where the new leader of the Sanussi order, the future King Idris, was advocating for independence. After the Emirate of Cyrenaica was established in 1949, its newly recognized leader, Idris al-Sanussi, appointed Omar Mansour as the prime minister. When Libya was unified as a state in 1952, Omar Mansour became the head of the Senate of the Kingdom of Libya. In 1951, at the age of seventy-one, Omar Mansour had a second son, the future Professor Mansour El-Kikhia. Omar's older son, Fathi, became a minister of justice in the new government and was instrumental in establishing closer ties with the Turkish Republic.[29] Omar Mansour died in 1962.

'Arap Kaymakam'

Sadullah Koloğlu, from Derna in eastern Libya, was enrolled in the School for Tribes in 1894 at the age of ten. His great-grandfather, born in Karaman in the centre of Anatolia, was sent as a soldier to Egypt in 1798 under the command of Mehmed Ali. As outlined above the Kuloğlu appellation was not exclusive to this family. Every couple of years, around 1,000 young boys were dispatched from Izmir to the various port towns of North Africa. The Kuloğlu families constituted the ruling elites of Libya, Tunis and Algeria for several centuries.

After fighting in Egypt, Sadullah Koloğlu's great-grandfather was appointed to Derna, which is close to Alexandria. His grandson, Hacı Mabruk, was Sadullah's father.[30] At the time of Sadullah's birth in 1884, the Koloğlu tribe boasted an armed force of over 500 men and acted as the local rulers of Derna. Sadullah had seventeen siblings. In 1911, when the Italians attacked Tripoli, Enver Paşa set up his camp in Derna and befriended Hacı Mabruk. After the Italians defeated the Ottomans, Hacı Mabruk migrated to Mecca, where he passed away. His wife Zeynep, who was of Turkish origin, and her children then moved to Tarsus, a town in southern Anatolia.

The Koloğlu tribe used to supply the Ottoman palace with ghee from Derna.[31] Hacı Mabruk travelled to Istanbul in 1893 with his son Sadullah, where he met Sultan Abdülhamid at the ceremonial Friday prayers. The sultan suggested that Sadullah attend the School for Tribes, and he was admitted at an early age because he already knew Turkish. Thus, in 1894, Sadullah was sent to Istanbul accompanied by a black servant on the vessel *Inayet* together with Omar Mansour. Sadullah's son Orhan Koloğlu wrote a book about his father, titled *Arap Kaymakam*.

According to his testament, the sultan organized the traditional royal picnic on the Kağıthane pastures for the School for Tribes on 22 May 1895. On this occasion, Sadullah delivered the following speech:

> My dear brothers: Although I am very young, I am full of awe and gratitude toward our beloved sultan, who commands the hearts of all and has made it possible for us to be here in this park today, which is akin to paradise. Our sultan, who has more compassion and mercy than our parents, has provided for all our needs and continues to grant us his beneficence every day. *Padişahım çok yaşa!*[32]

Sadullah was surprised that a fellow student, Abdussalam from Tripoli, was not only twenty years old, but also had two wives when he arrived at the school. Abdussalam frequently caused trouble in the school and escaped multiple times. There are several records in the archives about how the authorities tried

Life Stories – Libya 137

Figure 5.5 Book written by Orhan Koloğlu about his father's life.

to eject this unsuitable candidate. Abdussalam was first transferred to the military academy and shortly thereafter returned to his hometown.[33] Sadullah described the modernized district of Istanbul as the Republic of Pera – today's *Beyoğlu*. European innovations were displayed in this part of town, including toys and medications; women would roam freely without covering their faces; theatres and cabarets were abundant. Sadullah was impressed by the huge Western-style buildings of the Pera Palas and Tokatlıyan hotels. After graduating from the school, Sadullah continued his studies at the civil service academy and completed his degree in 1901 with high honours.

As intended, Sadullah returned to his home after graduation and began his career in the Ottoman administration. He was married and had three children. However, having lived in a metropolis like Istanbul, Sadullah was not content in Derna. He applied for a post closer to the capital, and in 1910 he was appointed to serve as the kaymakam of Buldan, an Anatolian town renowned for its carpet industry and close to Izmir. This transition was to greatly affect the life of Sadullah and his family, whose country was soon thereafter occupied by the Italians. In March 1913, Sadullah was transferred to Pınarhisar, a small town in the European region of the empire. It was here that he became known as the '*Arap Kaymakam*', a title he held for the rest of his career. The defeat of the Ottomans in the Balkans caused a flood of refugees to pour towards Istanbul, and Sadullah found Pınarhisar full of migrants. His first task was to settle these newcomers and establish order in his small town with the support of the gendarmerie.

The Balkan war and the havoc it created finally ended in October 1913, but during these difficult days Sadullah's wife died of tuberculosis. He then decided to send his three children to his mother and brother who had settled in Tarsus, and he turned into a workaholic, working from early morning hours until midnight. Sadullah first mobilized the local population to build a school, which was later named after him. For his efforts, he was awarded the Legion of Merit from the ministry in 1915 and the Medal of Honour in the following year. Meanwhile, the Gallipoli campaign was raging only 200 kilometres away.

In 1917, Sadullah was appointed *kaymakam* of Vize, a larger town close to Pınarhisar also in the European part of the empire. In 1919, he was transferred to another neighbouring town, Saray. Sadullah then decided to join Mustafa Kemal's independence movement and travelled to Ankara, the journey taking him more than one month.

He was given a temporary position in the newly formed Ministry of Interior, and after victory was secured, was appointed to Maçka as the kaymakam of the town. Maçka, was part of the Trabzon province on the Black Sea, and Sadullah's first task was to resettle the soldiers and guerrilla fighters, distribute

Kuvayı Milliyeci Arap Kaymakam Ankara'da

Figure 5.6 Sadullah Koloğlu in Ankara.

the lands left by the departing Greeks equitably and re-establish order in the town. The monks of the famous Greek Orthodox monastery, Sumela, quite close to Maçka, had evacuated in 1923, and Sadullah claimed that he recovered an antique golden cross from one of them and sent it to Ankara.[34] He was then transferred to Of, another township of Trabzon on the coast, where he organized a campaign against the animal plague that hit the town, and this time he received a medal from the government in Ankara.

The Of population liked their kaymakam and suggested that he marry a girl from the region, Refika, the daughter of Sakallı Eşref, a war hero who had served in the secret service. When Sadullah went to Istanbul to meet his future bride, Refika was surprised to hear that he had three children, but still agreed to marry him. They settled in Of and had two sons, Mabruk Doğan (named after Sadullah's father) and Eşref Orhan (after Refika's father). His last appointment in the region was to Sürmene, another coastal town, where he mobilized the population to build a town hall.[35]

In 1928, Sadullah was appointed to Kadınhan, Konya, but on 5 July 1929 a major flood struck the Of region, and he was recalled due to his familiarity with the area. Since this natural disaster caused the death of hundreds and the loss of homes for more than 10,000 people,[36] Sadullah supported the resettlement of the population to Sürmene and other regional towns. His hard work brought him a promotion to become deputy governor of Konya. In 1938, Sadullah became governor of Hakkari, the poorest city in Turkey even today, situated on the distant eastern borders with Iran and Iraq. Here Sadullah once again mobilized the locals to build several roads, seven schools and a modern bridge over the Zab river. After two years in Hakkari, Sadullah was appointed governor of Bingöl in 1940, another poor city in Eastern Anatolia. However, one year later he was forced into sudden early retirement, explaining this decision as a result of the abnormal wartime conditions. Without any other choice, the family moved to Tarsus, where Sadullah's brother was living, and Sadullah spent two years growing fruits and vegetables on family lands without much profit. When Sadullah was able to find a low-level job in Istanbul, the family moved back to the capital.

At this time, Libya was undergoing major changes, and Sadullah decided to return to his homeland to seek his fortune. In 1948, he travelled to Egypt and from there to Derna. After reuniting with his family, Sadullah moved to Benghazi, where he met Idris Sanussi. During the war, Idris Sanussi had supported the British with the intention of evicting the Italians from Libya. When the two men, both in their sixties, met, they developed a comradeship, and Idris Sanussi asked Sadullah to take an official position in the government of Cyrenaica. Sadullah, happy with his good fortune, requested that such an appointment be granted the official blessing of the Turkish Republic. Idris Sanussi wrote a letter to the British Embassy in Turkey and requested assistance in securing the services of the ex-governor. The British delivered this request to the Turkish government, which gave its approval, albeit with some astonishment.[37]

In 1949, the United Nations adopted a resolution stipulating that Libya should become an independent nation by 1952, with Idris Sanussi as king.

Arap Kaymakam - Türk başbakan Bingazi'de son istirahatgahına götürülüyor -1952

Figure 5.7 Photograph of funeral, Orhan Koloğlu, *Arab Kaymakam*, Aykırı, 2011, p. 200.

In the years leading up to independence, Idris honoured Sadullah with the position of prime minister of Cyrenaica, but Sadullah was unable to find agreement with the dominating British military commanders. Soon thereafter, Sadullah was assigned to the post of education and health minister. In 1952, when the new Libyan state was instituted and Tripoli was chosen as its capital, Sanussi offered Sadullah a lifetime position as senator in the new parliament. However, with his health failing, Sadullah turned the offer down and made plans to return to Turkey. But before he was able to travel, Sadullah died and was given a state funeral in Benghazi by the king.[38]

The sons of Sheikh Zafir and other Libyan students

A very special and prominent figure in Sultan Abdülhamid's entourage was Sheikh Zafir al-Madani. In his younger days, Sheikh Zafir had met Omar Mansour's grandfather, who had shown him a great deal of respect and hospitality. Therefore, when young Omar arrived in Istanbul, the Sheikh took care of him and introduced him to his own family. Sheikh Zafir then sent four of his sons (Abdusselam, Omar, Mahmud and Abu Bakr) to the School for Tribes. Below is Omar Mansour's description of Sheikh Zafir:

> Sheikh Zafir was a pious man who was appointed to high ranks by Sultan Abdülhamid. Sheikh Zafir refused to appear in formal clothes with silver and gold embroidery but only wore the regular caftan, robe and turban. It is well known that Abdülhamid admired the man's virtuousness and asceticism. He even exclusively addressed him as 'Şeyhim', meaning my sheikh. Upon Sheikh Zafir's death, Abdülhamid erected a shrine for him and prayed there, having never done such a thing for anyone else. One of Sheikh Zafir's sons, Husayn Beik, was married to the daughter of Emir Muhiddin Paşa al-Jazaeri, the son of Abdulqadir al-Jazaeri, the well-known Algerian leader.[39]

Sheikh Muhammad Zafir bin Muhammad Hasan al-Madani was born in Misrata, Libya in 1829. His grandfather was from one of the leading families of Medina, and his father, Muhammad Hasan al-Madani, went to Morocco to study under Mulay al-Arabi al-Darqawi, of the Shadhiliya order. On his return trip in 1823, Muhammad Hasan al-Madani decided to settle in Tripoli and established the Madaniya branch of the Shadhiliya order. Like his father, Muhammad Zafir travelled to complete his education, first to Tunis, then to Algeria and finally to Medina. Settling in his hometown Tripoli, Muhammad Zafir joined the Shadili order and took over its leadership upon his father's death in 1847, gradually expanding his network and his political power. In 1860, the Ottoman Governor of Tripoli, befriended Sheikh Muhammad Zafir and received approval from Istanbul to have him appointed as an instructor with a corresponding salary.[40] In 1870, Sheikh Zafir travelled to the capital and established a branch of the Shadhiliya order in Unkapanı. It was at this time that he met the young Abdülhamid, who was second in line to the Ottoman throne. Abdülhamid was taken by Sheikh Muhammad Zafir and joined his order. Apparently, Sheikh Zafir predicted that Abdülhamid would become sultan in 1876. After spending three years in Istanbul, the sheikh travelled to Medina and later returned to Libya. When Abdülhamid did indeed accede to the throne in 1876, as Sheikh Zafir had foreseen, he was invited to Istanbul and remained close to the sultan until his death in 1903.

In 1878, Sheikh Zafir suggested to Sultan Abdülhamid that he employ the services of the former leader and reformer of Tunis, Khayreddin Paşa. Following a short period of advisory duties, Khayreddin Paşa was appointed as the first and only Arab grand vizier of the Ottoman Empire at the end of the year. Although his tenure as grand vizier was not long, Khayreddin Paşa also remained in Istanbul until his death in 1890 and was frequently asked to submit written reports to the sultan on various issues. During the Urabi revolt and British occupation of Egypt in 1882, both Sheikh Zafir and Khayreddin Paşa acted as close advisors to the sultan. A letter from Abdülhamid to Urabi Paşa was sent by Sheikh Zafir, advising the Egyptian leader to dispatch letters only through trusted advisors.[41] In 1887 a second, larger centre for the Shadhiliya-Madaniya order was built very close to the Yıldız Palace in Serencebey, and was called the *Ertuğrul Tekkesi*, named after the founder of the Ottoman dynasty. Abdülhamid frequently visited this complex for the Friday prayers, and this centre also served as the place of daily worship for the soldiers of the Ertuğrul division, which were the personal guards of the sultan. When Sheikh Zafir passed away in 1903 the shrine was expanded and renovated to house the tomb of the deceased Sheikh.[42]

Next to the Tekke-Mosque complex one can still see today the large mansion which served as home to Sheikh Zafir and his large family and another mansion which was used as a guest house for dignitaries from Arab lands. All the expenses of these mansions were covered by the palace and meals were delivered regularly to the inhabitants and guests. Güngör Tekçe, one of the many great grandchildren of Sheikh Zafir, wrote his memories of the time he spent in one of the mansions from 1951 to 1970.[43] Below are photos of the buildings from the 1950s and today.

Tekçe recalls that Abdülhamid's daughter Ayşe Sultan used to visit the Zafir family often, along with many other intellectuals and artists.[44]

There are three documents in the Ottoman archives related to the sons of Sheikh Zafir who attended the School for Tribes. On 23 August 1898, Tahsin Paşa, chief scribe of Sultan Abdülhamid wrote to the grand vizier stating that Abdusselam, Omar, Mahmud and Abu Bakr, sons of Sheikh Zafir, were to be enrolled in the School for Tribes at the order of the sultan. Two days later, an internal memo was prepared by the Ministry of Education with instructions to prepare a letter to the Ministry of Military Schools on the matter, but for some reason, this letter took a long time to materialize. Finally on 20 September 1898, the archives show clear instructions to the Ministry of Military Schools regarding the enrolment of these four students, further stating that the quota for the school for the coming year should be reduced by four accordingly.[45]

Figure 5.8 The two Zafır mansions in the 1950s and today.

The matter also caught the attention of the local press, though after another significant delay and with the names of three sons only:

Sheikh Zafir's Sons Admitted to the Aşiret Mektebi

The sultan, shadow of God, has decreed that Bekir, Mahmud and Abdusselam, the three sons of the honorable Sheikh Zafir, head of the Shadhiliya order, are to be admitted and enrolled in the Aşiret Mektebi.[46]

After graduating from the school, the eldest son Abdusselam was appointed as a clerk in the Ministry of Interior's secretariat in 1903 and promoted in 1904.[47] The second son, Omar, was given several government posts in Istanbul before moving to Tripoli in 1924.[48] Mahmud did not complete his studies but moved to the Uskudar Idadi school. In 1905, he opted to go to Libya to serve as district administrator of Tabya with a salary of 500 kurus. Later he was appointed as district administrator of the Touareg region of Khoms in Libya.[49] Abu Bakr, the last son who came to be known as Bekir, became a doctor and served in the Darülaceze in Istanbul for many years.[50]

Some of the following students' names and careers were obtained from the civil service academy records, while the rest were culled either from archive documents and/or the *Tercüman-ı Hakikat* newspaper. It is worth noting that based on the available information, all of these students spent their lives in Libya.

1. Ali Nureddin: Son of Hacı Hamid Efendi, member of the Administrative Council of Ubeidat region of Benghazi, from the Ubeidat tribe. He was born in Derna in 1872. He graduated from the civil academy in 1897, with the degree of average. He started his career in the Benghazi Administration in 1897, was promoted to regional administrator in Dirsa in 1902 and in Bersis in 1906. He was dismissed in 1907, reason unknown.
2. Mukhtar: Son of Abubakr Sidqi Efendi, Khoms sanjak (differentiate from Homs in Syria) and born in Khoms in 1873. He graduated from the civil academy in 1897, with the degree of high honours. He started his career in the Tripoli administration in 1897, and moved to Jabal-i Garbi in 1902.
3. Muhammad Halifi: Son of Ahmad Efendi, one of the leaders of the Badr tribe of Benghazi and a merchant. He was born in 1879 in Benghazi. He graduated from the academy in 1901, with the degree of honours.

He started his career in the Benghazi administration in 1901, and was promoted to become a member of the Court of First Instance of Benghazi in 1907.
4. Muhammad Mukhtar: Son of Hacı Muhammad Kanan Bey, mutasarrif of Garzan. He was born in 1877 in Tripoli. He graduated from the academy in 1903. He started his career in the Tripoli administration in 1903, was transferred to Izmit in 1906 and was promoted to assistant at the Council of State in 1908. He then returned to Libya and became *kaymakam* of Ajilat (Tripoli) in 1911.
5. Mahmud: Son of Abdulhadi, leader of Arfa tribe from Benghazi. One of the first to arrive in the school, he is mentioned in a report by the minister of education on 13 October 1893, who visited the school found the boy sick. It was reported that he recovered the next day. No information about his career could be found.
6. Abduljalil: Son of Osman from the Baragith tribe of Benghazi. It is mentioned in the archive documents that he was expelled after the first year due to his poor performance.
7. Madi Garbil: The archive records show he continued his studies at the military academy. Professor Kikhia knew Madi Garbil and tried to contact his descendants in Tripoli without success.
8. Husayn Hosni: Son of Jabir, sheikh of the Varshefana tribe from Aziziyah, Tripoli. No documentation was found on him in the civil academy records, but the *Tercüman-ı Hakikat* newspaper reported that he graduated from this institution.

With eight additional names found in the archives and newspaper articles,[51] the total number of Libyan students identified reaches twenty-two. Perhaps an appropriate conclusion to this chapter is provided by Omar Mansour in his memoirs. Below is his perception of the School for Tribes and the Turkish-Arab relationship at that time:

> The Madrasat al-Ashair was established because the Ottoman government started to perceive the Arabs as a force to be reckoned with. The sultan wanted to imbue the Arab students with the Ottoman spirit. With a population of thirty million and four-fifths of the sultanate's area, Arabs at that time were the main constituent of the state. The Arabian Peninsula has an area that

is equal to a quarter of Europe. Being the connecting point between the East and West, in addition to its abundant natural resources that make it one of the richest areas, the peninsula had a great influence on political and economic affairs. Had God granted Sultan Abdülhamid more time and dependable men who appreciated the importance of such considerations, our sultanate would not have reached this unfortunate fate. If only the Arabs and Turks were together, our enemy could have been defeated and would have surrendered.

6

Life stories – Iraq

On 14 September 1892, Nusret Paşa, commander of the Sixth Army stationed in Baghdad, sent the following letter to the palace:

> Fahd Paşa, sheikh of one of the lofty and ancient tribes, the Saaduni's of the Muntafiq from Basra, who as a family have always been willing to serve our generous sultan[1] is desirous to send his son Abdulmuhsin Bey to the Hamidiye School to study sciences. Fahd Paşa has asked for permission that the long time slave of his son travel with and remain in the service of Abdulmuhsin Bey.[2]

As would be expected from the above missive, Abdulmuhsin was accepted to the School for Tribes and became part of the school's first group of students. Abdulmuhsin was given student identification number 30. On 18 October Nusret Paşa wrote another letter, this time on behalf of Abdulmuhsin and his classmate Hamid, who was the very first student enrolled in the school, and the son of Farhad Paşa of the powerful Shammar tribe from Baghdad. Given the special status of these two students and their families, Nusret Paşa had invited them to visit his family in Istanbul for the weekend, but apparently, the administration told the students that they were not allowed to leave the premises.[3] Nevertheless, the Saadun family must have been impressed with the training, and sent his younger brother Abdulkarim to the school along with Abdulmuhsin one year later.

The Saadun family had migrated from Mecca to southern Iraq before the Ottoman period and were renowned as descendants of the prophet, *Sayyid*'s. They became the leaders of the largely Shiite Muntafiq tribes, 'people of the camel', and were also famed for raising Arabian horses, which they exported to Iran and India.[4] The Saaduns maintained good relations with the East India

Company's representatives, who played an important role in the area since the end of the eighteenth century.[5]

In 1831, the Ottomans sent a large army to Iraq under the command of Ali Rıza Paşa, Governor of Aleppo, who displaced the Mamluk rulers and reestablished central authority in Baghdad and Basra. In 1848, a new army unit, later called the 6th Army, was organized in Baghdad. During the governorship of Namık Paşa, a census was conducted and telegraph lines were expanded within the province and also linked to Iran and India. In 1869, the Governor Midhat Paşa convinced Nasir Paşa, then head of the Saadun family, to build a new town called Nasiriya, to serve as the centre of the new administrative district of Muntafiq. Nasiriyya, named after its founder, is today the fourth largest city of Iraq. The introduction of steam navigation on the rivers gradually transformed the tribes of the region from subsistence living to a market-oriented economy. Nasir supported Midhat Paşa in his battles with the rebellious Shammar tribal leader Abdulkarim, who was taken prisoner in Muntafiq and later hanged. Abdulkarim's brother Farhan Paşa succeeded as the next leader of the Shammar tribe and settled accounts with Midhat Paşa, turning into a loyal Ottoman notable.[6] The Shammar were officially awarded large tracts of land to settle on and began paying taxes. It is interesting to note that the first student to be enrolled in the Aşiret Mektebi in 1892, as mentioned above, was the son of this same Farhan Paşa.

Midhat Paşa subsequently promoted Nasir Paşa to the governorship of Basra. At the time, Nasir Paşa was financing trade to Najd and Basra through his Jewish banker in Baghdad.[7] Many scholars have argued that the example of the Saadun family and other tribes illustrates that the urban and rural populations of the late Ottoman period were much more integrated economically than has been generally assumed. However, in 1876, the administration, displeased with his growing power, recalled Nasir to Istanbul where he was practically held hostage until his death in 1885.[8]

The Saadun family was large and not united, at times the members competed with each other for Ottoman appointments. Some went as far as outbidding each other as can be seen in the following telegram sent by Saleh Saadun to the palace in 1880:

> The Saadun family is not limited to Nasir and Mansour Paşa, who have plundered the population for eighteen years and filled their pockets. I have

recently been informed that the son of Nasir Paşa, Falih Paşa, has been nominated as the administrator of Muntafiq to replace Fahd Paşa against a payment of 1.6 million kuruş. I have expressed to Abdurrahman Paşa Governor of Basra my readiness to pay 5 million kuruş to serve in this post. I am writing to your exalted office to confirm I can present any guarantees required.[9]

Mansour Paşa, who had been ousted by his brother Nasir as head of the Muntafiq tribes, became an opponent of the Ottoman regime along with his son Saadun. After several years of fighting with the government forces, Mansour received a pardon from Sultan Abdülhamid in 1885; however, he was taken to Baghdad and forced to reside under surveillance until his death one year later.[10] In 1891, his son Saadun al-Saadun began a military campaign against his own family and against the state to regain control of the Muntafiq region. Like his father, he plundered many towns and tribes, but in 1904 he also received a pardon from the sultan through the intercession of Ibn Rashid from Najd.[11] Nevertheless, Saadun continued to assert his authority and subsequently clashed with the newly installed Committee of Union of Progress (CUP) in Istanbul. Below is the letter from the minister of interior to the grand vizier, in which the minister associates Saadun with Arab Izzat Holo Paşa, who ran Sultan Abdülhamid's spy network and escaped after the Young Turk revolution:

> Saadun bin Abd al-Saadun, who has only caused mischief and brigandage and is known to have sent horses as presents to the fugitive Izzat, managed to coax a monthly allowance of 400 kuruş from the Najd *sanjak*. As per attached letter received from Basra, we request your permission to terminate these payments.[12]

Saadun was finally captured and sent to Aleppo, where he died in 1911.[13] Interestingly, his son Ujaimi Saadun later joined the Ottoman army with his men in the famous battle of Kut al-Amarah, where the Ottomans defeated the British in 1915. Ujaimi continued to resist the British during the occupation, and in 1920 Allenby wrote to London emphasizing that Amir Faisal, who was then in Damascus, had no involvement with the Iraqi revolt or with Ujaimi:

> Ujaimi Saadun has in no way been assisted by Faisal's Government, who have no control over him, but he has collected a number of Baghdad officers of the Turkish army, who have been unable to find employment elsewhere.[14]

When the British later quelled the rebellion and fully occupied Iraq, Ujaimi Saadun moved to Turkey and supported Ataturk in the war of independence against the French. Ujaimi settled in Urfa, a town in the southeast of Turkey, where he passed away in 1960 as a local hero.

It is noteworthy that the British official records after the occupation of Iraq in 1918 testify to the establishment of a special boarding school in Basra for the sons of tribal sheikhs on the lines of Gordon College at Khartoum or the chiefs' colleges in India. Money for the sheikhs' college was reserved in every budget during the years 1920 to 1924. In the end the project was thought to be too costly.[15] There is no reference to the Aşiret Mektebi in the British records; however, the local tribes were undoubtedly aware of the parallel.

While Mansur Paşa's son Saadun was busy with his rebellion, other cousins of the family from Najd arrived in Istanbul in 1893 and were awarded the following honours and gifts by Sultan Abdulhamid:

> Abdullah al-Saadun who is stationed in Najd – Second degree Mecidi medal, a silver lined robe of honor, gold watch with chain. His son Sheikh Saadun who came to Istanbul – Third degree Mecidi medal, a silver lined robe of honor and 5,000 kuruş
>
> His other son Abdurrahman in Najd – Fourth degree Mecidi medal and a silver lined robe of honor
>
> Sheikh Ibad, who came to Istanbul with Saadun – Fourth degree Mecidi medal, a silver lined robe of honor and 2,500 kuruş
>
> Wife of Abdullah al-Saadun, thirty meters of cloth and one ring
>
> The three attendants who travelled with them, 1,000 kuruş each.[16]

Abdulmuhsin Saadun was born in 1879 and was thirteen years old when he arrived in Istanbul on 20 September 1892, with his fellow Iraqi students to attend the School for Tribes.[17] When the group returned to Iraq at the end of the first school year, their arrival was duly celebrated in the newspapers as follows:

> The six students from Baghdad and Basra provinces have arrived in their homes for the summer holidays and have expressed their deep gratitude to the sultan. Together with members of their tribes they have prayed for the well-being of the beneficent Caliph of all Muslims.[18]

Abdulmuhsin and his brother, the newly admitted Abdulkarim, were to leave Basra on 31 October 1893, to travel to Istanbul, according to a telegram sent to the Ministry of Education.[19] However, it appears that their departure was delayed to 25 November as is evident from further correspondence of the ministry.[20] The report card from 14 August 1894, shows that Abdulmuhsin, in the third (most advanced) class, received the grade *ala* (fair). Abdulkarim, in the second class, received the same. In October 1896, Abdulmuhsin and Abdulkarim both chose to enrol in the one-year training at the military academy. They graduated in August 1897 and received the honorific title aide-de-camps to the sultan.

Unlike their peers, and perhaps upon their own request, both brothers were assigned to duties in the capital within the military establishment, where in time they were promoted to senior captain rank. In June 1902, Abdulmuhsin wrote a petition conveying to the palace that he wished to be discharged from the army as he needed to settle inheritance matters with his relatives and, moreover, had not been in Basra for ten years (ever since he enrolled in the School for Tribes).[21] No reply was forthcoming, so Abdulmuhsin reapplied for permission to leave three months later. This second letter requests permission for both him and Abdulkarim to return home to manage their estates. The petition attached to this document carries both brothers' signatures and begs for at least one of them to be given home leave.[22]

Finally, on 12 January 1903, the palace granted Abdulmuhsin permission to return to Basra. The letter from the palace noted that the brothers' father had passed away and included Abdulmuhsin's earlier request, in which he wrote dramatically that he had graduated from the School for Tribes and the military academy, was a slave of the sultan who would never accept to be freed,[23] and had been in Istanbul for ten years and thus had not been able to join his father at his deathbed.[24]

Several years later, in June 1910, the grand vizier sent a letter to the minister of war stating that the resignation of Abdulmuhsin Efendi of the Sixth Army of Baghdad had been accepted. The letter stated explicitly that Abdulmuhsin would not be eligible to return to the army or make any claims regarding his pension.[25] At the end of 1910, the Muntafiq representative in the Third Ottoman Parliament Refet Senevi Efendi passed away. In the by-elections held

Figure 6.1 Abdulmuhsin and Abdulkarim as aide-de-camps of the sultan (*yaver-i hazret-i şehriyari*).

in May 1911, Abdulmuhsin Saadun was elected to replace him. The minister of interior wrote to the president of the parliament on 13 May 1911 as follows:

> Attached please find telegram from Basra confirming the election of Abdulmuhsin Saadun, son of Fahd Paşa, as the member of parliament to represent Muntafiq.[26]

The Third Parliament was dissolved in January; therefore, in his first term Abdulmuhsin served for a total of eight months. After elections were held, the Fourth Parliament convened in April 1912, and Abdulmuhsin, who was re-elected, returned to Istanbul for his second term. Surprisingly one of Abdulmuhsin's classmates in the Aşiret Mektebi, Mehmed Hamza, was also elected to the parliament from Muntafiq in the same year. Mehmed Hamza had been enrolled in the school in 1892 and came from the Van province. In fact, he was the fourth Kurdish student in the school (after the three Cibran family members from Bitlis). He came from the Mekri tribe of Şemseki, located in Hakkari, the southeastern tip of Turkey. The Mekri tribe traced its roots to Iran. Mehmet Hamza was the son of Huseyin Bey, and grandson of Davuthan Bey, chief of the tribe.

Upon graduation, Mehmet Hamza chose to attend the civil service academy and therefore was separated from his friend Abdulmuhsin. Subsequently, he was assigned to serve in the administration of his hometown, Van. He then obtained a transfer to Bursa, a large city much closer to the capital. He later served in various towns as district administrator. In the parliamentary 1912 elections, Mehmed Hamza was elected as a Turkish (added to the records to indicate he was not an Arab) representative of Muntafiq of the Basra province along with his classmate Abdulmuhsin. It would be reasonable to assume that the Saadun family, the leaders of the region, vouched for Mehmed Hamza. In any case, the close links between classmates continued.

The Fourth Parliament was dispersed only four months later due to the Balkan wars. Mehmed Hamza returned to the lands of his ancestors and became kaymakam of Hoşab in the Van province (well known for its ancient fort).[27] However, at the end of 1915, he became the administrator of the Muntafiq region of Basra and once again joined his classmate. In the next year, Mehmed Hamza was transferred to Karbala, but returned to Muntafiq in 1917. When the British occupied southern Iraq, he moved to Istanbul where he passed away in 1921, ending a long-standing relationship between the two graduates of the Aşiret Mektebi.

Although many sources claim that Abdulmuhsin served for a total ten years in the Ottoman Parliament, this is not the case. The Fifth Parliament, which was functional during the war years, consisted exclusively of the Committee of Union and Progress appointees and did not include Abdulmuhsin. His term in office was, therefore, limited to a total of one year in the Third and Fourth Parliaments. His disagreements with the CUP were such that in 1915 the governor of Baghdad sent a ciphered telegram to the minister of interior, Talat Bey (later Paşa), as follows:

> Abdulmuhsin Bey, member of parliament from Muntafiq, should not be trusted under any circumstances, and all his actions should be under surveillance.[28]

The Office of General Security immediately transmitted the same message to the police administration of Istanbul.[29] Thus, Abdulmuhsin Saadun had gone from being an aide-de-camp of the sultan and a member of parliament to persona non grata in the Ottoman Empire under the CUP.

On 6 November 1914, only one day after the Allies declared war on the Ottoman Empire, the British entered the port of Faw in southern Iraq. They occupied Basra two weeks later. In 1917, they marched into Baghdad. The widespread popular revolt of 1920, when the Sunni and Shiite, the townsmen and tribes, all joined forces against the invaders, was quelled by British heavy aerial bombing all around the country. On 23 August 1921, the British decided to proclaim Faisal, son of Sharif Husayn, who had lost his throne in Damascus, king of the new state of Iraq, which consisted of the Ottoman provinces of Baghdad and Basra. Faisal became the 'sovereign of a state that was itself not sovereign'.[30]

Abdulmuhsin Saadun returned to Iraq at the end of 1921, and in March 1922, upon the suggestion of the British, was named the minister of justice in the second cabinet of Abdurrahman Kaylani.[31] After the elderly Kaylani resigned as a result of Shiite protests over the Anglo-Iraqi treaty, the well-educated and ambitious Abdulmuhsin became prime minister on 18 November 1922. He was charged with organizing the elections for the first constituent assembly, which was expected to ratify the treaty with Britain. During this turbulent period, Abdulmuhsin was able to successfully conclude negotiations with Ibn Saud to demarcate the borders between Najd and Iraq. The British agreed to reduce the Anglo-Iraqi treaty period from twenty to four years to mollify public opinion, and Abdulmuhsin utilized the local press to advocate a national roadmap to self-rule. However, the Shiite clerics insisted on boycotting the upcoming elections, and despite the reservations of the king and the British, Abdulmuhsin applied harsh military measures, exiled thirty-four prominent Shiite leaders to Iran and put another fifty under surveillance. His success disturbed King Faisal, who began to accuse Abdulmuhsin of responsibility for the financial crisis the country was undergoing, whereupon the prime minister had to resign.[32]

King Faisal appointed Jafar al-Askari to form the next cabinet and the constituent assembly was opened on 27 March 1924. 'Of the ninety-nine members who made up the Iraqi constituent assembly of 1924, no fewer than thirty-four were sheikhs and aghas.'[33] Abdulmuhsin Saadun was elected president of the assembly. However, the delegates remained bitterly opposed to ratifying the treaty with Britain. On 10 June as the deadline announced by London approached, Askari and Saadun managed to convene the assembly with a quorum of sixty-nine. Although only thirty-seven members voted in favour of the treaty, it was thereby officially ratified, and a major showdown was averted. The constituent assembly then promulgated the new Iraqi constitution, despite the fact that many Iraqis were opposed to it and argued that the Turkish constitution was a more liberal document.[34] Finally, the assembly also ratified the electoral law, putting in place most of the legal framework of the new state of Iraq.

On 26 June 1925, Abdulmuhsin Saadun was appointed as prime minister for the second time. This time, his initial mission was to hold parliamentary elections.[35] After the fanfare of the opening ceremonies of the parliament was completed, the prime minister organized a new political party, the Progress Party (*Hizb al-Takaddum*), which commanded a majority in parliament. This was perhaps the highest point in Saadun's career. His brother Abdulkarim was elected to serve in the senate at this time.[36] On 20 August 1925, several notables and landowners, including Abdulkarim and Talib al-Naqib, met in Basra and 'discussed the question of doing away with the king and setting up a republic under the protection of the British with Abdulmuhsin Saadun as president.'[37]

The next issue on Abdulmuhsin's agenda was the Mosul question. The First World War had ended in the Middle East with the signing of the Mudros Armistice on 30 October 1918. This did not stop the British from occupying Mosul on November 3. Therefore, the Turkish side insisted on its legal and rightful claim to the region.[38] Although Turkey signed the Lausanne peace treaty in 1923, the Mosul question could not be resolved and was left to the mediation of the League of Nations. For Faisal and Saadun, the incorporation of Mosul into the new Iraqi state was critical, as can be seen in their statements:

> Prime minister Abdulmuhsin Saadun asserted that Mosul was the 'head' of the 'body' of the Iraqi nation, and King Faysal declared that the Mosul question was 'a life or death matter for our beloved country'.[39]

According to his colleague and relative by marriage, Tawfik al-Suwaidi, Saadun's long-standing and intimate knowledge of the Ottoman Empire made him suspicious of the political and territorial claims of the nascent Turkish Republic over Iraq:

> As for his foreign policy, Saadun was known for his fierce and stringent policy towards Turkey. Although he spent most of his life in Istanbul and had strong connections with the Turkish people as he mastered the Turkish language, he believed that the prime risk to Iraq was 'Turkey', especially that the Turkish mentality would not easily submit to the fact that Iraq, which once belonged to their empire, was no longer theirs.[40]

The League of Nations eventually decided that Mosul should be part of Iraq. The decision was binding for all parties, and consequently a treaty with the Turkish Republic was signed on 26 June 1926, which certified the borders between the two countries and made Mosul a province of Iraq. However, Turkey was guaranteed to receive 10 per cent of the oil revenues of Mosul.[41] During this period, the British had also managed to sign a treaty with the government to give exclusive rights of exploration and production of oil to the Iraq Petroleum Company, which was a subsidiary of the British oil companies. Faisal was weary of the growing influence of Saadun (in collusion with the British) and managed to arrange the defeat of Saadun's candidate for speaker of the assembly in November, whereupon the prime minister once again left his post.[42]

One year later, on 14 November 1927, Abdulmuhsin Saadun was called upon to form his third cabinet. He was charged with overseeing the national elections yet another time and managed to command a majority in the new parliament. The novelty of this parliament was the inclusion of many Shiites as a step towards reconciliation. Although the Shiite leaders dubbed him as 'Sir Abdulmuhsin, who would not object to anything the British did',[43] it was in this period, that Saadun began to resist the demands of the British high commissioner. Abdulmuhsin Saadun was adamantly opposed to the extension of the military cooperation agreement, which would force Iraq to continuously finance the British military presence in their country. Abdulmuhsin also took the portfolio of the Defense Ministry in January 1928. 'In the closing year of his life, to the surprise of friend and foe, Abdulmuhsin altered course. He took the side of the king against the high commissioner on a number of outstanding issues.'[44]

The archives in Istanbul reveal that Abdulmuhsin requested the Ministry of Foreign Affairs of the Turkish Republic to provide him with documentation about dates of his service in the Ottoman Empire in June 1928, which would be included in his retirement calculations in Iraq, indicating his plans for the future.[45] In December 1928, Henry Dobbs, the High Commissioner, wrote to London that Abdulmuhsin's 'education in Constantinople had infected him with a townsman's ideas', confirming the rift between the two sides.[46] Below is an altercation between them regarding the extension of the military treaty:

> Dobbs: Let's assume that the military treaty has come to an end, what are you going to do about the Turkish risk? Especially that you have no means to defend yourselves. Do you not think that you are risking your independence by requesting its termination?
>
> Saadun replied: I am not convinced that Britain is sending thousands of its sons to the desert to protect the Iraqis from the Turks. I believe that Britain is doing that for its own sake. And to prove that we are not afraid of facing the Turks by ourselves, we ask you to withdraw your forces; you will then see that nothing will happen to us.[47]

Not surprisingly, Britain refused to make any concessions to Iraq. The impasse led in January 1929 to Abdülmuhsin's resignation and Dobbs's departure.[48]

However, no progress could be achieved by the succeeding government and the new High Commissioner Gilbert Clayton, either. Thus, on 19 September 1929, Saadun was once again asked to take over the role of prime minister for a fourth and final time. This time, he seemed fortunate, because the recently elected British Labour government had agreed to recommend Iraq's entry into the League of Nations as an independent state in 1932. He included prominent nationalists like Yasin al-Hashimi and Naji al-Suwaidi as well as the Shiite spokesman Abdalhusayn Chalabi in his cabinet.[49]

However, the sudden death of Gilbert Clayton and King Faisal's preference to work with his own team left Abdulmuhsin Saadun in a weakened position. In a speech on 6 November he stated: 'A nation that seeks a liberation has to prepare for it. This should not be mere empty talk. It has to be done by real deeds and sacrifices.'[50]

Figure 6.2 Abdulmuhsin, Prime Minister of Iraq.

Losing hope of solving the difficult problems of Iraq, unable to win the confidence of King Faisal, depressed and lonely, he committed suicide on 13 November, leaving behind the following note to his son written in Ottoman Turkish:

> Forgive me, my dearest son Ali, for my crime. I have grown weary of this life. The nation expects service, the English refuse. I have no supporters. The Iraqis who call for independence are weak and helpless. They do not appreciate the advice of men of honour like myself. They think that I am a traitor to my country and a slave of the English. What a calamity. I am devoted to my country and bore disdain and humiliations for this beloved land of my forefathers. My last will is that you take care of your young siblings who will be orphaned, and remain loyal to King Faisal and his descendants.[51]

The Saadun family remained one of the largest landowners in Iraq.[52] Unlike most leaders from the era of the monarchy, Abdulmuhsin Saadun, who served as Prime Minister four times between 1922 and 1929, was recognized by the later regimes as one of the builders of the state of Iraq. His name was given to one of the main streets of Baghdad, where his statue was also prominently displayed. Sadly, the statue was plundered during the recent civil war but has now been restored in the same location.

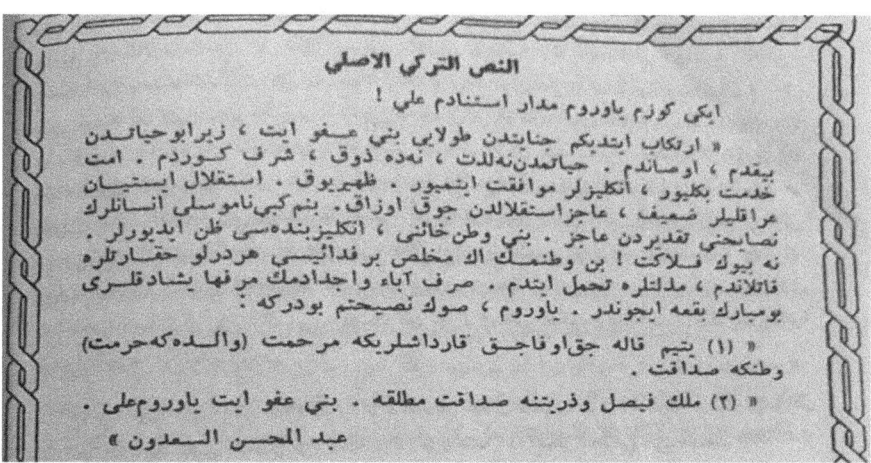

Figure 6.3 Suicide note of Abdulmuhsin in Ottoman Turkish.

Conclusion

In June 1892, Sultan Abdülhamid II issued a decree declaring that a special school for the sons of Arab tribal leaders would be established in Istanbul. This unique project was designed to extend the tentacles of the Ottoman state to the most remote frontiers and cultivate the loyalty of the unruly Arab tribes. The school was inaugurated on the Prophet's birthday, 4 October 1892 and in the following fifteen years around 500 students from distant parts of the empire were educated in the capital at the state's expense. Many of the young men who completed the five-year programme of the School for Tribes attended the special one-year training either in the military or in the civil service academy before embarking on their careers.

I contend, based on the evidence presented in the preceding chapters that the Imperial School for Tribes was an ambitious, important and successful project initiated and executed by the Ottoman state. A comparative analysis of the profiles of some of the graduates (Ramadan Shallash, Fahd al-Atrash, the Merhebis, Omar Mansour, Sadullah Koloğlu and Abdulmuhsin Saadun) illustrates that the school produced well-educated and well-rounded notables. The students came from powerful families, some going back several centuries. Their prominent backgrounds, their strong personalities and the rigorous training they received in the capital of the empire enabled the graduates to take on leadership roles in their future lives.

After graduating from the school, Ramadan Shallash and Abdulmuhsin Saadun attended the military academy and served in the Ottoman army, while the others examined in this study completed their training at the civil academy and served as administrators in the Ottoman bureaucracy. Koloğlu, Atrash, Shallash and the Merhebis were employed in the Balkan and Anatolian territories of the empire for many years as Arab administrators or army officers. Omar Mansour and Abdulmuhsin Saadun were both elected to the Ottoman Parliament after 1908. Most of these figures were involved in the armed conflicts between the Ottoman Empire and the Western powers. Kologlu was imprisoned by the invading Greeks, and Omar Mansour fought the French, Italians and British. Ramadan Shallash became famous for taking British soldiers hostage in Deir ez-Zor, and later also rebelled against the French invading forces in Syria. The Atrash were among the leaders of the Great Syrian revolution.

Once the French and British authorities were established in the Middle East, the local notables were obliged to position themselves in the new power structure. The Merhebis were probably among the earliest converts and secured themselves important positions within the French Mandate and the Lebanese republic. Ramadan Shallash, realizing the futility of resistance, attempted to mediate between the French and the Syrians in 1926. The British supported Abdulmuhsin Saadun as a well-educated leader who served as prime minister of Iraq four times between 1922 and 1929. During the Second World War, the Atrash joined the Allies and entered Damascus with General de Gaulle. Sadullah Kologlu and Omar Mansour took part in the foundation of the new state of Libya under King Idris Sanussi after 1948. The limited sample examined in this work indicates that the graduates of the school became an important part of the elites of their region, remained loyal to the Ottoman Empire until its demise and thereafter took on leadership roles in the Middle East.

If the school was successful, then why was it closed down? There are two common explanations offered by many commentators. The first is that the school was a very expensive enterprise. The transportation of students from and to the hinterlands was both costly and cumbersome, in addition, each student was given a monthly stipend. The second factor which affected the decision to close down the School for Tribes was the construction of many new schools in the provinces during the Hamidian period. Sending their sons to these closer locations became an attractive option for tribal leaders.

The Ottoman archives reveal to us a less evident but important reason for the termination of the School for Tribes. Below is a letter sent to Istanbul by Nazım Paşa, Governor of Syria in 1898, while the school was still operational. After praising the institution, Nazım Paşa stated that a large number of tribes were roaming the countryside and proposed assigning twelve tutors to them as follows:

> In order to fortify the nomadic tribes with Islamic principles and train them in the teachings of the Quran, we suggest to assign tutors to join them with a salary of 250 kuruş. This will honor the tribes and prevent the penetration of pernicious foreigners. The tutors should be vetted by the local administration and the religious bodies and should be forceful and knowledgeable. We believe it would be beneficial to assign one tutor to the Jahaya tribe and another to the Munayit tribe. For the Haitab and Bani Sakher tribes, two tutors would be required for each. For the larger tribes of Balqa and Ben-i Atiye, three tutors would be accompanying each clan. According to this allocation, the total cost would be a negligible amount of 3,000 kuruş, and with such meager funds, we could spread the light of Islam in our region. We hope you will find our proposal acceptable and instruct the Sublime Porte accordingly.[1]

Nazım Paşa correctly argued that the School for Tribes could enrol only forty students every year, while with much lower budgets hundreds could be given a basic education close to their families. Although there is no evidence that Nazım Paşa's scheme was implemented, in the following decades the concept of 'mobile tribal schools' reappeared frequently. The grand vizier sent the letter below to the minister of education in May 1909, after the school was closed down, attesting to an interesting and rather ambitious project for the tribes:

> Rashid Nasir from Najd and Abdurrahman Ilyas Paşa from Medina presented a treatise to the council of ministers regarding the reformation of the Arabian peninsula and obtaining the loyalty of the tribes. The Council accordingly agreed to open, as a first step, ten tribal schools in the region. As we had informed you on 18 March 1909, the following budget was allocated for this project: Two preachers and ten tutors (two women and eight men), who are familiar with the ways of these clans, will be employed with a budget of 6,300 kuruş per month. Abdurrahman Ilyas Paşa will oversee the selection and also supervise the training process by periodically visiting the schools. He will be assigned a monthly salary of 2,000 kuruş. It appears that no progress has been made on this matter, which should be now acted upon promptly.[2]

A similar correspondence occurred around the same period between Baghdad and the capital. The governor sent a report about his plans for the province, which included the establishment of a school for tribes (*Aşiret Mektebi*) in Baghdad. The minister of education replied on 25 May 1909 that such a boarding school would not be beneficial unless the tribal students first received an elementary education. The minister added that it had been decided to establish mobile tribal schools (*Seyyar Aşiret Mektepleri*) in the region instead.[3] Although there is no evidence of the establishment of the mobile units in Baghdad at that time, all the above documents disclose the new outlook of the Ottoman Administration towards training the tribal population.

Another attempt to establish a school for tribes occurred in 1916, during the First World War.[4] After Enver Paşa returned from his trip to Syria and Hijaz, the government issued a decree on 24 May 1916 to open a primary school for the tribes of Arabia (*Medrese-i Aşair*) next to the city of Madain-i Salih, which was also one of the stations of the Hijaz railway. The three-year curriculum was similar to the primary schools of the empire and thirty sons of tribal leaders would be recruited each year. Upon graduation, they would continue their education in the high schools of Medina or Jerusalem. Although the detailed preparation never saw the light of day, this project also reconfirms the consensus that the primary education for tribes was best provided in their own regions.

In 1933, the Turkish Republic decided to institute a system of mobile tribal schools (*Seyyar Aşiret Mektepleri*). The *Vakit* newspaper announced the launch of a government programme to mollify the rebellious Kurds in the mountainous eastern parts of Turkey by commissioning a group of educators who would roam the rural areas and educate the tribes. The prime minister's office confirmed the allocation of a budget to cover the expenses of these tutors.

Although it is not clear how long this system was sustained, all of these efforts reveal that the authorities reached the following consensus: It would be more sensible to teach the alphabet to the tribal children close to their habitat. The promising students could then continue their education in the towns and cities of the empire.

In my view, another unpublicized reason for the closure of the school is related to the mission and the recruitment process. The foundation documents repeatedly and clearly state that the School for Tribes was

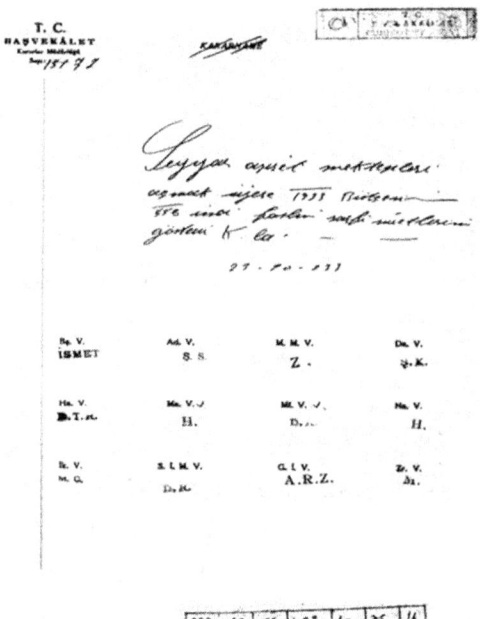

Figure 7.1 *Vakit* newspaper, 28 May 1933 and Turkish Republic Cabinet memorandum regarding mobile training for tribes, 23 October 1933.

established for the sons of Arab tribal leaders.[5] However, in reality, from the first year onwards, students from other parts of the empire were admitted to the school. Had the recruitment been restricted to the Arabs, it would have been easier to instruct and control the student body. The rivalry and infighting between the two main groups – the Arabs and Kurds – continued throughout the school's fifteen years of existence. A sound analysis of the matter could have resulted in opening another similar institution for the Kurds. The initial mission of a school dedicated to Arabs would have enabled a better education for a more cohesive group and perhaps multiplied the benefits of the school for the state.

The system of recruitment was not efficiently or effectively organized, either. It should be noted that at the time of the school's founding, the Ottoman Empire had accumulated a significant amount of information about the tribes. There were estimates about how many tents each subgroup possessed, and how, in several locations, the tribes were organized into federations. The names of the chiefs of the largest and most powerful tribes were well known by the provincial authorities as well as by the palace. One would have expected a systematic approach to recruitment, which was clearly lacking. The only example that came close was the first recruitment effort in Baghdad, where the local administration reported that four prominent tribes were targeted, and one student was selected from among the sons of the sheikhs of each of these tribes. Unfortunately, all four of these students left the school after the first year and Baghdad failed to send students in the subsequent period.

During the school's fifteen-year existence, the contribution of the Ministry of Education to the recruitment process was merely to announce the numerical quotas of students to be admitted from each region, which was dictated by the palace. Once the quotas were determined, the recruitment process was left to the discretion of the provincial authorities, with uneven results. The quotas were rarely met, whether by region or by number. Another flaw in the recruitment process was revealed in 1899, when an inspection showed that while many students came from nomadic backgrounds, they had moved to urban centres, due either to the careers of their fathers or to their own primary education. These students were transferred to other schools, and the provinces were warned that only students living in rural areas were to be selected in the future. In short, the selection of students to the School for Tribes was a difficult process and could not be executed according to the initial blueprint designed at the inception of the school.

Finally, the reactions of the tribal leaders to the venture were not as expected. While some Arab provinces were not responsive to this project at all, recruitment from the other provinces was erratic. The struggle to bring in students from the Hijaz was abandoned after the first year. Mosul was another province that was deleted from the targeted locations after a couple of years. Despite the offer of an excellent education, accommodation, transportation and a stipend, only 70 per cent of the quota could be filled throughout the lifespan of the school. In summary, the dilution of the original mission and the difficulties of recruitment must have led to a lack of enthusiasm for the school which facilitated its closure.

Another critical factor in the decline of the performance of the school was the erosion of talented leadership. The top administrators of the school who were involved in the conceptual framework of the School for Tribes were replaced three years after its foundation. The minister of education, Zühdü Paşa, who was very well educated, served in Europe and later as minister of finance and minister of public works, had carefully orchestrated the foundation of the school. However, in 1895 the management of the school was transferred to Zeki Paşa, the minister of military schools. Unlike Zühdü Paşa, who was committed to create a new generation of loyal and educated Arab subjects, Zeki Paşa's top priority was to maintain safety and security within the walls of the school.

The same pattern of deterioration is evident in the qualifications of the directors of the school. Recai Efendi and Ali Nazima were both immersed in the world of education. As stated earlier, Recai Efendi was instrumental in building the Islamic curriculum in all state schools, while Nazima wrote seventy-five textbooks during his lifetime. They defined the regulations, prepared the curriculum, and Nazima, especially, was involved in all the details of the school. However, Recai Efendi's tenure in the school lasted only some months, and in 1895, Ali Nazima was also moved back to the civil service academy. The subsequent directors lacked the vision of these founding leaders.

Overall, the fortunes of the school reflect the change in the stature of Sultan Abdülhamid. At the time of the school's inauguration in 1892, the sultan was ascendant, and he probably reached the apogee of his reign at the time of his victory over the Greeks in 1897. After the turn of the century, internal and external forces contrived to weaken Sultan Abdülhamid, who gradually came to be labelled as a recluse. Gone were the days when he would drive past the School for Tribes and send extravagant gifts to the tutors and the students. The event related in Omar Mansour's memoirs, in which the students were invited to the Dolmabahçe Palace for the reception given in honour of Kaiser Wilhelm in 1898, was probably never repeated. Moreover, the enrolment on the sultan's orders of Albanians and Javanese after 1902 signifies the vacillations in the palace regarding the mission of the school. It should be noted that in 1907 Sultan Abdülhamid had already been on the throne for thirty-one years. Given all these considerations, I argue that the Ottoman administrators suggested to the sultan in 1907 that the school had served its purpose in its fifteen years of existence and should be converted to a regular high school.

Despite these shortcomings, the history of the School for Tribes underlines the fact that the Ottoman Empire of the late nineteenth and early twentieth centuries was far from a defunct state as is commonly assumed, but rather fully functional and capable of initiating long-term projects and seeing them through. The reach of the empire extended to its furthest corners: from Van in Anatolia in the East to Hadramut in Yemen in the South and Jalu in Libya in the West. The state was able to initiate such a complex undertaking in the very short time span of three months and sustain it for fifteen years. The Ministry of Interior instructed the governors of the provinces to assign officers for recruitment; gendarmes were ordered to escort young sons of tribal chiefs from diverse locations to the capital and back (sixty students in 1892, but around 200 after the fourth year). The Ministry of Education mobilized resources to develop a special curriculum and select high calibre tutors. When disciplinary issues arose, the Ministry of Military Schools was co-opted to oversee the school. The bureaucracy of the empire organized a special one-year course for the students at the civil service academy and created a unique breed of district administrators. Similarly, the military apparatus devised a special training programme for the graduates and then assigned them to their homelands as officers. All of these activities were meticulously noted in the public records, most of which are now available online. Therefore, the School for Tribes is one example that illustrates how the Ottoman Empire in its twilight continued to be a sovereign power acting successfully within its vast territory and mobilizing previously untapped resources.

The archival material pertaining to the school communicates a second resonant message: the very rhetoric of these documents speaks volumes to the sheer power of the Shadow of God; that is, the sultan/caliph. The divine rights of kings were meticulously guarded in Europe for centuries and the Ottoman rulers were careful to position themselves vis-a-vis their Western counterparts, proud to be one of the longest ruling dynasties in the world. Sultan Abdülhamid was a grand master of ceremonies; every Friday the sultan's procession to the communal prayers was organized as a major public event. From its first days, the school was envisioned as an institution which would instil awe and loyalty for the sultan/caliph in the minds of the most remote subjects of the empire. The inauguration ceremony of the school was planned on the birthdate of the Prophet, celebrated as a holy day by all Muslims. The school was characterized as being 'proud to be under the protection and supervision of the Exalted Caliph', a phrase repeated in most documents and newspaper articles.[6]

Another aspect of the Hamidian regime reflected by the School for Tribes experiment is the significant role of the press. There is no question that after the revolution of 1908, freedom of the press intensified, and newspapers proliferated all over the empire. However, during his reign, Sultan Abdülhamid utilized the press as an effective and controlled medium to disseminate information and influence public opinion. One of the first measures taken at the inception of the school was to instruct the Ministry of Education to publish the announcement of its founding in the newspapers. This announcement in Istanbul was quickly followed by ones in the newspapers in all the provincial capitals. On 15 September 1892, the *Zawra'* newspaper of Baghdad reported that the four students who had been admitted to the school and would be leaving for Istanbul were received by the governor and that subsequently a banquet on the Tigris was organized on the eve of their departure. Similarly, the *Sana'a* newspaper of Yemen published several articles about the school. The *Tercüman-ı Hakikat* newspaper of Istanbul regularly informed the public on even the most minute operational activities of school. *Thamarat al-Fünun* newspaper of Beirut was another active promoter of the school.

Finally, the School for Tribes embodies a unique method of promoting upward mobility and talent recruitment within the Ottoman Empire. The case of the janissaries is quite well known, as promising young men from the European provinces were selected and trained not only for the military but also for administrative and academic positions; many grand viziers came from janissary stock. Similarly, the School for Tribes enabled youngsters from far away regions to discover the world at a very early age and return home to build themselves significant careers. As portraits in this study demonstrate, graduates of the school became prime ministers and army commanders in Libya, Iraq, Syria and Lebanon and their descendants played significant roles in their societies. A majority of the graduates served in middle-level governmental or military posts in the last days of the empire. Some of them returned to Turkey after the foundation of the republic, while many remained in their homelands as well-educated and respected citizens.

As explained in the previous chapters, the School for Tribes was officially abolished and the Kabataş high school was opened in the Esma Sultan Palace buildings in 1908. In the last year of its existence, the number of students in the school was below 150 and probably closer to 100. When the Kabataş high school became operational as a day school for students living in the vicinity, seven grades were established, with 276 students enrolled in the first year. In 1913, a primary school was added, and the school was renamed Kabataş Sultanisi. After the foundation of the Turkish Republic, the name was changed to Kabataş Erkek Lisesi. In 1929, due to the further expansion of the school, it was moved to its current beautiful and extensive location on the Bosphorus. Today Kabataş Erkek Lisesi is one of the best high schools in Turkey. The premises of the School for Tribes were then converted briefly into a health clinic and later became a vocational high school, the Kabataş Mesleki ve Teknik Lisesi, which is still functional today.

When I visited the premises of the School for Tribes in 2019, I was pleased to see that the original building was restored by the Istanbul Municipality according to the drawings found in the archives.

I discovered that a new building was constructed in the spacious gardens of the Esma Sultan Palace in 1990 to host yet another high school, Fındıklı Meslek ve Teknik Anadolu Lisesi. The locally elected authority had settled in a corner of the grounds where the original dining hall of the school was located, which still needs refurbishing. These three schools which have replaced the school today have around 2,500 students in total.

Figure 7.2 The Aşiret Mektebi building today – Restored according to original drawings.

On 22 November 2020, I received a surprising email from a friend who had emigrated to Canada and who had heard that I was working on the school:

> I am one of the graduates of the School for Tribes. I completed my studies at the school in its 91st year, in 1983. At that time, we had some knowledge about the history of our school (Kabataş Erkek Lisesi) but were not much interested. Looking back, I can say that the original mission of the school was not changed much. Most of my classmates were talented young boys from the provinces, who qualified in the competive national entrance examination. Our school was a preferred destination for families around the country who aspired that their children become part of the administrative and urban elites.[7]

Thus, in a sense, the legacy of the School for Tribes, which was converted into the Kabataş Erkek Lisesi, lives on. In the twenty-first century, the tribes still play an important role in the Middle East. Although many members of the tribal families have settled in urban environments, the strong ties among them are retained. The School for Tribes stands out as an early hub for talented and select young men from the diverse tribes of the Ottoman Empire, who were moulded into 'Men for All Seasons' and left their imprint on the 'Last Ottoman Generation'.

'Nomads took from civilization only what was needful, depending instead on their native intelligence, enterprise and initiative. They were eager to trade off a constricted existence in an urban setting for the freedom of their massive desert domains, hallowed by time and sanctified by immemorial tradition and customs.'

Samir Seikaly, 'Tribes in Late Ottoman Syria: Local Representations', in *Archivium Ottomanicum* 34, Harassowitz Verlag, 2017, pp. 224–5.

Notes

Introduction

1. *Vaka-i Hayriye* (The Auspicious Event) and the *Asakir-i Mansure-i Muhammadiye* (The Mohammedan Victorious Army) are still recognized as the founding blocks of the modern Turkish army.
2. Karen Barkey, *Empire of Difference: The Ottomans in Comparative Perspective*, Cambridge, 2008, p.292.
3. Eugene Rogan, *Frontiers of the State in the Late Ottoman Empire, Trans Jordan, 1850–1921,* Cambridge, 1999, p.13.
4. Hasan Kayalı, *Arab and Young Turks: Ottomanism, Arabism and Islamism in the Ottoman Empire, 1908–1918*, Berkeley, 1997, p.33.
5. Rogan, *Frontiers of the State in the Late Ottoman Empire*.
6. *Mekteb-i Harbiye*.
7. *Mekatib-i Rüşdiye Nezareti*.
8. *Maarif-i Umumiye Nezareti* – Akşin Somel, *The Modernization of Public Education in the Ottoman Empire, 1839–1908*, Brill, 2001, p.43.
9. *Mekteb-i Mülkiye*.
10. The university was called *Darülfünun,* meaning the house of sciences.
11. *Maarif-i Umumi Nizamnamesi*.
12. 'Daire-i medeniyete dahil olan milel ve akvam.'
13. Benjamin Fortna, *The Imperial Classroom Islam, the State and Education in the Late Ottoman Empire*, Oxford, 2002, p.11.
14. Engin D. Akarlı, 'The Problems of External Pressures, Power Struggles and Budgetary Deficits under Abdülhamid II', Princeton University, unpublished dissertation, 1976, p.1.
15. *Maarif Hisse Ianesi* was collected with the *Öşr,* the classical agriculture tax.
16. *Dar-ül Muallimin*.
17. Engin Akarlı, 'Abdülhamid II's Attempts to Integrate Arabs into the Ottoman System', in *Palestine in the Late Ottoman Period*, ed. David Kushner, Brill, 1986, p.81.

18 M. Talha Çiçek, *Negotiating Empire in the Middle East: Ottomans and Arab Nomads in the Modern Era, 1840–1914*, Cambridge, 2021, p.167.
19 Ibrahim Sivrikaya, 'Osmanlı İmparatorluğu İdaresindeki Aşiretlerin Eğitimi ve İlk Aşiret Mektebi', *Belgelerle Türk Tarihi Dergisi*, cilt 11- sayı 63, 1972, p.24.
20 Eugene Rogan, 'Aşiret Mektebi: Abdülhamid II's School for Tribes (1892–1907)', *Int. J. Middle East Studies* 28, 1996, p.83. Rogan describes the Aşiret Mektebi as 'an experiment in social engineering… an instrument to advance the state-sanctioned supranational identities of Ottomanism and Pan-Islamism among the marginal communities inhabiting the frontiers of its Arab and Anatolian provinces.'
21 Alişan Akpınar, *Osmanlı Devletinde Aşiret Mektebi*, Göçebe, 1997.
22 Alişan Akpınar and Eugene Rogan, *Aşiret, Mektep, Devlet*, Aram, 2001, p.55.
23 Ussama Makdisi, 'Ottoman Orientalism', *The American Historical Review* 107, June 2002, pp.768–96 and Selim Deringil 'They Live in a State of Nomadism and Savagery: The Late Ottoman Empire and the Post-Colonial Debate', *Comparative Studies in Society and History* 45, no. 2, April 2003, pp.311–42.
24 Enver Ziya Karal, *Osmanlı Tarihi*, Türk Tarih Kurumu, 1983, p.401, Hasan Ali Kocer, *Türkiye'de Modern Eğitimin Doğuşu ve Gelişmesi (1773–1923)*, Milli Eğitim Basımevi, 1970, p.157.
25 Michael Provence, *The Last Ottoman Generation and the Making of the Modern Middle East*, Cambridge, 2017, p.27.
26 Fortna, *Imperial Classroom*, p.215.
27 Ibid., p.216.
28 Corinne Blake, 'Training Arab-Ottoman Bureaucrats: Syrian Graduates of the Mülkiye Mektebi, 1890–1920', unpublished dissertation, Princeton Univ., 1991, p.278.
29 Benedict Anderson, *Imagined Communities: Reflections on the Origin and Spread of Nationalism*, Verso, 1983, p.140.

Chapter 1

1 Ibrahim Şirin, 'Münif Pasa'nın Tahran'dan Gönderdiği Devlet İşleriyle Ilgili Layihası ve Düşündürdükleri', *Turkish Studies* 3-4, Summer 2008, pp.759–71. Münif Paşa was educated in Cairo and Damascus and studied Arabic, Persian and French. In 1853, he joined the Translation Bureau of the Sublime Porte. Münif Paşa then worked in the Berlin Embassy, where he learnt

German. In 1895, he was sent to Tehran for a second term. He then retired to his home in Istanbul.
2   *Mecmua-i Fünun.*
3   The recommendations in the treatise begin with an emphasis on the rule of law and the establishment of a law school. Münif Paşa highlighted the significance of economic improvements and active foreign relations.
4   *Tercüman-ı Hakikat*, 18 July 1890.
5   Osman Ergin, *Türkiye Maarif Tarihi*, Cilt 3, Maarif Matbaası, 1941, p.975.
6   Selçuk Akşin Somel, 'Osman Nuri Paşa'nın 17 Temmuz 1885 Tarihli Hicaz Raporu', *Ankara Univ. Tarih Araştırmaları Dergisi*, 18, 1996/5, pp.1–38.
7   Metin Hülagu, 'Hacı Osman Nuri Paşa, Hayatı ve Faaliyetleri, 1840-1898', *Ankara Univ. OTAM dergisi*, 5, 1994/5, pp.1–9.
8   'İşte esasen emr ü ferman-ı hikmet beyan-ı hazret-i hilafetpenahiden bil-iktibas'.
9   'Bela-yı cehalet'.
10 Ottoman Archives, DH MKT 1964-79-1-1 and A DVN MKL-33-17-1, 22 June 1892.
11 Ottoman Archives, BEO 28-2029-1, 29 June 1892.
12 Ottoman Archives, BEO 28-2029-2, 29 June 1892.
13 'Tebligat-ı Resmiye – Matbuat Idare-i behiyesinden'.
14 *Tercüman-ı Hakikat*, 3 June 1892.
15 Ottoman Archives, DH-MKT-1971-125, 3 July 1892.
16 Ottoman Archives, BEO 30-2219-1, 7 July 1892.
17 *Nizamname.*
18 Ottoman Archives, I.MMS-131-564-6-1, 25 July 1892.
19 *Tercüman-ı Hakikat*, 15 August 1892. The Hamidiye regiments were cavalry units established in the eastern provinces in 1890.
20 *Tercüman-ı Hakikat*, 20 September 1892.
21 Ottoman Archives, Y-PRK-DH-5-60-1/same doc Y-MTV-67-90-1, 18 September 1892.
22 Memoirs of Omar Mansour.
23 Hagop Mıntzuri, *Istanbul Anıları*, Tarih Vakfı, 1998 (Armenian book published in 1984), p.41.
24 Ismayıl Hakkı Baltacıoglu, *Hayatım*, Dünya Yayınları, 1998, p.28. It is interesting that the population living in the environs had little knowledge about the school and rumours about the students abounded.
25 *Tercüman-ı Hakikat*, 11 October 1892.
26 *Tercüman-ı Hakikat*, 17 October 1892.

27 *Talimatname-i Dahiliye.*
28 Ottoman Archives, Y-MTV-73-99-1 and 99-2-(1 through 6), 3 January 1893.
29 '*Nezafet ve taharet*'.
30 Ottoman Archives, Y-MTV-76-88-1-1, 3 April 1893 and 8 April 1893 (response written on same document).
31 *Tercüman-ı Hakikat*, 4 June 1893, '*Kağıthane mesire yeri.*'
32 *Tercüman-ı Hakikat*, 31 May 1894.
33 The grand vizier himself wrote that the price of the purchase would be 9.000 liras with 3.000 paid upfront and the balance in monthly installments of 500 liras.
34 Ottoman Archives, BEO 218-16320-1, 12 June 1893.
35 Ottoman Archives, BEO 30-2219-2, 13 October 1893.
36 Ottoman Archives, I-HUS-34-126-1-1, 8 February 1895.
37 Ottoman Archives, Y-MTV-114-80, 7 February 1895.
38 Ottoman Archives, MF-MKT 339-36-6, 12 July 1896.
39 Ottoman Archives, MF-MKT 339-36-1, 1 October 1896.
40 *Sınıf-ı Mahsus.*
41 Ottoman Archives, I-HUS-49-127-1, 1 October 1896.
42 Ottoman Archives, MF IBT 202-116-1, 1 October 1896.
43 *Tercüman-ı Hakikat*, 27 December 1896.
44 Ottoman Archives, I-SE-9-46-1, 2 January 1897.
45 *Tercüman-ı Hakikat*, 16 September 1897.
46 I would like to thank Professor John Meloy, Chair of AUB History and Archeology Department, for discovering the full identity of Benedictsen.
47 *Tercüman-ı Hakikat*, 12 December 1897.
48 Matthias Bjørnlund, 'Karen Jeppe, Aage Meyer Benedictsen, and the Ottoman Armenians: National Survival in Imperial and Colonial Settings', www.researchgate.net/publication/237490456, 2008.
49 *Tercüman-ı Hakikat*, 22 October 1905.
50 Ottoman Archives, Y-A-RES-134-17, 13 December 1905.
51 Ottoman Archives, MF-MKT 909-29-1-1 and MF-MKT 675-83-1-1, 25 January 1906. Darulhayr-ı Ali was a boarding school inaugurated in 1903 for orphans.
52 Ottoman Archives, MF MKT 1004-26-1, 19 May 1907.
53 *Tercüman-ı Hakikat*, 30 August 1907.
54 Ottoman Archives, Y-PRK-TKM-50-51-1-1 and HR-SYS 198-23-3, November 1907. The claim that there were no applicants is obviously a fabrication.
55 Ottoman Archives, Y-PRK-TKM-50-51-2, 30 November 1907.
56 Rogan, 'Aşiret Mektebi', p.100.

57 Ottoman Archives, DH-MKT-1244-42-1-2, 13 January 1908.
58 Ottoman Archives, I-HUS-163-35-2-1, 17 February 1908.
59 Ottoman Archives, BEO 3252-243857-1-1 and Y-PRK-MF 2-88-1-1, 18 February 1908. Most of the missionary schools including Robert College were in this vicinity and had started attracting Muslim student.
60 Ottoman Archives, BEO 3255-244115-4-1, 19 February 1908. '*mektep lağv olunmuşdur*'.
61 The first Director of Kabataş high school was Hasan Tahsin Ayni, who was one of the tutors of the Aşiret Mektebi students in the civil service academy.

Chapter 2

1   *Tercüman-ı Hakikat*, 18 August 1892, based on *Sana'a* newspaper of Yemen.
2   Ottoman Archives, Y-MTV-67-90-2-1, 9 August 1892.
3   *Zawra'* article reproduced in *Tercüman-ı Hakikat*, 15 September 1892. Chief secretary – *mektupçu*.
4   *Tercüman-ı Hakikat*, 18 August 1892.
5   Ottoman Archives, Y-PRK-UM-25-21-11, 29 August 1892.
6   Ottoman Archives, BEO 66-488-2, 6 September 1892.
7   Ottoman Archives, BEO 66-4880-1, 9 September 1892.
8   '*Ahlak ve terbiyelerince derkar olan mugayeret*'.
9   Alişan Akpınar, *Osmanlı Devletinde Aşiret Mektebi*, Göçebe Yayınları, 1997, p.38–9 and Ottoman Archives Y-A-HUS 267-68-1 and 68-2, 29 November 1982 and 4 December 1892.
10 *Tercüman-ı Hakikat*, 13 September 1892.
11 Ottoman Archives, Y-PRK-DH-5-60-1-1, Same doc Y-MTV-67-90-1, 18 September 1892.
12 *Tercüman-ı Hakikat*, 20 September 1892.
13 *Tercüman-ı Hakikat*, 26 September 1892 and 3 October 1892. One day before the inauguration, the fourth student from Trablusgarb, who had got ill and left in the hospital in Crete, also arrived at the school.
14 *Tercüman-ı Hakikat*, 4 October 1892.
15 Ottoman Archives, Y-A-HUS-265-99-2-1, 23 September 1892 and Y-A-HUS-265-99-1-1, 9 October 1892.
16 Ottoman Archives, Y-A-HUS-266-111-2-1, 7 November 1892, Y-A-HUS-266-111-1-1, 9 November 1892 and Y-PRK-BŞK-28-63-1-1, 10 December 1892.

17 *Tercüman-ı Hakikat*, 18 October 1892.
18 *Tercüman-ı Hakikat*, 10 November 1892.
19 *Tercüman-ı Hakikat*, 12 November 1892.
20 Ottoman Archives, MF-MKT 154-99-1, 10 November 1892. Telegram from the Vali of Beirut about the sons of the Dandashli tribe.
21 *Tercüman-ı Hakikat*, 27 December 1892.
22 *Tercüman-ı Hakikat*, 15 June 1893. The government clearly announced a quota for forty students; it is, not clear why the newspaper mentions sixty.
23 Ottoman Archives, MF-IBT-33-98-1, 12 September 1893 – this document is related to the dispatch of Muhammad Hattab from Hawran/Syria, brother of Sheikh Rahil of the Türki tribe; the first three students were given ID numbers 63–65.
24 Ottoman Archives, MF-MKT 190-14-1, 29 October 1893.
25 Ottoman Archives, MF-MKT 193-18-1, 31 October 1893.
26 Ottoman Archives, MF-MKT 192-78-1, 14 January 1894. '*Kürt ve Arab'ın ihtilaf-ı mizac ve meşrepleri cihetiyle*'.
27 Ottoman Archives, BEO 419- 31414, 6 June 1894, draft of minister's letter.
28 Ottoman Archives, BEO 419- 31414-2-1, 11 June 1894.
29 '*Terbiye ve tahsile müstaid ve cismen tebeddülatı havaiye mütehammil*'.
30 *Tercüman-ı Hakikat*, 13 August 1894.
31 Ottoman Archives, MF-MKT 234-50-1, 22 August 1894. '*Hamepira-yi ta'zim ve tekrim olan emirname-i sami-i cenab-ı sadaretpenahileri hüküm-ü alisine tevfikan*'.
32 Ottoman Archives, MF-MKT 202-51-1 and 51-2, 11 March 1894 and 15 March 1894. These documents include a letter of the Vali of Syria stating that Fayez from the Leca tribe was the son of Feyiz Aga, who commanded a loyal Sunni force of one hundred men in Jabal Druze and therefore deserved priority in admission.
33 Ottoman Archives, MF-MKT 234-50-5, 23 October 1894.
34 *Tercüman-ı Hakikat*, 1 October 1894 and 11 October 1894.
35 Ottoman Archives, MF-MKT 246-32-1 and 32-2, 28 November 1894; BEO 557-41720-1-2, 23 January 1895 and Tercüman-ı Hakikat, 1 January 1895.
36 Ottoman Archives, BEO 419-31414-2-1, 11 June 1894, *Tercüman-ı Hakikat* 13 August 1895, BEO 775-58103-1-1, 5 May 1886, *Tercüman-ı Hakikat*, 27 May 1899, MF-MKT 557-22-1, 9 May 1901, BEO 2336-175191-1-1, 18 May 1904, MF-MKT 902-37-1, 25 November 1905, BEO 3126-234376-1-1, 15 August 1907.
37 In 1899, a student with ID number 247 was transferred to the civil service academy. This is another indication that the total population must have exceeded 450.

38 Total target was 625 for fifteen years, and the assumed intake of 450 brings the ratio to 72 per cent.
39 Ottoman Archives, MF-IBT-30-47-1-1, 4 September 1892. '*İşbu lutf-u celil-i Cenab-ı Zillullahiyi bir nimet-i cihan-kıymet olmak üzere kemal-i şükran ile tahdis ve takdis ederek.*'
40 Ottoman Archives, MF-MKT 366-50-1, 19 July 1897.
41 Ottoman Archives, MF-MKT 400-53-1, 18 January 1898 and MF-MKT 399-2-9, 7 April 1898.
42 Ottoman Archives, MF-MKT 399-2-7, 18 May 1898, MF-MKT 400-53-2, 3 June 1898, MF-MKT 399-2-13, 7 June 1898 and MF-MKT 400-53-3, 7 June 1898.
43 Ottoman Archives, MF-MKT 423-34-1, 17 August 1898 and six consecutive letters.
44 Ottoman Archives, MF-MKT 472-1-1, 16 October 1899 and DH-MKT-2258-35-1, 17 October 1899.
45 Ottoman Archives, MF-MKT 533-20-3, 23 October 1900 and MF-MKT-533-20-15, 1 November 1900.
46 In 1898, Naum Paşa had vouched for four members of the same family. Ottoman archives, DH-MKT-1206-45-1-1, 14 June 1907.
47 Ottoman Archives, MF-MKT 1018-53-1 and 4, 19 August 1907 and 28 August 1907.
48 *Tercüman-ı Hakikat*, 12 September 1899.
49 Ottoman Archives, BEO 3126-234376-1-1, 15 August 1907.
50 *Tercüman-ı Hakikat*, 12 September 1892. As noted previously, he arrived one day before inauguration.
51 Ottoman Archives, BEO 309-23125-1, 9 November 1893.
52 Ottoman Archives, MF-MKT 414-52-1, 31 July 1898 (Despatch of Seyfunnasr and Hasan from Benghazi); DH-MKT-2094-52-1, 22 August 1898 and *Tercüman-ı Hakikat*, 21 August 1898.
53 Ottoman Archives, MF-MKT 417-3-4, 23 August 1898.
54 Ottoman Archives, MF-MKT 684-20-1, 11 February 1903, MF-MKT 738-25-1, 24 September 1903 and MF-MKT 754-42-1, 28 December 1903.
55 Ottoman Archives, BEO 471-35303-1-1, 6 September 1894. *Tercüman-ı Hakikat*, 17 November 1894. He replaced a student from Benghazi who had left and received ID #44.
56 Ottoman Archives, Y-MTV 295-115-1, 9 March 1907 and ML-EEM 587-46-1-1, 11 March 1907.
57 *Tercüman-ı Hakikat*, 1 January 1899.

58 Ottoman Archives, MF-MKT 469-13-1, 13-2, 13-3, 13-4-1, 13-4-2 and 13-5, from 19 July to 30 November 1899.
59 Ottoman Archives, MF-MKT 466-36-6, 4 September 1898, MF-MKT 466-36-7, 11 September 1898 and MF-MKT 466-36-1, 11 December 1898.
60 Ottoman Archives, MF-MKT 533-20-1/5/7/13, 8 July 1900 and 11 July 1900.
61 Ottoman Archives, MF-MKT 592-22-1, 30 November 1901.
62 Ottoman Archives, MF-MKT 732-4-1 and 5, 8 August 1903 and 26 January 1904.
63 Ottoman Archives, MF-MKT 797-65, 2 August 1904 and 798-24-1 through 24-14, from 8 May 1905 to 10 October 1905.
64 Ottoman Archives, I-HUS-98-16-1, 28 June 1902.
65 Nathalie Clayer, 'The Albanian Students of the Mekteb-i Mülkiye, Social Networks and Trends of Thought', in *Late Ottoman Society, the Intellectual Legacy*, ed. Elisabeth Özdalga, Routledge, 2005, p.289–309. Two of these graduates became prime ministers of Albania, after Albania became independent. (Suleiman Bey Delvina and Mehdi Frasheri).
66 Ottoman Archives, MF-MKT 653-38-1, 12 August 1902.
67 Ottoman Archives, Y-MTV-233-83-1, 17 August 1902 and DH-MKT-565-28-1, 24 August 1902.
68 Ottoman Archives, I MF 8-32-4-1, 23 September 1902.
69 *Tercüman-ı Hakikat*, 24 September 1902.
70 Ottoman Archives, DH-MKT-931-11-1, 8 February 1905 and DH-MKT-983-45-1, 45-2, 45-3 and 45-4 from 15 March 1905 to 30 August 1905; MF-MKT 906-5-1-1 and 1-2, 13 December 1905 and 30 December 1905.
71 Ottoman Archives, I MF-13-9-1-1, 17 December 1906.
72 Ottoman Archives, MF-MKT 161-94-1, 28 February 1893.
73 Ottoman Archives, BEO 860-64427-1 and 64427-2, 26 October 1896 and 31 October 1896.
74 Ottoman Archives, MF-MKT 721-20-1 through 21, from 28 July 1903 to 20 October 1903.
75 *Tercüman-ı Hakikat*, 27 January 1905.
76 Ottoman Archives, MF-MKT 173-118-1, 10 July 1893. An earlier undated draft is also available MF-MKT 173-118-3 and the stamp of the Aşiret Mektebi can be seen in this document.
77 Ottoman Archives, BEO 654-49037-1-1, 15 July 1895.
78 *Tercüman-ı Hakikat*, 1 November 1895 and 12 November 1895.
79 *Tercüman-ı Hakikat*, 23 November 1895.

80 *Tercüman-ı Hakikat*, 8 September 1897, Ottoman Archives, MF-MKT 370-55-011, 11 September 1897 and *Tercüman-ı Hakikat*, 7 December 1897.
81 *Tercüman-ı Hakikat*, 29 June 1900, 6 July 1900 and 30 July 1900.
82 Ottoman Archives, MF-MKT 447-42-1 and 447-42-2, 28 March 1899.
83 *Tercüman-ı Hakikat*, 25 June 1899.
84 *Tercüman-ı Hakikat*, 23 July 1897.
85 Ottoman Archives, Y-PRK-BŞK-54-49-1-1, 6 October 1897.
86 Ottoman Archives, Y-PRK-ASK-137-24-1, 9 April 1898.
87 Eugene Rogan, Aşiret Mektebi, p.97. Rogan describes the reminiscences of Alois Musil in the region in 1908.
88 Ottoman Archives, I-HUS-63-102-1 and I-HUS-63-50-1, both dated 10 April 1898.
89 *Tercüman-ı Hakikat*, 16 April 1898.
90 *Tercüman-ı Hakikat*, 21 April 1898.
91 Mücellidoğlu Ali Çankaya, *Yeni Mülkiye Tarihi ve Mülkiyeliler*, II. Cild, Mars Matbaası, 1969.
92 *Tercüman-ı Hakikat*, 16 March 1899.
93 *Tercüman-ı Hakikat*, 8 April 1900 and 14 May 1900 also Ottoman Archives, I. TAL 211-60-1, 18 April 1900.
94 *Tercüman-ı Hakikat* 17 July 1901, 29 July 1901 and 16 August 1901.
95 Ottoman Archives, I-TAL-257-58-1, 14 August 1901.
96 Ottoman Archives, Y-MTV-228-98-2-1, 6 February 1902.
97 *Tercüman-ı Hakikat*, 18 January 1904.
98 Ottoman Archives, Y-A-RES-134-17-5-1, 24 May 1905.
99 *Tercüman-ı Hakikat*, 21 September 1906.
100 Ottoman Archives, Y-MTV-301-74-1, 21 August 1907.

Chapter 3

1 Although many accounts including Fortna give his birth as 1840, his official biography states that he was born on 7 December 1852, Ottoman Archives, DH SAID 42-146-289.
2 My paper on this school was published in *Sahn-ı Seman'dan Darülfunun'a V*, ed., Ahmet Hamdi Furat, Zeytinburnu Belediyesi, 2021.
3 His appointment as assistant director is recorded as 1881 in Çankaya, *Yeni Mülkiye Tarihi ve Mülkiyeliler*, p.829; however, I have followed the date in his official biography.

4   The Galatasaray Sultani was opened in 1868, the French Minister of Education Duruy prepared the curriculum.
5   Ottoman Archive, Y-MTV-25-2-3, no date, but before March 1887.
6   Fortna, *Imperial Classroom*, p.111.
7   Akşin Somel, *Osmanlıda Eğitimin Modernleşmesi*, İletişim Yayınları, 2010, pp.228–9.
8   Fortna, *Imperial Classroom*, p.215. 'Ilm-i Ahlak and Fıkh'.
9   Hikmet Yavuzyiğit, *Mülkiye Tarihi*, Mülkiyeliler Birliği Yayınları, 1999, p.25.
10   Fortna, *Imperial Classroom*, p.53.
11   Letter written to the Christian Missionary Society by Robert Cust on 5 February 1888, in Rogan, *Frontiers of the State in the Late Ottoman Empire*, p.146.
12   Çankaya, *Yeni Mülkiye Tarihi ve Mülkiyeliler*, p.830. MF-MKT 99-83-1, 1 July 1888 contains information about the pilgrimage of Recai and Zihni.
13   Ottoman Archives, BEO 77-5771-1, 26 September 1892.
14   Ottoman Archives, BEO 79-5908-1, 29 September 1982.
15   Ottoman Archives, SAID 42-146-289 and I-HUS-4-51-1, 3 October 1892.
16   *Tercüman-ı Hakikat*, 17 October 1892.
17   Ottoman Archives, DH-SAID 77-77-149.
18   Gökçe Özder-Didem Ardalı Büyükarman, 'Osmanlı Devletinin Son Yıllarında Yaşamış Bir Eğitimci: Ali Nazima', *Turkish Studies dergisi* 12, no. 15, 2016, pp.511–24.
19   Ottoman Archives, Y A RES 61-12-6-1, 9 October 1892. This curriculum vitae was prepared before his appointment to the school.
20   Ottoman Archives, Y-MTV-102-88, 14 August 1894.
21   Ottoman Archives, BEO 576-43175-1, 21 February 1895, Nazima appointed assistant director with a salary of 2.500 kuruş.
22   *Idman*, 1886.
23   Ottoman Archives, MF-MKT 347-23-1, 21 December 1896. Ban issued by Süreyya Paşa, chief scribe of the sultan.
24   *Çocuklar Bahçesi*, 1888.
25   *Bak ve Öğren*, 1912.
26   *10 Temmuz, Malumat-ı Medeniye*.
27   Cüneyd Okay, *Meşrutiyet Çocukları*, Bordo Kitaplar, 2000, p.17.
28   *Inas Darülfünunu*.
29   Çankaya, *Yeni Mülkiye Tarihi ve Mülkiyeliler*, p.943.
30   Ibid.
31   I would like to thank Professor Michael Provence for pointing out the relationship with the renowned Jerusalem Huseini family. Taher Efendi al-

Husseini was Grand Mufti of Jerusalem from 1860 until 1908 and his son Muhammad Amin was a leader in Mandatory Palestine. Abdulmuhsin was clearly related to them which may explain his appointment to the School for Tribes at its inception.

32 Ottoman Archives, DH SAID 10-172-2-343.
33 *'Mukdim ve gayur bendegan'*.
34 Ottoman Archives, MF-MKT 360-24-1, 15 June 1896 and MF-MKT 360-24-2, 22 July 1896.
35 *Tercüman-ı Hakikat*, 16 September 1897.
36 Ottoman Archives, BEO 1596-119655-1, 14 December 1900. *'Hilaf-ı sadakat hal ve hareketi anlaşıldığından.'*
37 Ottoman Archives, I-DH 1381-40-1, 16 December 1900.
38 Ottoman Archives, BEO 1617-121234-3, 1 February 1901. *'Elde akçem kalmadığı cihetle son derece sefaletde kaldım.'*
39 Ottoman Archives, BEO 1617-121234-2, 3 February 1901, I-DH 1381-40-3, 6 February 1901, DH-MKT-2450-75, 9 February 1901, BEO 1617-121234-1, 11 February 1901 and MF-MKT 551-25, 13 April 1901.
40 Ottoman Archives, I-MF 6-52-1-1, 14 December 1900.
41 Ottoman Archives, BEO 2303-172695-1, 30 March 1904, MF-MKT 898-62-1-1, 26 November 1905.
42 Ottoman Archives, MF-MKT 898-62-1-2, 26 November 1905 and MF-MKT 939-3-1, 27 June 1906.
43 *Tercüman-ı Hakikat*, 14 September 1906. Abdülhamid began a large-scale donation campaign to build the Hijaz railway and almost one-third was financed in this manner. Officials were encouraged to donate.
44 Ottoman Archives, Y-MTV-293-7, 17 January 1907.
45 Ottoman Archives, MF-MKT 211-15-1, 9 June 1894.
46 Ottoman Archives, Y-MTV-102-88-3-1, 14 August 1894.
47 Akpınar, *Osmanlı Devletinde Aşiret Mektebi*, pp.97–101.
48 *Tercüman-ı Hakikat*, 12 December 1897, his visit was discussed in Chapter 1.
49 *Malumat-ı Mütenevvia*.
50 Ottoman Archives, MF-MKT 439-30-1-1, 28 February 1899.
51 *Tercüman-ı Hakikat*, 16 May 1902.
52 Atatürk Library Collection, Maarif Salnamesi, 1903.
53 Omar Mansour, Memoirs.
54 Ottoman Archives, Y-A-RES-112-59-1-2, attached to a group of docs from 10 June 1901.
55 Ottoman Archives, Y-MTV-161-95-1-1, 29 June 1897.

56 Ottoman Archives, MF-MKT 340-7-1-1, 15 October 1896. '*Misafireten birinci seneye konularak, hiç bir ders ile meşgul edilmedikleri anlaşıldığı*'.
57 Ottoman Archives, MF-MKT 340-7-1-2, 18 October 1896 and Çankaya, *Yeni Mülkiye Tarihi ve Mülkiyeliler*, p.290.
58 *Mecelle, Idari Kavanin ve Usul-u Idare-i Mülkiye*.
59 Selim Deringil, *The Well Protected Domains*, I.B.Tauris, 1999, p.103 and p.109.
60 Omar Mansour, Memoirs.

Chapter 4

1 Fruma Zachs, *The Making of a Syrian Identity*, Brill, 2005, p.69.
2 Ibid., p.117.
3 Eugene Rogan, 'Instant Communication: The Impact of the Telegraph in Ottoman Syria', in *The Syrian Land: Processes of Integration and Fragmentation*, ed. Thomas Philipp and Birgit Schaebler, Franz Steiner, 1998, p.117.
4 Chatham House, *Kurdish and Syrian Regime Forces Take Very Different Routes to Control Deir ez-Zor,* December 2017.
5 Rudayna Baalbaky and Ahmad Mhidi, *Tribes and the Rule of the Islamic State: The Case of the Syrian city of Deir Ez-Zor*, AUB Policy Institute, 2018.
6 Idris Bostan, 'Zor Sancağının İmar ve Islahı ile Alakalı Üç Layiha', *The Journal of Ottoman Studies* 6, 1986, pp.163–220. Bostan notes that Deir ez-Zor was often mixed up with Şehr-i Zor and therefore the name of the latter was changed to Kirkuk in 1893.
7 Norman Lewis, *Nomads and Settlers in Syria and Jordan, 1800–1980*, Cambridge, 1987, p.30.
8 Ibid., pp.170–1 and p.196.
9 Bostan, 'Zor Sancağının İmar ve Islahı ile Alakalı Üç Layiha', p.220. 'hal-i bedavet ve vahşiyette bulunan aşair-i urban.... lezzet-i hükümet ve nimet-i medeniyeti alarak... her tarafça teessüs ve takarrur etmekde olan emr-i maarif ve turuk ve meabir inşaatı gibi müessesat-ı hayriye...'
10 Ottoman Archives, Y-PRK-DH-5-60-1 (same text appears in Y-MTV-67-90-1), 18 September 1892.
11 Ottoman Archives, BEO 205-15354-3, 16 May 1893.
12 Ottoman Archives, BEO 419-31414-2-1, 11 June 1894.
13 Ottoman Archives, Y-MTV-102-88-3, 14 August 1894.

14 Ottoman Archives, Y-MTV-114-80, 7 February 1895. Also mentioned in the memoirs of Omar Mansour.
15 Michael Provence, 'A Man of the Frontier, Ramadan Shallash and the Making of the Post-Ottoman Arab East', in *Age of Rogues, Rebels, Revolutionaries and Racketeers at the Frontiers of Empires*, ed. Ramazan Öztan – Alp Yenen, Edinborough, 2021, p.7.
16 Michael Provence, 'Ottoman Modernity, Colonialism and Insurgency in the Interwar Arab East', in *International Journal of Middle East Studies* 43, May 2011, p.212.
17 *Al-Muntada al-Adabi*.
18 James Gelvin, *Divided Loyalties, Nationalism and Mass Politics in Syria at the Close of Empire*, Univ. of California, 1998, p.66. Al-Nadi al-Arabi.
19 Provence, 'A Man of the Frontier, Ramadan Shallash and the Making of the Post-Ottoman Arab East', p.9.
20 Eliezer Tauber, *Arab Movements in World War I*, Frank Cass, 1993, p.111.
21 Talha Çiçek, *War and State Formation in Syria, Cemal Paşa's Governorate during World War I, 1914–1917*, Routledge, 2014, p.116.
22 Provence, 'A Man of the Frontier, Ramadan Shallash and the Making of the Post-Ottoman Arab East', p.11.
23 Eliezer Tauber, *The Formation of Modern Syria and Iraq*, Frank Cass, 1995, p.226.
24 Eliezer Tauber, 'The Struggle for Deir Ez-Zur:The Determination of Borders between Syria and Iraq', *Journal of Middle East Studies* 23, August 1991, p.363.
25 Tauber, *The Formation of Modern Syria and Iraq*, p.195.
26 Katharina Lange, 'Heroic Faces, Disruptive Deeds: Remembering the Tribal Shaykh on the Syrian Euphrates', in *Nomadic Societies in the Middle East and North Africa*, ed. Dawn Chatty, Brill, 2006, p.945.
27 Tauber, *The Formation of Modern Syria and Iraq*, p.369.
28 Ibid.
29 Gelvin, *Divided Loyalties, Nationalism and Mass Politics in Syria at the Close of Empire*, p.175.
30 Mukhlis had deserted the Ottoman army in 1915 to join the British in Iraq; then he went to Hijaz and became part of the Sharifian army. (Tauber, *Arab Movements in World War I*, p.110).
31 Lewis, *Nomads and Settlers in Syria and Jordan, 1800–1980*, p.153.
32 Michael Provence, *The Great Syrian Revolt and the Rise of Arab Nationalism*, University of Texas, 2005, p.13.

33 Ibid., pp.82–3.
34 Michael Provence, 'A Man of the Frontier, Ramadan Shallash and the Making of the Post-Ottoman Arab East', p.15, letter obtained from CADN (Nantes), carton 1704, BR 241, 5 December 1925, annex 1.
35 Philip Khoury, *Syria and the French Mandate: The Politics of Arab Nationalism, 1920–1945*, Princeton University Press, 1987, p.176.
36 Daniel Neep, *Occupying Syria under the French Mandate: Insurgency, Space and State Formation*, Cambridge University Press, 2012, p.62.
37 Provence, *The Great Syrian Revolt and the Rise of Arab Nationalism*, p.116.
38 *Filistin*, 6 November 1925.
39 *Filistin*, 9 February 1926.
40 Provence, *The Great Syrian Revolt and the Rise of Arab Nationalism*, p.134.
41 *Filistin*, 5 February 1926.
42 *Filistin*, 23 November 1926.
43 Abu Husayn, 'The Long Rebellion: The Druzes and the Ottomans, 1516–1697', Archivum Ottomanicum, 2001, pp.165–91.
44 Kamal Salibi, *The Modern History of Lebanon, Salibi*, Caravan Books, 2004, p.109.
45 Kamal Salibi, *The Druze Realities and Perceptions*, Druze Heritage Foundation, 2006, pp.130–1.
46 Thomas Philipp and Birgit Schaebler, eds. *The Syrian Land: Processes of Integration and Fragmentation, Bilad al-Sham from the 18th to the 20th Century*, Franz Steiner, 1998, p.333.
47 Lewis, *Nomads and Settlers in Syria and Jordan 1800–1980*, p.87 and Linda Schilcher, *Families in Politics, Damascene Factions and Estates of the 18th and 19th Centuries,* Franz Steiner, 1985, p.102.
48 Ottoman Archives, A-MKT-NZD-422-55 and A-MKT-MHM-294-39-3-1, 11 February 1864 attest that the Ottoman Governor of Syria Mehmed Rüşdü sent three squadrons to the mountain. Miralay Ahmad was given the task of investigating a murder of a relative of Faysal al-Shaalan of the neighbouring Ruwala tribe.
49 Abdul Rahim Abu Husayn, *Beyn al-Markaz wa al-Atraf, Hawran fi al-Wathaiq al-Uthmaniyyah, 1842–1918*, Druze Heritage Foundation, 2015, p.34.
50 Philipp and Schaebler, *The Syrian Land*, p.333.
51 Ibid., p.338. Ottoman Archives, YEE 104-70-1, 27 November 1887, describes how Yahya al-Atrash was approached by the French and refused to cooperate.
52 Abu Husayn, *Beyn al-Markaz wa al-Atraf*, p.38.

53 Ottoman Archives, BEO 180-13448-3-1, 8 April 1893.
54 Ottoman Archives, BEO 180-13448-2-1, 30 March 1893.
55 Ottoman Archives, I-DH 01317- 53-3-1, 21 October 1894 and I-DH 01317- 53-4-1 appointment of Shibli dated 17 November 1894. Sultan's confirmation I-DH 01317- 53-5-1, 21 November 1894.
56 *Tercüman-ı Hakikat*, 13 May 1894.
57 Ottoman Archives, Y-MTV-102-88-3-3, August 1894.
58 This earlier student was Darwish from Basra. Archive document Y-MTV-79-182-2-1, 10 July 1893 states that 'Darwish (#13) is above the age allowed and married and has a child; he also caused other students to misbehave and should not be allowed to return.'
59 *Tercüman-ı Hakikat*, 16 March 1899. The names of the students admitted to Mülkiye were Fahreddin- Diyarbakır, Fayez-Syria, Omer Mansur-Benghazi, Halil-Hawran, Faris-Syria, Ahsen-Yemen, Fahd-Jabal Druze and Yusuf-Jabal Druze.
60 Ottoman Archives, I. TAL 211-60-1, 18 April 1900.
61 *Tercüman-ı Hakikat*, 14 May 1900.
62 Ottoman Archives, DH MKT 02478-46-1, 30 April 1901
63 Ottoman Archives, I.HB 76-43-2-1/76-43-3-1/76-43-5-1, 10 February 1911.
64 Michael Provence, 'Druze Shaykhs, Arab Nationalists and Grain Merchants', in *The Druze, Realities and Perceptions*, ed. Kamal Salibi, Druze Heritage Foundation, 2006, p.145.
65 Ottoman Archives, BEO 3873-290460, 27 March 1911.
66 Provence, 'Druze Shaykhs, Arab Nationalists and Grain Merchants', p.146.
67 Ottoman Archives, DH ŞFR 451-105-1, 3 December 1914.
68 Ottoman Archives, BEO 4473 335-428, 9 June 1917.
69 Ottoman Archives, DH EUM 4.ŞB 18-2, 16 March 1918.
70 Ottoman Archives, DUIT 46-98, 9.4.1918 and BEO 4511-338-271, 12 April 1918.
71 Ottoman Archives, DHR ŞFR 86-202-1, 18 April 1918.
72 Ottoman Archives, I DUIT 48-27, 1 August 1919.
73 Sharifa Zuhur, *Asmahan's Secrets, Woman, War and Song*, University of Texas at Austin, 2000, p.166.
74 Giraud is reported to have gone to Saladin's tomb after occupying Damascus, where he declared the victory of the cross over the crescent.
75 Khoury, *Syria and the French Mandate: The Politics of Arab Nationalism, 1920–1945*, p.249.
76 Provence, *The Great Syrian Revolt and the Rise of Arab Nationalism*, p.57.
77 Ibid., p.41, taken from the memoirs of Said al-As.

78 This document is available in Muhammad al-Tabai's book p.151 according to Zuhur, *Asmahan's Secrets, Woman, War and Song*, p.166.
79 One of the Roman Emperors (Severus Alexander) was born there (Arca Caesarea, Phonecia) in 208 AD.
80 Michael Gilsenan, *Lords of the Lebanese Marches, Violence and Narrative in an Arab Society*, Univ. of California, 1996, p.71.
81 Ottoman Archives, A_DVNSMHM-d page no 117 line 322, reference found in Abdul Rahim Abu Husayn, *The View From Istanbul, Ottoman Lebanon and the Druze Emirate*, I.B.Tauris, 2003, p.108.
82 I would like to thank Sadallah Walid Merhebi for sharing with me his meticulously detailed research on the family genealogy and for directing me to Michael Gilsenan's book.
83 *Osman Paşazade Mehmed Paşa el Muhammad ahfadından Abud Bey*, as he is referred to in the Ottoman documents.
84 Ottoman Archives, BEO 1014-76043-1-1, 30 October 1897. Sadallah Walid Merhebi shared with me a photograph of the three cousins taken in Istanbul with their names written on the back. The fourth younger boy, Adham, another cousin, was also sent to Istanbul but not accepted due to his age.
85 Gilsenan, *Lords of the Lebanese Marches, Violence and Narrative in an Arab Society*, p.172.
86 Ottoman Archives, BEO 21-1518-1-2, 7 June 1892.
87 Ottoman Archives, Y-MTV-75-231-1-1, 16 March 1893.
88 Ottoman Archives, I-TAL-106-119-1/2 and 3, 27 October 1896.
89 Ottoman Archives, I-TAL-249-76-1-1, 5 May 1901.
90 Gilsenan, *Lords of the Lebanese Marches, Violence and Narrative in an Arab Society*, p.9.
91 Ottoman Archives, AE-SMHD-II-42-2769-1-1, 8 April 1915.
92 Gilsenan, *Lords of the Lebanese Marches, Violence and Narrative in an Arab Society*, p.93 and p.337.
93 Interestingly, the widow of Aboud lent one of her houses in Berqayel to Michael Gilsenan during his one year residence in Akkar in 1971 for his anthropological research.
94 Ottoman archives, MF-MKT 1065-13-1-1, 21 June 1908.
95 Ottoman archives, MF-MKT 1065-13-1-2, 26 June 1908.
96 Ottoman archives, MF-MKT 1065-13-2-2, 9 July 1908.
97 Ali Çankaya Mücellitoğlu, *Mülkiye Tarihi ve Mülkiyeliler, 1860–1949, Cilt 1 ve 2*, Örnek, 1954, p.509.

98 Mustafa's first wife was Turkish, but they had no children. In Hasbaya, he met and married a Shihabi princess named Amira Fariza who bore him two sons, Amir and Zeyd, and a daughter, Sabah. Sadallah Walid Merhebi interviewed Sabah in 2019.
99 Thanks to Sadallah Merhebi.
100 Blake, *Training Arab-Ottoman Bureaucrats*, p.285.

Chapter 5

1 Ali Abdullatif Ahmida, *The Making of Modern Libya: State Formation, Colonization and Resistance, 1830–1932*, SUNY, 1994, p.26.
2 Anna Baldinetti, *The Origins of the Libyan Nation, Colonial Legacy, Exile and the Emergence of a New Nation State*, Routledge, 2010, p.2.
3 Dirk Wandewalle, *A History of Modern Libya*, Cambridge, 2006, p.18 and Mostafa Minawi, *The Ottoman Scramble for Africa*, Stanford University Press, 2016, p.13. Minawi has described the Ottoman efforts in Libya as follows: 'Frontiers are zones of interaction where cultural, geographical and political boundaries are blurred as the central imperial state tries to balance stability with state hegemony.'
4 Ali Abdullatif Ahmida, *The Making of Modern Libya*, p.15.
5 Baldinetti, *The Origins of the Libyan Nation, Colonial Legacy, Exile and the Emergence of a New Nation State*, p.29.
6 Ali Abdullatif Ahmida, *The Making of Modern Libya*, p.85. Mansour al-Kikhia and Abu Bakr Haduth became *mudir* (administrator) in their regions, while Salim Dghaim and Ali Paşa Ubaydat became district administrators.
7 Wandewalle, *A History of Modern Libya*, p.18. and Mostafa Minawi, *The Ottoman Scramble for Africa*, p.19.
8 Ali Abdullatif Ahmida, *The Making of Modern Libya*, p.73 and 87. In 1856 al-Sanussi described the ways to cope with the West as follows: 'Does a bird have a mind or not?' They replied, 'No.' Al-Sanussi went on: 'Yet he puts his eggs on the top of a remote mountain so no fox or wolf can get them. Does the Yarbu (a big desert rat) have a mind or not?' His followers replied, 'No.' Al-Sanussi answered: 'Yet he digs many routes in his tunnel to escape snakes. Thus, be aware of the black snake which will come to you and point in an east-west direction.'
9 E.E. Evans-Pritchard, *The Sanussi of Cyrenaica*, Oxford University Press, 1949 (reprint 1973), p.91. Pritchard states that the decree of Abdulmecid was 'brought from Istanbul by Sidi Abd al-Rahim al-Maghbub, who had been sent to obtain

an audience with the sultan... A second decree was issued by Abdulaziz and delivered by Sidi Abu al-Qasim al-Isawi' confirming tax exemption and rights to collect a religious tithe. Muhammad Tandoğan, *Büyük Sahrada Son Osmanlı Tebaası Tevarikler*, Türk Tarih Kurumu, 2018, p.240. Tandogan claims the move to the South was based upon an understanding with the Ottomans after the first visit of Sadiq al-Mouayad to Muhammad Sanussi in 1887.

10   Baldinetti, *The Origins of the Libyan Nation, Colonial Legacy, Exile and the Emergence of a New Nation State*, p.32.
11   Wandewalle, *A History of Modern Libya*, p.18 and Mostafa Minawi, *The Ottoman Scramble for Africa*, p.18.
12   Ali Abdullatif Ahmida, *The Making of Modern Libya*, p.58.
13   Anthony Cachia, *Libya under the Second Ottoman Occupation (1835–1911)*, Gov. Press-Tripoli, 1945, p.46 and Hamiyet Sezer, 'II.Abdülhamit Döneminde Osmanlı'da Vilayet Yönetiminde Düzenleme Gayretleri – Trablusgarp Örneği ve Ahmet Rasim Paşa', *www.eskieserler.com*, pp.170–5. In 1891, Ahmad Rasim wrote a comprehensive report about his achievements in the previous ten years, including how he increased the tax base and a list of the 4.000 buildings he erected.
14   Tandoğan, *Büyük Sahrada Son Osmanlı Tebaası Tevarikler*, p.240.
15   Memoirs.
16   Ibid.
17   Ibid.
18   Fatmagül Demirel, *Dolmabahçe ve Yıldız Saraylarında Son Ziyaretler, Son Ziyafetler*, Doğan, 2007, p.53. It is reported that the kaiser's royal yacht the Hohenzollern was equipped for the trip with 8,400 bottles of beer, 4,700 bottles of champagne and 5,000 bottles of wine.
19   Ostrich feathers were an important export item from Libya to Europe at that time.
20   Description of Mülkiye tutors: 'Ainzade Hasan Tahsin Beik, was the economics teacher; Abdulrahman Sharaf, the ethics and Arab history teacher; and Sheikh Ismail Hakkı Beik the theology teacher. Sheikh Ismail was a Turk who mastered the Arabic language. He used to recite al-Akhtal's poem which says: "It is the heart which is the source of speech, as God had made the tongue speak what is inside the heart". Sheikh Ismail was the first Turk whom I ever heard reciting Arabic poetry.' Hasan Tahsin later became first director of the Kabataş Idadi school, which was established in place of the Aşiret Mektebi.

21 Ottoman Archives, DH MKT 2421-17-1, 28 August 1900, ministry of interior instruction for payment of his salary. Another document reveals that payment was mistakenly sent to Deir ez-Zor and would be forwarded to Benghazi seventeen months later! DH MKT 2587-72-1, 11 February 1902. Clearly, Omar was not short of funds.
22 Evans-Pritchard, *The Sanussi of Cyrenaica*, pp.99–100. Mansour does not mention the fee, which is explained in Pritchard's account.
23 Sadiq Paşa belonged to the powerful Azm family and was appointed to several posts by Sultan Abdülhamid.
24 Sadık El-Müeyyed Azmzade, *Afrika Sahra-yı Kebirinde Seyahat*, Çamlıca, 2008 (first ed. 1898), p.15, 79, 95. Author refers to Omar's father as 'mu'tebarandan Izzatlü Mansur Efendi el Kahiye' and recounts several conversations with him during the long journey.
25 Evans-Pritchard, *The Sanussi of Cyrenaica*, p.102. According to Pritchard the district administrator Kailani Lataiwish, who was a member of the Sanussi tribe of the Magharba, could be sent to Kufra only in 1910.
26 Sultan Abdülhamid may have known about the visit of Omar's father with Sadık Paşa to al-Mahdi and assumed it was the father who made the second trip as well. There was no mention of the School for Tribes perhaps because the school was closed at this time.
27 Celal Tevfik Karasapan, *Libya – Trablusgarb, Bingazi ve Fizan*, Resimli Posta, 1960, pp.177–9.
28 *Al-Muqattam, Al-Munir, Lisan Al-Hal, Al-Mufid and Al-Hadara*.
29 Celal Tevfik Karasapan, *Libya – Tripoli, Benghazi ve Fizan*, Resimli Posta, 1960, p.361.
30 Sadullah Koloğlu's son Orhan became a journalist and a historian who published ninety books, one of which was a biography of his father, titled *Arap Kaymakam*. I was fortunate to meet Orhan Koloğlu before he passed away in 2019, and he very lucidly narrated some of the reminiscences of his father.
31 Orhan Koloğlu remembered this product as olive oil, but the archives record that Derna's valuable product was ghee, a special kind of butter.
32 Orhan Koloğlu, *Arab Kaymakam*, Aykırı, 2011, p.16.
33 Ottoman Archives, I-HUS-9-19-1-1, 21 February 1893.
34 Koloğlu, *Arab Kaymakam*, p.103.
35 Ibid., p.110.
36 Muzaffer Baskaya, '1929 of-Sürmene Felaketi ve Bölgeye Etkileri', *Karadeniz İncelemeleri Dergisi* 18, 2015, pp.177–96.

37 Koloğlu, *Arab Kaymakam*, p.159.
38 The Cyrenaican flag used between 1949 and 1951 was identical to the Turkish flag, but with a black background in place of red. Idris Sanussi recruited many other people from Turkey in his administration. King Idris was overthrown by Kaddafi while he was in Turkey for medical treatment in 1969 and died in Cairo in 1983, at the age of ninety-four.
39 Memoirs of Omar Mansour. Abdelqadir's son Emir Ali travelled to Libya in 1911 supporting the fight against the Italian invasion, where he met French journalist Georges Remond, *Trablusgarb Savaşı ve Enver Paşa*, trans. Idil Cihangir, Doğu, 2019 (first ed. 1913), p.143.
40 Tufan Ş. Buzpınar, 'Dersaadette bir Arap Şeyhi: Şeyh Muhammad Zafir ve Sultan Abdülhamid ile İlişkileri', *Akademik Araştırmalar Dergisi* 12, November 2010–April 2011, p.214.
41 Tufan Ş. Buzpınar, 'Dersaadette bir Arap Şeyhi: Şeyh Muhammad Zafir ve Sultan Abdülhamid ile İlişkileri', *Akademik Araştırmalar Dergisi* 12, November 2010–April 2011, p.218.
42 Abdülhamid asked Raimondo D'Aranco, the chief architect of the empire who specialized in art-nouveau 'stile floreale' buildings, fashionable at the time, to renovate the Tekke and build the tomb of his favourite Sheikh.
43 In Gökçe's words: 'One of the larger gardens of the mansions was called "*Irem bağı*", referring to the gardens of paradise. Varieties and colors of roses, tulips, carnations, daffodils, geraniums, jasmines, judas and jujube trees and many other beautiful plants adorned the garden. There was a pond whose frame was decorated with gold leaves, a small tree made of silver with jeweled birds perched on its branches, and palm trees coated with copper plates. There were mechanical birds which started singing when they detected that somebody was coming close.'
44 Güngör Tekçe, *Zafir Konağında Bir Tuhaf Zaman*, YKY, 2007, pp.73–5. One of the brothers, Mehmet Ali Laga, became a well-known painter and a friend of future prime minister Ecevit's mother Nazlı, who also was an artist and visited the mansion often.
45 Ottoman Archives, MF-MKT 417-3-4, 23 August 1898.
46 *Tercüman-ı Hakikat*, 4 March 1899.
47 Ottoman Archives, I-HUS-107-121, 11 July 1903 and BEO 2384-178782, 6 August 1904.
48 Neslihan Ağdas, *II. Abdülhamit'in Kuzey Afrika Siyaseti: Şeyh Zafir ve Ertuğrul Tekkesi*, Masters Thesis, Marmara University, 2015, p.27.

49 Ibid., p.32.
50 Tekce tells the tale of Bekir's wife, who was called 'Feraşet Vekili', and the young boy thought she was related to a minister. Apparently this was a hereditary title for families who were given the honour to sweep the Kaaba in Mecca and they performed this duty through a proxy or '*vekil*'.
51 Tripoli: Khalil, son of Muftah, Zintan tribe; Hafiz Ali, son of Abdülqadir, Tawalib tribe from Hums; Hadar, son of Said al-Najaf, Khuwawata tribe from Hums; Muhammad, son of Mustafa, Zemameta tribe; Suleiman, son of Izzat, Usqa tribe; Muhammad, son of Hamza, Usqa tribe; Benghazi, Husayn Nuri, son of Muhammad, Baragith tribe; Salih, from Nefsi Benghazi.

Chapter 6

1 '*Familyaca uğur-u mekarim-mevfur-ı padişahide hüsn-ü hidmet ve sadakat etmeye hahişger*'.
2 Ottoman Archives, BOA Y-MTV-69-88-1-1, 14 September 1892.
3 Ottoman Archives, BOA Y-MTV-69-88-2-1, 18 November 1892.
4 Hanna Batatu, *The Old Social Classes and the Revolutionary Movements of Iraq*, Princeton University Press, 1978, p.68 and Samira Haj, The Problems of Tribalism: The case of nineteenth-century Iraqi history, *Social History* 16–1, 1991, p.53 (FN). In 1694, Sheikh Mani' al-Saadun occupied and ruled Basra for some years. Sheikh Thuwayni, the great-grandfather of Abdulmuhsin and Abdulkarim Saadun and 'the founder of *Suq al-Shuyukh,* was known for his travels through Kuwait, Gharraf and Basra with tents of goods and merchants'.
5 Giorgio Levi Della Vida and Peter Sluglett, al-Muntafiq, in *Encyclopaedia of Islam, Second Edition*. During my research I was able to make contact with Abdulellah al-Saadun in Riyad, who directed me to Abdulkarim's grandson Nasser Tawfik Abdul Karim al-Saadun in Amman. Nasir al-Saadun kindly sent me a book on his family as well as some documents.
6 Ali Haydar Midhat, *The Life of Midhat Paşa*, John Murray, London, 1903, pp.58–9.
7 Samira Haj, *The Problems of Tribalism*, p.53.
8 Hala Fattah and Candan Badem, 'The Sultan and the Rebel: Saadun al-Mansur's Revolt in the Muntafiq, 1891–1911', *Int. J. Middle East Studies* 45, 2013, p.681. Kamal Abdal Rahman Salman, 'The Ottoman and British Policies toward Iraqi Tribes, 1831–1920', unpublished Ph.D. dissertation, Univ of Utah, 1992, p.155.
9 Ottoman Archives, BOA Y-MTV-AZJ 4-42-1, 27 December 1880.

10   Gökhan Çetinsaya, *The Ottoman Administration of Iraq, 1890–1908*, Routledge, 2006, p.89.
11   Ibid., p.91.
12   Ottoman Archives, DH-MKT-2850-38-1, 20 June 1909.
13   Fattah and Badem, 'The Sultan and the Rebel', p.688.
14   Jafaar Paşa al-Askari, *A Soldier's Story: From Ottoman Rule to Independent Iraq*, Arabian Publishing, 2003, p.181.
15   Hanna Batatu, *The Old Social Classes and the Revolutionary Movements of Iraq*, Princeton University Press, 1978, p.93. Batatu refers to Great Britain, Reports of the Administration, 1918–1924. The India Punjab Chiefs' College was established in 1868, then moved to Lahore in 1886 and is now known as Aitchison College. Gordon College of Khartoum was founded in 1902 to train bureaucrats, and later became the University of Khartoum.
16   Ottoman archives, Y. PRK. BŞK 31-72-1, 13 July 1893 – Letter from chief scribe of Sultan, Süreyya Paşa.
17   *Tercüman-ı Hakikat*, 20 September 1892.
18   *Tercüman-ı Hakikat*, 23 October 1893.
19   Ottoman Archives, MF-MKT 193-18-1, 31 October 1893.
20   Ottoman Archives, MF-MKT 189-179-1, 16 December 1893.
21   Ottoman Archives, Y-MTV-231-113-1, 24 June 1902.
22   Ottoman Archives, Y-MTV-234-48-1, 9 September 1902.
23   '*Azad kabul etmez bir köleleriyim*'.
24   Ottoman Archives, Y-MTV-238-70-1, 12 January 1903. In Imarat al-Muntafiq, wa Athariha fi Tarikh Al-Iraq wa Al-Mintiqa, 2017, by Hamid al-Sadoun, the attendance of the brothers at the school is portrayed as an instruction from the centre, to keep them as hostages in the capital, p.309.
25   Ottoman Archives, BEO 3769-282628-1, 23 June 1910.
26   Ottoman Archives, DH SYS 49-44-1, 13 May 1911.
27   Mücellidoğlu Ali Çankaya, *Mülkiye Tarihi ve Mülkiyeliler*, II. Cild, Örnek Matbaası, 1954, p.357.
28   Ottoman Archives, DH ŞFR 464-70-1, 10 March 1915.
29   Ottoman Archives, DH EUM 1.Şb. 2-35-1, 10 March 1915.
30   Charles Tripp, A History of Iraq, Cambridge, 2000, p.49.
31   Karol Sorby Jr, 'The Role of Abdalmuhsin as-Saadun in Iraqi Politics in the 1920's', *Asian and African Studies* 24, no 1, 2015, p.104.
32   The dates of Saadun's first term as prime minister are 18 November 1922, through 21 November 1923 (12 months).

33 Hanna Batatu, *The Old Social Classes and the Revolutionary Movements of Iraq*, Princeton University Press, 1978, p.95.
34 Toby Dodge, *Inventing Iraq: The Failure of Nation Building and a History Denied*, Columbia University Press, 2003, p.52.
35 Karol Sorby Jr, 'The Role of Abdalmuhsin as-Saadun in Iraqi Politics in the 1920's', *Asian and African Studies* 24, no. 1, 2015, p.113.
36 Hamid al-Sadoun, Imarat al-Muntafiq, wa Athariha fi Tarikh Al-Iraq wa Al-Mintiqa, 2017, p.309.
37 Hanna Batatu, *The Old Social Classes and the Revolutionary Movements of Iraq*, Princeton University Press, 1978, p.189.
38 Interestingly, in the Sykes-Picot agreement, Mosul was designated to be under the French sphere of influence.
39 Sara Pursley, 'Lines Drawn on an Empty Map: Iraq's Borders and the Legend of the Artificial State (Part 2)', *Jadaliyya*, 2 June 2015.
40 Tawfik al-Suwaidi, *Muthakkirati, My Reminiscences*, Dar al-Hikma, 1969, p.177.
41 Although there are many views on this matter, it appears that in 1954, a lump sum final payment was received and the agreement was terminated.
42 The dates of Saadun's second term as prime minister are 26 June 1925, through 1 November 1926 (sixteen months).
43 Hanna Batatu, *The Old Social Classes and the Revolutionary Movements of Iraq*, Princeton University Press, 1978, p.331.
44 Hanna Batatu, *The Old Social Classes and the Revolutionary Movements of Iraq*, Princeton, 1978, p.191.
45 Turkish Republic Archives, 30-10-4-24-42-1, 24 June 1928.
46 Toby Dodge, *Inventing Iraq: The Failure of Nation Building and a History Denied*, Columbia University Press, 2003, p.49.
47 Tawfik al-Suwaidi, *Muthakkirati, My Reminiscences*, Dar al-Hikma, 1969, p.180.
48 Karol Sorby Jr, 'The Role of Abdalmuhsin as-Saadun in Iraqi Politics in the 1920's', *Asian and African Studies* 24, no. 4, 2015, p.119. The dates of Saadun's third term as prime minister are from 14 January 1928 to 20 January 1929 (12 months).
49 Peter Sluglett, *Britain in Iraq, Contriving King and Country*, I.B. Tauris, 2007, p.121.
50 Mir Basri, *Alem al-Siyasiya fi Al-Iraq Al-Hadith*, Dar al Hikma, 2004, p.224.
51 The dates of Saadun's fourth term as prime minister are from 19 September 1929 to 13 November 1929.

52 Hanna Batatu, *The Old Social Classes and the Revolutionary Movements of Iraq*, Princeton University Press, 1978, p.58 and 157, figures obtained from the Iraqi Ministry of Planning report. In addition to their large estates in Muntafiq, it was calculated in 1958 that the Saadun family owned 219,765 dunums in Kut, Basra, Hillal and Mosul, ranking them among the first three landowners of the country.

Conclusion

1 Ottoman Archives, Y-PRK-UM-44-84-1-1, 26 December 1898.
2 Ottoman Archives, BEO 3552-266387-1-1, 20 May 1909.
3 Ottoman Archives, DH MKT 2826-57-1, 25 May 1909.
4 Hasan Yıldız, 'II. Meşrutiyet Döneminde Akim Kalmış Bir Eğitim Projesi: Medrese-i Aşâir', *Belleten, Türk Tarih Kurumu* 296, 2019, pp.289–308.
5 '*Evlad-ı aşair-i urban*'.
6 '*Nezaret-i maneviye-i hazret-i hilafetpenahileriyle mübahi*' – a phrase oft repeated in documents/newspapers.
7 Thanks to Emre Yılmaz.

Bibliography

Primary Sources

Arşiv Belgelerine Göre Osmanlı Eğitiminde Modernleşme, Başbakanlık Devlet Arşivleri, 2014.
Documents of the Merhebi family provided by Sadullah Merhebi.
Filistin, Palestine newspaper, 1920–2.
Handwritten diary of Omar Mansour, 1919.
Ottoman Archives, Kağıthane, Istanbul.
Servet-i Fünun periodical online, 1892–1907.
Tanzimat'tan Cumhuriyet'e Modernleşme Sürecinde Eğitim Istatistikleri, 1839–1924, Başbakanlık, 2000.
Tercüman-i Hakikat newspaper online, 1892–1907.
Thamarat al-Fünun, Beirut newspaper, 1892–1907.

Books

Abu Husayn, Abdul Rahim. *The View from Istanbul, Ottoman Lebanon and the Druze Emirate*, I.B. Tauris, 2003.
Abu Husayn, Abdul Rahim. *Beyn al-Markaz wa al-Atraf, Hawran fi al-Wathaiq al-Uthmaniyyah, 1842–1918*, Druze Heritage Foundation, 2015.
Ağdaş, Neslihan. *II. Abdülhamit'in Kuzey Afrika Siyaseti: Şeyh Zafir ve Ertuğrul Tekkesi*, Masters Thesis, Marmara University, 2015.
Ağırakça, Gülsüm Pehlivan. *Mekteplerde Ahlak Eğitim ve Öğretimi, 1839–1923*, Çamlıca, 2013.
Ahmida, Ali Abdullatif. *The Making of Modern Libya: State Formation, Colonization and Resistance, 1830–1932*, SUNY, 1994.
Akarlı, Engin Deniz. 'The Problems of External Pressures, Power Struggles and Budgetary Deficits under Abdülhamid II', Princeton University, unpublished dissertation, 1976.
Akarlı, Engin Deniz. *The Long Peace, Ottoman Lebanon, 1861–1920*, University of California Press, 1993.

Akbayar, Nuri. *Osmanlı Yer Adları Sözlüğü*, Tarih Vakfı, 2001.
Akpınar, Alişan. *Osmanlı Devletinde Aşiret Mektebi*, Göçebe, 1997.
Akpınar, Alişan and Eugene Rogan. *Aşiret, Mektep, Devlet*, Aram, 2001.
Aksoy, Özgönül. *Osmanlı Devri Istanbul Sıbyan Mektebleri Üzerine bir İnceleme*, İTÜ Mimarlık, 1968.
Aksun, Ziya Nur. *II. Abdülhamid Han*, Ötüken, 2010.
Akyıldız, Ali. *Osmanlı Bürokrasisi ve Modernleşme*, Iletisim, 2004.
Akyüz, Yahya. *Türk Eğitim Tarihi (Başlangıçtan 1999'a)*, Alfa, 1999.
Allen, Roger. *Spies, Scandals & Sultans: The First English Translation of Egyptian Ibrahim al-Muwaylihi's Ma Hunalik*, Rowman and Littlefield, 2008.
Anderson, Benedict. *Imagined Communities: Reflections on the Origin and Spread of Nationalism*, Verso, 1983.
Anderson, Lisa. *The State and Social Transformation in Tunisia and Libya, 1830–1930*, Princeton University Press, 1986.
El-Ariss, Tarek. *Trials of Arab Modernity*, Fordham, 2013.
Armağan, Mustafa. *Abdülhamid'in Kurtlarla Dansı*, Ufuk Kitap, 2006.
Arslan, Emir Şekib. *Ittihatçı Bir Arap Aydınının Anıları*, Klasik, 2005.
Avcıoğlu, Doğan. *Türkiye'nin Düzeni*, Bilgi, 1968.
Aydın, Suavi and Erdal Çiftçi. *Imparatorluğun Son Aşiret Sayımı, Fihristü'l Aşair*, Iletişim, 2021.
Ayni, Mehmed Ali. *Darülfünun Tarihi*, Istanbul Darülfünunu, 1927.
Balcı, Ramazan. *Osmanlı'nın Doğu Siyaseti*, Hazine, 2000.
Baldinetti, Anna. *The Origins of the Libyan Nation, Colonial Legacy, Exile and the Emergence of a New Nation State*, Routledge, 2010.
Balkış, Mehmed Nuri and Mahmud Naci. *Tripoli*, ed. Ahmet Kavas, Tarihçi, 2012 (First edition 1912).
Baltacıoğlu, Ismayıl Hakkı. *Hayatım*, Dünya Yayıncılık, 1998.
Barakat, Nora. *An Empty Land? Nomads and Property Administration in Hamidian Syria*, Phd Dissertation, UC Berkley, 2015.
Barkey, Karen. *Empire of Difference: The Ottomans in Comparative Perspective*, Cambridge, 2008.
Basri, Mir. *Alim al-Siyasiya fi Al-Iraq Al-Hadith*, Dar al Hikma, 2004.
Batatu, Hanna. *The Old Social Classes and the Revolutionary Movements of Iraq*, Princeton, 1978.
Baykurt, Cami. *Tripoli'dan Sahra-yı Kebire Doğru*, Özgü Yayınları, 2011 (First published in 1906).
Berker, Aziz. *Türkiyede Ilk Ogrenim 1839–1908*, Milli Egitim Basımevi, 1945.
Berkes, Niyazi. *Türkiye'de Çağdaşlaşma*, 1945.
Berktay, Halil and Suraiya Faroqhi. *New Approaches to State and Peasant in Ottoman History*, Routledge, 2017.

Bilgenoğlu, Ali. *Osmanlı Devletinde Arap Milliyetçi Cemiyetleri*, Yeniden Müdafaa-i Hukuk, 2007.

Blake, Corinne. 'Training Arab-Ottoman Bureaucrats: Syrian Graduates of the Mülkiye Mektebi, 1890-1920', unpublished dissertation, Princeton University. 1991.

Blumi, Isa. *Rethinking the Late Ottoman Empire: A Comparative Social and Political History of Albania and Yemen, 1878-1918*, ISIS, 2003.

Bölükbaşı, Faruk. *II. Abdülhamid Devrinde Mali İdare*, Osmanlı Bankası, 2005.

Bozdağ, İsmet. *Abdülhamid'in Hatıra Defteri*, Kervan, 1975.

Brown, Carl L. *The Surest Path to Knowledge by Khayr al-Din al-Tunisi*, Harvard, 1967.

Brown, Carl L., ed. *Imperial Legacy: The Ottoman Imprint on the Balkans and the Middle East*, Columbia University Press, 1996.

Buheiry, Marwan. *Intellectual Life in the Arab East, 1890-1939*, AUB, 1981.

Büssow, Johann. *Hamidian Palestine: Politics and Society in the District of Jerusalem 1872-1908*, Brill, 2011.

Buzpınar, Tufan. *Hilafet ve Saltanat, II. Abdülhamid Döneminde Halifelik ve Araplar*, Alfa, 2016.

Cachia, Anthony. *Libya under The Second Ottoman Occupation (1835-1911)*, Gov. Press-Tripoli, 1945.

Candemir, Murat. *Bab-ı Ali Evrak Odası*, Akademi Titiz, 2017.

Ceylan, Ebubekir. *The Ottoman Origins of Modern Iraq*, I.B. Tauris, 2011.

Chatty, Dawn, ed. *Nomadic Societies in the Middle East and North Africa*, Brill, 2006.

Chowdhury, Rashed. 'Pan-Islamism and Modernisation during the Reign of Sultan Abdülhamid II, 1876-1909', Unpublished dissertation, McGill, 2011.

Coleman, James, ed. *Education and Political Development*, Princeton University Press, 1965.

Cleveland, William L. *The Making of an Arab Nationalist: Ottomanism and Arabism in the Life and Thought of Sati al-Husri*, Princeton University Press, 1971.

Çaycı, Abdurrahman. *Büyük Sahra'da Türk-Fransız Rekabeti (1858-1911)*, Atatürk Üniv., 1970.

Çetin, Atilla. *Tunuslu Hayreddin Paşa*, TC Kültür Bakanlığı, 1999.

Çetiner, Selahattin. *Çöküş Yılları*, Remzi Kitabevi, 2008.

Çetinsaya, Gökhan. *Ottoman Administration of Iraq, 1890-1908*, University of Manchester, 1994.

Çiçek, M. Talha. *War and State Formation in Syria, Cemal Paşa's Governorate during World War I, 1914-1917*, Routledge, 2014.

Çiçek, M. Talha. *Negotiating Empire in the Middle East: Ottomans and Arab Nomads in the Modern Era, 1840-1914*, Cambridge University Press, 2021.

Danişmend, Ismail Hami. *Izahlı Osmanlı Tarihi*, Cilt 4, Türkiye Yayınevi, 1972.

Davison, Roderic. *Reform in the Ottoman Empire, 1856-1876*, Princeton University Press, 1963.

Dawn, Ernest. *From Ottomanism to Arabism, Essays on the Origins of Arab Nationalism*, University of Illinois, 1973.
Demirel, Fatmagül. *Dolmabahçe ve Yıldız Saraylarında Son Ziyaretler, Son Ziyafetler*, Doğan, 2007.
Deringil, Selim. *The Well Protected Domains*, I.B. Tauris, 1999-reprint 2004.
Dodge, Toby. *Inventing Iraq: The Failure of Nation Building and a History Denied*, Columbia University Press, 2003.
Dohaish, Abdullatif Abdullah. 'A Critical and Comparative Study of the History of Education in the Hijaz during the Periods of Ottoman and Sharifian Rule between 1869–1925', unpublished dissertation, Leeds University, 1974.
Douwes, Dick. *The Ottomans in Syria: A History of Justice and Oppression*, I.B.Tauris, 2000.
Dukhan, Haian. *State and Tribes in Syria: Informal Alliances and Conflict Patterns*, Routledge, 2018.
Duman, Esmer. *Osmanlı Arşiv Belgeleri Işığında Aşiret Mektebi*, Masters Thesis, Van University, 2019.
Emrence, Cem. *Remapping the Ottoman Middle East, Imperial Bureaucracy and Islam*, I.B. Tauris, 2016.
Engin, Vahdettin. *II. Abdülhamid ve Dış Politika*, Yeditepe Yayınevi, 2005.
Eraslan, Cezmi. *II. Abdülhamid ve Islam Birliği*, 1876–1908, Ötüken, 1992.
Ergin, Osman Nuri. *Türkiye Maarif Tarihi*, Maarif Matbaası, 1940–1945.
Ess, John Van. *Meet the Arab*, John Day, 1943.
Evans-Pritchard, E.E. *The Sanussi of Cyrenaica*, Oxford University Press, 1949-reprint 1973.
Facey, William and Najdat Fathi Safwat, eds. *A Soldier's Story: From Ottoman Rule to Independent Iraq: The Memoirs of Jafar Paşa Al-Askari (1885–1936)*, Arabian Publishing, 2003.
Farah, Ceasar E. *Arabs and Ottomans: A Checkered Relationship*, ISIS, 2002.
Farah, Ceasar E. *Abdülhamid II and the Muslim World*, Isar, 2008.
Faroqhi, Suraiya. *Approaching Ottoman History: An Introduction to the Sources*, Cambridge, 1999.
Findley, Carter V. *Ottoman Civil Officialdom. A Social History*, Princeton, 1989.
Findley, Carter V. *Turkey, Islam, Nationalism and Modernity*, Yale, 2010.
Firro, Kais. *A History of the Druzes*, Brill, 1992.
Firro, Kais. 'The Ottoman Reforms and Jabal al-Druze, 1860–1914', in *Ottoman Reform and Muslim Regeneration*, eds. Weissmann Zachs, I.B. Tauris, 2005.
Fortna, Benjamin. *Imperial Classroom. Islam, the State and Education in the Late Ottoman Empire*, Oxford University Press, 2002.
Le Gall, Michel F. *Paşas, Bedouins and Notables: Ottoman Administration in Tripoli and Benghazi, 1881–1902*, phd diss., Princeton University Press, 1986.

Gelvin, James. *Divided Loyalties, Nationalism and Mass Politics in Syria at the Close of Empire*, University of California, 1998.

Georgeon, Francois. *Sultan Abdülhamid*, İletisim, 2003.

Gibb, H.A.R. and Harold Bowen. *Islamic Society and the West*, Oxford University Press, 1957.

Gilsenan, Michael. *Lords of the Lebanese Marches, Violence and Narrative in an Arab Society*, University of California, 1996.

Gör, Emre. *Abdülhamid Döneminde Istihbarat*, Kitap Yayınvevi, 2019.

Gross, Max L. 'Ottoman Rule in the Province of Damascus, 1860–1909', unpublished dissertation, Georgetown, 1979.

Haddad, William and William Ochsenwald, eds. *Nationalism in a Non-National State*, Ohio State University, 1977.

Haj, Samira. *Reconfiguring Islamic Tradition: Reform, Rationality and Modernity*, Stanford University Press, 2009.

Halabi, Abbas. *The Druze: A New Cultural and Historical Appreciation*, Ithaca, 2015.

Hallaq, Wael B. *The Impossible State: Islam, Politics and Modernity's Moral Predicament*, Columbia University Press, 2014.

Hanioğlu, Şükrü. *A Brief History of the Late Ottoman Empire*, Princeton University Press, 2008.

Al-Hasani, Abd al-Razzaq. *Tarikh al-Wizarat al-Iraqiya, II, Dar ül Şüyun el Thakafiya*, Iraq, 1988.

Haslip, Joan. *The Sultan*, Cassell, 1958.

Hathaway, Jane. *The Arab Lands under Ottoman Rule, 1516–1800*, Pearson, 2008.

Hocaoğlu, Mehmet. *Abdülhamid Han'ın Muhtıraları*, Türkiyat, 1989.

Hourani, Albert. *The Emergence of the Modern Middle East*, University of California, 1981.

Hülagu, Metin. *Sultan Abdülhamid'in Sürgün Günleri*, Pan, 2003.

Imbert, Paul. *Osmanlı Imparatorluğunda Yenileşme Hareketleri*, Havass, 1909 (Translated 1981).

Inal, Ibnulemin Mahmut Kemal. *Osmanlı Devrinde Son Sadrazamlar*, Maarif Matbaası, 1940–1953.

Inalcık, Halil and Donald Quartet. *An Economic and Social History of the Ottoman Empire, 1300–1914*, Cambridge University Press, 1994.

Ince, Mehmet. *Sultan II. Abdülhamid Han'ın Şeyhi Muhammad Zafir el-Madani'nin Hayatı*, Şazeli Yayınları, 2015.

Irtem, Suleiman Kani. *Bilinmeyen Abdülhamid*, Temel Yayınları, 2003.

Issawi, Charles, ed. *The Economic History of the Middle East, 1800–1914*, Chicago, 1966.

Issawi, Charles, ed. *The Economic History of Turkey, 1800–1914*, Columbia University Press, 1982.

Itzkowitz, Norman. *Ottoman Empire and Islamic Tradition*, Alfred Knopf, 1972.

Jabbur, Jibrail S. *The Bedouins and the Desert, Aspects of Nomadic Life in the Arab East*, SUNY, 1995.
Kafadar, Osman. *Türk Eğitim Düşüncesinde Batılılaşma*, Vadi, 1997.
Kansu, Aykut. *1908 Devrimi*, Iletişim, 2015.
Kansu, Nafi Atıf. *Türkiye Maarif Tarihi*, 1931.
Karal, Enver Ziya. *Osmanlı Tarihi*, Türk Tarih Kurumu, 1983.
Karasapan, Celal Tevfik. *Libya – Tripoli, Benghazi ve Fizan*, Resimli Posta, 1960.
Karateke, Hakan. *Padişahım Çok Yaşa, Osmanlı İmparatorluğunun Son Yüz Yılında Merasimler*, Kitap Yayınevi, 2004.
Karpat, Kemal. *The Politicization of Islam. Reconstructing Identity, State, Faith and Community in the Late Ottoman State*, Oxford University Press, 2001.
Kasaba, Resat. *A Moveable Empire: Ottoman Nomads, Migrants, and Refugees (Studies in Modernity and National Identity)*, University of Washington, 2009.
Kavas, Ahmet. *Osmanlı-Afrika İlişkileri*, Tasam, 2006.
Kayalı, Hasan. *Arabs and Young Turks: Ottomanism, Arabism and Islamism in the Ottoman Empire, 1908–1918*, University of California Press, 1997.
Kayalı, Hasan, *Imperial Resilience: The Great War's End, Ottoman Longevity, and Incidental Nations*, University of California, 2021.
Kazamias, Andreas. *Education and the Quest for Modernity in Turkey*, University of Chicago Press, 1966.
Kedourie, Elie. *Arabic Political Memoirs and Other Studies*, Frank Cass, 1974.
Kemali, Ali. *Sultan Aziz'in Mısır ve Avrupa Seyahati*, Ahmet Saitoğlu Kitabevi, 1944.
Khalidi, Ismail and A. Pelt Raghib, eds. *Constitutional Development in Libya*, Khayat's College, 1956.
Khazanov, Anatoly. *Nomads and the Outside World*, University of Wisconsin, 1983.
Khoury, Philip. *Urban Notables and Arab Nationalism: The Politics of Damascus 1860–1920*, Cambridge University Press, 1983.
Khoury, Philip. *Syria and the French Mandate: The Politics of Arab Nationalism, 1920–1945*, Princeton University Press, 1987.
Khoury, Philip and Joseph Kostner, eds. *Tribes and State Formation in the Middle East*, University of California, 1990.
El-Kikhia, Mansour O. *Libya's Qaddafi: The Politics of Contradiction*, University of Florida, 1997.
Kırmızı, Abdulhamit. *Abdülhamid'in Valileri 1895–1908*, Klasik, 2007.
Kısakürek, Necip Fazıl. *Ulu Hakan*, 1965-reprint 2003.
Klein, Janet. *The Margins of Empire, Kurdish Militias in the Ottoman Tribal Zone*, Stanford University Press, 2011.
Kocabaş, Suleiman. *Sultan II. Abdülhamid – Şahsiyeti ve Politikası*, Vatan, 1995.

Koçer, Hasan Ali. *Türkiye'de Modern Eğitimin Doğuşu ve Gelişmesi (1773–1923)*, Milli Eğitim Basımevi, 1970.
Kodaman, Bayram. *Abdülhamid Devri Eğitim Sistemi*, Türk Tarih Kurumu, 1988.
Koloğlu, Orhan. *Avrupa'nın Kıskacında Abdülhamit*, Iletişim, 1998.
Koloğlu, Orhan. *Osmanlı Meclislerinde Libya ve Libyalılar*, Boyut, 2003.
Koloğlu, Orhan. *Abdülhamid Gerçeği*, Artı Yayın, 2005.
Koloğlu, Orhan. *Türk-Arap Ilişkileri Tarihi*, Tarihçi, 2007.
Koloğlu, Orhan. *Arab Kaymakam*, Aykiri Yayinlari, 2011.
Kuneralp, Sinan. *Son Dönem Osmanlı Erkan ve Ricali, 1839–1922*, ISIS, 1999.
Kurşun, Zekeriya. *Necid ve Ahsa'da Osmanlı Hakimiyeti: Vehhabi Hareketi ve Suud Devletinin Ortaya Çıkışı*, T. Tarih Kurumu, 1998.
Kurşun, Zekeriya. *Basra Körfezinde Osmanlı-Ingiliz Çekişmesi: Katar'da Osmanlılar, 1871–1916*, T. Tarih Kurumu, 2004.
Kurşun, Zekeriya. *Afrika'nın Asil Göçerleri Tuaregler*, Taşmektep, 2015.
Kurtcephe, Israfil and Mustafa Balcıoğlu. *Kara Harb Okulu Tarihi*, Kara Harb Okulu, 1991.
Kurzman, Charles, ed. *Modernist Islam, 1840–1940*, Oxford University Press, 2002.
Lancaster, William. *The Rwala Bedouin Today*, Waveland, 1997.
Landau, Jacob M. *The Politics of Pan-Islam, Ideology and Organization*, Oxford University Press, 1990.
Landau, Jacob M. *Exploring Ottoman and Turkish History*, Hurst, 2004.
Lewis, Bernard. *The Emergence of Modern Turkey*, Oxford University Press, 1968.
Lewis, Norman N. *Nomads and Settlers in Syria and Jordan 1800–1980*, Cambridge University Press, 1987.
Longrigg, Stephen H. *Iraq, 1900 to 1950, A Political, Social and Economic History*, Oxford University Press, 1956.
Nafi, Mahmud Cevad Ibnus-Seyh. *Maarif-i Umumiye Nezareti. Tarihçe, Teşkilat ve İcraatı*, Matbaa-i Amire, 1920.
Maoz, Moshe, Joseph Ginat and Onn Winckler, eds. *Modern Syria: From Ottoman Rule to Pivotal Role in the Middle East*, Sussex Press, 1999.
Mardin, Şerif. *The Genesis of Young Ottoman Thought*, Princeton University Press, 1962.
Marr, Phebe. *A Modern History of Iraq*, Wesrview, 2004.
Masters, Bruce. *The Arabs of the Ottoman Empire, 1516–1918*, Cambridge University Press, 2013.
McCarthy, Justin. *The Ottoman Peoples and the End of Empire*, Oxford University Press, 2001.
Mestyan, Adam. *Arab Patriotism: The Ideology and Culture of Power in Late Ottoman Egypt*, Princeton University Press, 2017.

Midhat, Ali Haydar. *The Life of Midhat Paşa*, John Murray, 1903-reprinted by Andesite Press.

Minawi, Mostafa. *The Ottoman Scramble for Africa*, Stanford University Press, 2016.

Moubayed, Sami. *Damascus between Democracy and Dictatorship*, University Press of America, 2000.

Mousa, Suleiman. *T.E. Lawrence: An Arab View*, Oxford University Press, 1966.

Mücellitoğlu, Ali Çankaya. *Mülkiye Tarihi ve Mülkiyeliler, 1860–1949, Cilt 1 ve 2*, Örnek, 1954.

Mücellitoğlu, Ali Çankaya. *Yeni Mülkiye Tarihi ve Mülkiyeliler*, Mars, 1969.

El-Müeyyed, Sadık Azmzade. *Afrika Sahra-yı Kebirinde Seyahat*, Çamlıca, 2008 (First edition 1898).

Mümtaz, Ahmet Semih. *Sultan II. Abdülhamid ve Zamanı*, Kapı, 2008.

Mümtaz, Ahmet Semih. *Abdülhamid'in Kara Kutusu Arab Izzat Holo Paşa'nın Günlükleri*, İş Bankası, 2018.

Mundy, Martha and Basim Musallam, eds. *The Transformation of Nomadic Society in the Arab East*, Cambridge, 2000.

Naci, Mahmud and Mehmed Nuri. *Trablusgarb*, ed. Ahmet Kavas. Tarihçi, 2012 (First edition 1916).

Nazima, Ali. *Hazine-i Kıraat*, ed. Gökçe Özder, Büyüyen Ay, 2020 (First published 1912).

Nuri, Osman. *Bilinmeyen Abdülhamid*, Temel Yayınları, 2017.

Ochsenwald, William. *Religion, Economy and State in Ottoman-Arab History*, ISIS, 1998.

Orhonlu, Cengiz. *Osmanlı Imparatorluğunda Aşiretlerin Iskanı*, Eren, 1987.

Osmanoğlu, Ayşe. *Babam Sultan Abdülhamid*, Selis Kitaplar, 1960-reprint 1994.

Owen, Roger. *The Middle East in the World Economy, 1800–1914*, I.B. Tauris, 2002.

Özbek, Nadir. *Osmanlı Imparatorlugunda Sosyal Devlet. Siyaset, Iktidar ve Meşruiyet (1876–1914)*, Iletişim, 2003.

Özdalga, Elizabeth, ed. *Late Ottoman Society: The Intellectual Legacy*, Routledge, 2005.

Özköse, Qadir. *Muhammad Senûsî: Hayatı, Eserleri, Hareketi*, İnsan Yayınları, 2000.

Pamuk, Şevket. *The Ottoman Empire and European Capitalism, 1820–1913*, Cambridge University Press, 1987.

Parvus, Alexander Helphand. *Türkiye'nin Can Damarı: Devlet-i Osmaniyyenin Borçları ve Islahı*, Türk Yurdu Kütüphanesi, 1330.

Paşa, Tahsin, *Abdülhamit ve Yıldız Hatıraları*, Muallim Ahmet Halit Kitaphanesi, 1931.

Philipp, Thomas and Birgit Schaebler, eds. *The Syrian Land: Processes of Integration and Fragmentation, Bilad al-Sham from the 18th to the 20th Century*, Franz Steiner, 1998.

Provence, Michael. *The Great Syrian Revolt and the Rise of Arab Nationalism*, University of Texas, 2005.

Provence, Michael. *The Last Ottoman Generation and the Making of the Modern Middle East*, Cambridge University Press, 2017.

Quataert, Donald. *Social Disintegration and Popular Resistance in the Ottoman Empire, 1881–1908*, New York University, 1983.

Quataert, Donald. 'Ottoman Reform and Agriculture in Anatolia, 1876–1908', Unpublished dissertation, UCLA, 1973.

Quataert, Donald and Baki Tezcan, eds. *Beyond Dominant Paradigms in Ottoman and Middle Eastern/North African Studies: A Tribute to Rifa'at Abou-El-Haj*, ISAM, 2010.

Al-Qaysi, Abdul Wahhab Abbas. 'The Impact of Modernization on Iraqi Society during the Ottoman Era: A Study of Intellectual Development in Iraq, 1869–1917', unpublished dissertation, University of Michigan, 1958.

Al-Rasheed, Madawi. *Politics in an Arabian Oasis: The Rashidi Tribal Dynasty*, Bloomsbury, 1997.

Remond, Georges. *Trablusgarb Savaşı ve Enver Paşa*, trans. Idil Cihangir, Doğu, 2019 (First edition 1913).

Rogan, Eugene. *The Frontiers of the State in the Late Ottoman Empire, Trans Jordan, 1850–1921*, Cambridge University Press, 1999.

Rogan, Eugene, ed. *Outside in: On the Margins of the Modern Middle East*, I.B. Tauris, 2002.

Rogan, Eugene. *The Fall of the Ottomans*, Penguin, 2016.

Rogan, Eugene and Tareq Tell, eds. *Village, Steppe and State: The Social Origins of Modern Jordan*, Bloomsbury, 1994.

Al-Sadoun, Hamid. *Imarat al-Muntafiq, wa Athariha fi Tarikh Al-Iraq wa Al-Mintiqa*, Al-Thakera, Iraq, 2017.

Said Paşa, Mehmet. *Said Paşa'nın Hatıratı*, Sabah, 1912.

Sakaoğlu, Necdet. *Osmanlı Eğitim Tarihi*, Iletisim, 1991.

Salibi, Kamal. *The Modern History of Lebanon*, Caravan Books, 1965.

Salibi, Kamal, ed. *The Druze, Realities and Perceptions*, Druze Heritage Foundation, 2006.

Salman, Hacı. *İdadi Mektepleri'nin Tarihsel Gelişimi*, Masters Thesis, Ankara University, 2005.

Schaebler, Birgit and Leif Stenberg, eds. *Globalization and the Muslim World*, Syracuse, 2004.

Schilcher, Linda. *Families in Politics, Damascene Factions and Estates of the 18th and 19th Centuries*, Franz Steiner, 1985.

Şehbenderzade, Filibeli Ahmad Hilmi. *Senusiler ve Sultan Abdülhamid*, Ses Yayınları, 1992 (First edition 1908).

Selim, Sabit. *Rehnuma-i Muallimin. Sıbyan Mekteblerine Mahsus Usul-i Tedrisiyye*, Ozege, 1874.

Sharabi, Hisham. *Arab Intellectuals and the West: The Formative Years 1875–1914*, Baltimore, 1970.

Shaw, Stanford. *History of the Ottoman Empire and Modern Turkey*, Cambridge University Press, 1985.
Sluglett, Peter. *Britain in Iraq, Contriving King and Country*, I.B. Tauris, 2007.
Somel, Selçuk Akşin. *The Modernization of Public Education in the Ottoman Empire, 1839-1908*, Brill, 2001.
Al-Suwaidi, Tawfik. *Muthakkirati: My Reminiscences*, Dar al-Hikma, 1969.
Szyliowicz, Joseph. *Education and Modernization in the Middle East*, Ithaca, 1973.
Tandoğan, Muhammad. *Büyük Sahrada Son Osmanlı Tebaası Tevarikler*, Türk Tarih Kurumu, 2018.
Tauber, Eliezer. *The Arab Movements in World War I*, Frank Kass, 2006.
Tepedelenlioğlu, Nizamettin Nazif. *Sultan II. Abdülhamid*, Bedir Yayınları, 1945.
Tepedelenlioğlu, Nizamettin Nazif. *The Formation of Modern Syria and Iraq*, Frank Cass, 1995.
Tekçe, Güngör. *Zafir Konağında Bir Tuhaf Zaman*, Yapı Kredi Yayınları, 2007.
Tibawi, A.L. *Islamic Education: Its Traditions and Modernization into the Arab National Systems*, New York, 1972.
Tripp, Charles. *A History of Iraq*, Cambridge University Press, 2005.
Tosun, Mehmet, ed. *21. Yüzyılda Sultan II. Abdülhamid'e Bakış*, Acar, 2003.
Türkay, Cevdet. *Başbakanlık Arşiv Belgelerine Göre Osmanlı Imparatorluğunda Oymak, Aşiret ve Cemaatler*, Tercüman, 1979.
Uğurlu, Nurer. *Padişah II. Abdülhamid'in Hatıra Defteri*, Örgün Yayınevi, 2009.
Unat, Faik Reşit. *Türkiye Eğitim Sisteminin Gelişmesine Tarihi bir Bakış*, Milli Eğitim Bakanlığı, 1964.
Üner, Mehmet Emin. *Aşiret, Eşkiya ve Devlet*, Yalın, 2009.
Vandewalle, Dirk. *A History of Modern Libya*, Cambridge University Press, 2006.
Weismann, Itzchak and Fruma Zachs, eds. *Ottoman Reform and Muslim Regeneration, Studies in Honour of Butrus Abu-Manneh*, I.B. Tauris, 2005.
Williamson, B. *Education and Social Change in Egypt and Turkey. A Study in Historical Sociology*, Macmillan, 1987.
Yavuzyiğit, Hikmet. *Mülkiye Tarihi 1859-1999*, Mülkiyeliler Birliği, 1999.
Yazbak, Mahmoud. *Haifa in the Late Ottoman Period, 1864-1914: A Muslim Town in Transition*, Brill, 1998.
Young, Hubert. *The Independent Arab*, John Murray, 1933.
Yücel, Hasan Ali. *Türkiye'de Orta Öğretim*, Milli Eğitim Bakanlığı, 1938.
Zachs, Fruma. *The Making of a Syrian Identity, Intellectuals and Merchants in Nineteenth Century Beirut*, Brill, 2005.
Zeine, Zeine N. *The Emergence of Arab Nationalism, with a Background Study of Arab-Turkish Relations in the Near East*, Caravan Books, 1958-reprint 1976.
Ziadeh, Nicola. *Sanussiya: A Study of a Revivalist Movement in Islam*, Brill, 1958.

Zuhur, Sharifa. *Asmahan's Secrets, Woman, War and Song*, University of Texas at Austin, 2000.

Zuhur, Sharifa, ed. *Colors of Enchantment, Theater, Dance, Music and the Visual Arts of the Middle East*, AUC Press, 2001.

Zurcher, Erik J. *Turkey, a Modern History*, I.B. Tauris, 1993.

Articles

Abu Husayn, Abdul Rahim. 'The Long Rebellion: The Druzes and the Ottomans, 1516-1697', *Archivum Ottomanicum*, 2001, pp.165-93.

Abu Husayn, Abdul Rahim. 'Ambivalent Siblings: Evolving Arab Perceptions of the Turkish Republic', published in *Derin Tarih*, January 2017, pp.78-83.

Abu-Manneh, B. 'Sultan Abdülhamid and Sheikh Abulhuda Al-Sayyadi', *Middle Eastern Studies* 15, May 1979, pp.131-53.

Akarli, Engin Deniz. 'Friction and Discord within the Ottoman Government under Abdülhamid II', *Boğaziçi Üniversitesi Dergisi* 7, 1979, pp.3-26.

Akarli, Engin Deniz. 'Abdülhamid II's Attempts to Integrate Arabs into the Ottoman System', in *Palestine in the Late Ottoman Period*, ed. David Kushner, Brill, 1986, pp.74-89.

Akarli, Engin Deniz. 'The Tangled End of an Empire: Ottoman Encounters with the West and Problems of Westernization - An Overview', *Comparative Studies of South Asia, Africa and the Middle East* 26, no. 3, 2006, pp.353-66.

Aymalı, Ömer. 'Abdülhamid'in Aşiret Mektebi', Tarih Dosyası/Dünya Bülteni, dunyabulteni.net.

Başkaya, Muzaffer. '1929 Of-Sürmene Felaketi ve Bölgeye Etkileri', *Karadeniz İncelemeleri Dergisi* 18, 2015, pp.177-96.

Boyar, Ebru. 'The Press and the Palace: The Two-way Relationship between Abdülhamid II and the Press, 1876-1908', *Bulletin of SOAS* 69, no. 3, 2006, pp.417-32.

Büssow, Johann, Kurt Franz and Stefan Leder. 'The Arab East and the Bedouin Component in Modern History: Emerging Perspectives on the Arid Lands as a Social Space', *Journal of the Economic and Social History of the Orient* 58, no. 1/2, 2015.

Buzpınar, Tufan Ş. 'Dersaadette bir Arap Şeyhi: Şeyh Muhammad Zafir ve Sultan Abdülhamid ile İlişkileri', *Akademik Araştırmalar Dergisi* 12, November 2010-April 2011, pp.213-25.

Çapa, Mesut. 'Osmanlı İmparatorluğu'ndan Türkiye Cumhuriyeti'ne Geçiş Sürecinde Türkiye'de Tarih Öğretiminin Tarihçesi', *Trakya Üniversitesi Edebiyat Fakültesi Dergisi* 2, no. 3, January 2012, pp.1-28.

Cioeta, Donald J. 'Islamic Benevolent Societies and Public Education in Syria, 1875-1882', *Islamic Quarterly* 26, January 1982, pp.40-55.

Clayer, Nathalie. 'The Albanian Students of the Mekteb-i Mülkiye, Social Networks and Trends of Thought', in *Late Ottoman Society, The Intellectual Legacy*, ed. Elisabeth Özdalga, Routledge, 2005, pp.289-339.

Danso, Martin and Mekki Uludag. 'Aşiret Mektebi ve Ozellikleri', *Batman Univ. Journal of Life Sciences* 1, 2012, pp.775-80.

Deringil, Selim. 'They Live in a State of Nomadism and Savagery: The Late Ottoman Empire and the Post-Colonial Debate', *Comparative Studies in Society and History* 45, no. 2, April 2003, pp.311-42.

Farah, Ceasar E. 'Reassessing Sultan Abdülhamid II's Islamic Policy', *Archivum Ottomanicum* 14, 1995-1996, pp.191-212.

Farah, Ceasar E. 'Arab Supporters of Sultan Abdülhamid II, Izzat al-Abid', *Archivum Ottomanicum* 15, 1997, pp.189-219.

Fontana, Guiditta. 'Creating Nations, Establishing States: Ethno-Religious Heterogeneity and the British Creation of Iraq in 1919-23', *Middle Eastern Studies* 46, no. 1, 2010, pp.1-16.

Fortna, Benjamin C. 'Islamic Morality in Late Ottoman "Secular" Schools', *Int. Jour. of Middle East Studies* 32, August 2000, pp.369-93.

Fortna, Benjamin C. 'Education and Autobiography at the End of the Ottoman Empire', *Die Welt des Islams*, New Series 41, no. 1, 2001, pp.1-31.

Fortna, Benjamin C. 'Remapping the Ottoman Muslim Identity in the Hamidian Era: The Role of Cartographic Artifacts', in *Muslim Traditions and Modern Techniques of Power*, ed. Arnando Salvatore, Verlag Munster, 2001, pp.45-55.

Fortna, Benjamin C. 'Change in the School Maps of the Late Ottoman Empire', *Imago Mundi* 57, 2005, pp.23-34.

Fortna, Benjamin C. 'The Reign of Abdülhamid II', in *The Cambridge History of Turkey, Part I*, ed. Reşat Kasaba, Cambridge, 2008, pp.38-61.

Gündüz, Mustafa. *Tanzimattan Cumhuriyete Eğitim Sisteminin Finansmanı*, NWSA *Education Sciences* (Journal of New World Sciences Academy), 2010, pp.1658-69.

Haj, Samira. 'The Problems of Tribalism: The Case of the Nineteenth Century Iraqi History', *Social History* 16, January 1991, pp.45-58.

Haydarani, Sıddık. 'Aşiret Mektebi ve Aşiret Alayları', *Yakın Tarihimiz*, Cilt 2, 1963.

Hourani, Albert. 'How Should We Write the History of the Middle East?', *Int. J. Middle East Studies* 23, 1991, pp.125-36.

Hülagu, Metin. 'Hacı Osman Nuri Paşa, Hayatı ve Faaliyetleri, 1840-1898', *Ankara Univ OTAM dergisi*, 1994/5.

Inal, Ibnulemin Mahmut Kemal, 'Abdülhamid-i Saninin Notları', *Turk Tarih Encumeni Mecmuası*, 1926, pp.13–15.
Karpat, Kemal. 'The Transformation of the Ottoman State, 1789–1909', *Int. J. of Middle East Studies* 3, June 1972, pp.243–81.
Kasaba, Reşat. 'Do States Always Favor Statis? The Changing Status of Tribes in the Ottoman Empire', in *Boundaries and Belonging, States and Societies in the Struggle to Shape Identities and Local Practices*, ed. Joel S. Migdal, Cambridge, 2004, pp.27–48.
Keddie, Nikkie R. 'The Pan-Islamic Appeal: Afghani and Abdülhamid II', *Middle Eastern Studies* 3, October 1966, pp.46–67.
Khoury, Philip. 'A Reinterpretation of the Origins and Aims of the Great Syrian Revolt', in *Arab Civilization: Challenges and Responses, Studies in Honor of Constantin Zurayk*, eds. G.N. Atiyeh and I. Oweiss, SUNY, 1988.
Kodaman, Bayram. 'II. Abdülhamid ve Aşiret Mektebi', *Türk Kültürü Araştırmaları Dergisi*, Cilt XV, Sayı 1–2, 1976.
Kodaman, Bayram. 'Aşiret Mekteb-i Humayunu', Diyanet Vakfı, *Islam Ansiklopedisi*, Cilt 4, 1993.
Koksal, Yonca. 'Coercion and Mediation: Centralization and Sedentarization of Tribes in the Ottoman Empire', *Middle Eastern Studies* 42, May 2006, pp.469–91.
Kuhn, Thomas. 'Ordering the Past of Ottoman Yemen, 1872–1914', *Turcica* 34, 2002, pp.189–220.
Kuhn, Thomas. 'Shaping and Reshaping Colonial Ottomanism: Contesting Boundaries of Difference and Integration in Ottoman Yemen, 1872–1919', *Comparative Studies of South Asia, Africa and the Middle East* 27, 2007, pp.315–31.
Lange, Katharina. 'Heroic Faces, Disruptive Deeds: Remembering the Tribal Shaykh on the Syrian Euphrates', in *Nomadic Societies in the Middle East and North Africa*, ed. Dawn Chatty, Brill, 2006, pp.940–65.
Lewis, Bernard. 'The Ottoman Archives as a Source for the History of the Arab Lands', *The Journal of the Royal Asiatic Society of Great Britain and Ireland* 3, 1951, pp.139–55.
Makdisi, Ussama. 'Ottoman Orientalism', *The American Historical Review* 107, June 2002, pp.768–96.
Mardin, Şerif. 'Center Periphery Relations: A Key to Turkish Politics?', *Daedalus* 102, 1973.
Mikhail, Alan and Christine Philliou. 'The Ottoman Empire and the Imperial Turn', *Comparative Studies in Society and History* 54, October 2012, pp.721–45.
Minawi, Mostafa. 'Beyond Rhetoric: Reassessing Bedouin-Ottoman Relations along the Route of the Hijaz Telegraph Line at the End of the Nineteenth Century', *Journal of the Economic and Social History of the Orient* 58, 2015, pp.75–104.

Mohammadpour, Ahmad and Kamal Soleimani. 'Interrogating the Tribal: The Aporia of "Tribalism" in the Sociological Study of the Middle East', *The British Journal of Sociology* 0, 2019, pp.1-26.

Orhan, Sibel. 'Alman Imparatoru II. Wilhelm'in Weltpolitik Siyaseti Çerçevesinde Osmanlı Topraklarını Ikinci Ziyareti (1898)', *Tarih Kültür ve Sanat Arastırmaları Dergisi* 7, 2018.

Özder, Gökçe and Didem Ardalı Büyükarman. 'Osmanlı Devleti'nin Son Yıllarında Yaşamış Bir Eğitimci: Ali Nazima', *Turkish Studies* 12, no. 15, dx.doi.org/10.7827/11723, pp.511-24.

Provence, Michael. 'Ottoman Modernity, Colonialism and Insurgency in the Interwar Arab East', *International Journal of Middle East Studies* 43, May 2011, pp.205-25.

Provence, Michael. 'Late Ottoman State Education', in *Religion, Ethnicity and Contested Nationhood in the Former Ottoman Space*, ed. Jorgen Nielsen, Brill 2012, pp.116-27.

Provence, Michael. 'Ottoman Modernity, Colonialism and Insurgency in the Interwar Arab East', *International Journal of Middle East Studies* 43, May 2011, pp.205-25.

Provence, Michael. 'A Man of the Frontier: Ramadan Shallash and the Making of the Post-Ottoman Arab East', in *Age of Rogues, Rebels, Revolutionaries and Racketeers at the Frontiers of Empires*, eds. Ramazan Hakkı Öztan and Alp Yenen, Edinburgh, 2021, pp.333-54.

Rogan, Eugene. 'Aşiret Mektebi: Abdülhamid II's School for Tribes (1892-1907)', *Int. J. Middle East Studies* 28, 1996, pp.83-107.

Sakaoğlu, Necdet. 'Aşiret Mektebi', *İstanbul Ansiklopedisi*, Cilt I, 1993.

Salibi, Kamal S. 'Middle Eastern Parallels: Syria-Iraq-Arabia in Ottoman Times', *Middle Eastern Studies* 15, January 1979, pp.70-81.

Schaebler, Birgit. 'State(s) Power and the Druzes: Integration and the Struggle for Social Control (1838-1949)', in *The Syrian Land: Processes of Integration and Fragmentation*, eds. Thomas Philipp and Birgit Schaelbler, Franz Steiner Verlag, 1998, pp.331-68.

Schaebler, Birgit. 'From Urban Notables to "Noble Arabs": Shifting Discourses in the Emergence of Nationalism in the Arab East, 1910-1916', in *From the Syrian Land to the States of Syria and Lebanon*, eds. Thomas Philipp and Christopher Schumann, Wurzburg 2004, pp.175-98.

Schilcher, Linda. 'The Hauran Conflicts of the 1860's: A Chapter in the Rural History of Modern Syria', *The International Journal of the Middle East Studies* 13, no. 2, 1981.

Seikaly, Samir. 'Tribes in Late Ottoman Syria: Local Representations', *Archivum Ottomanicum* 34, 2017, pp.221-9.

Sezer, Hamiyet. 'II.Abdülhamit Döneminde Osmanlı'da Vilayet Yönetiminde Düzenleme Gayretleri - Trablusgarp Örneği ve Ahmet Rasim Paşa', www.eskieserler.com.

Sivrikaya, Ibrahim. 'Osmanlı İmparatorluğu İdaresindeki Aşiretlerin Eğitimi ve İlk Aşiret Mektebi', *Belgelerle Türk Tarihi Dergisi*, Cilt 11- sayı 63, 1972, pp.17–24.

Şirin, Ibrahim. 'Munif Pasa'nin Tahran'dan Gonderdigi Devlet Isleri ile ilgili Layihasi ve Dusundurdukleri', *Turkish Studies* 3-4, Summer 2008, pp.759–71.

Somel, Selçuk Akşin. 'Abdulhamit Devri Egitim Tarihciligine Bir Bakis: 1980 Sonrasinda Tasra Maarifi ve Gayri Muslim Mekteplerinin Historiografik Bir Analizi', in *Alman Türk Tesadüfleri: Kemal Beydilli'ye Armağan*, eds. Hedda Reindl-Kiel and Seyfi Kenan, EB Verlag, Berlin 2013, pp.571–92.

Somel, Selçuk Akşin. 'Osman Nuri Paşa'nın 17 Temmuz 1885 Tarihli Hicaz Raporu', *Ankara Üniv. DTC Tarih Dergisi*, Cilt 18, Sayı 29, 1996, pp.1–38.

Sorby Jr, Karol. 'The Role of Abdalmuhsin as-Saadun in Iraqi politics in the 1920's', *Asian and African Studies* 24, no. 1, 2015.

Stone, Lawrence. 'Prosopography', *Daedalus* 100, 1971, pp.46–79.

Topuzkanamış, Ersoy. 'Osmanlı Dönemi Ilk Modern Idadi Programlarında Türkçe Eğitimi: 1892 yılı örneği', *Tarihin Peşinde - Uluslararası Tarih Ve Sosyal Araştırmalar Dergisi* 19, 2018, pp.185–226.

Türkmen, Zekeriya. 'Sultan II. Abdülhamid Döneminde Mekteb-i Harbiye-i Şahane', *Osmanlı Istanbulu* IV, Sempozyum 2016, pp.931–54.

Watts, Tracy. 'The British Military Occupation of Cyrenaica, 1942–1949', *Transactions of the Grotius Society* 37, 1951, pp.69–81.

Wick, Alexis. 'Sailing the Modern Episteme, Al-Tahtawi on the Mediterranean', *Comparative Studies in Society and History* 34, no. 2, 2014, pp.405–17.

Yıldız, Hasan. 'II. Meşrutiyet Döneminde Akim Kalmış Bir Eğitim Projesi: Medrese-i Aşâir', *Belleten* 296, 2019, pp.289–308.

Index

Abdülaziz, Sultan 3, 4, 192
Abdülhamid II, Sultan 3-9, 11-14, 19, 35-6, 47-8, 51, 75, 78, 80, 88, 92-3, 107, 114-15, 122, 125-6, 128, 132, 134-6, 141-3, 147, 151-2, 163, 169-71
Akkar 10, 46, 113-14, 116-17
Albania 9, 51-2, 60, 170
Aleppo 2, 12, 18, 27, 35, 37, 39-40, 42, 43, 44-5, 47, 50, 53, 57, 92-5, 97, 101, 122, 150-1
Algeria 124, 136, 142
Ali Nazima 21-4, 43, 77-8, 80-1, 84, 87, 169
Anderson, Benedict 7
Aneze tribe 40, 45, 57, 59, 93, 96
Arabia 1, 2, 12, 97, 124, 146, 149, 165-6
Asir 41, 44
Askari, Jafar 157
Asmahan 10, 112-13
Atrash 10, 42, 58, 98-9, 102, 106-13, 122, 130, 163-4

Baghdad 2, 18, 27, 35-6, 39-40, 42-5, 49, 54-5, 60, 93, 96, 105, 149-53, 156, 161, 166, 168, 171
Balkans 2-4, 45, 51-2, 88, 92, 94, 109, 123, 138, 155, 163
Basra 2, 4, 10, 18, 35, 39-45, 49, 52-5, 94, 135, 149, 150-3, 155-7
Beirut 2, 40, 45-6, 54, 77, 81, 86, 101, 103-5, 110, 117-18, 120, 122, 126, 171
Benghazi 31, 35, 40, 42-4, 48, 57, 81, 86-7, 124, 126, 128, 131-2, 134-5, 140-1, 145-6
Bitlis 37, 50, 55, 155
Blake, Corinne 7, 122
Busaraya tribe 92-3

Cibran 38, 57, 155
Civil Service Academy, Mülkiye 3, 7, 10, 28-31, 51, 56-60, 75-8, 81, 87, 108-9, 117, 120, 122, 126, 145, 155, 163, 170
Committee of Union and Progress 110, 151, 156
Cyrenaica 135, 140-1

Damascus 2, 12, 39, 45, 47, 55, 58-9, 83, 92, 94-100, 105-6, 109-11, 113, 120, 122-3, 129-30, 151, 156, 164
Darüşşafaka 31, 52
Deir ez-Zor 9, 18, 27, 35, 38-40, 42-5, 55, 92-7, 101, 104-5, 111, 129, 164
Deringil, Selim 88, 176, 186, 202, 210
Derna 124, 128, 131, 134, 136, 138, 140, 145
Diyarbakır 35, 37, 40-1, 50, 82, 93
Druze 10, 42, 45, 47, 98-9, 102, 105-7, 109-12, 130

Egypt 13, 52, 91, 93, 105, 112-13, 123-5, 134-6, 140, 143
England, English (Great Britain) 6, 76, 88, 125, 161
Enver Paşa 95, 136, 166
Erzurum 29, 30, 37, 40, 50-1, 54-5, 117
Esma Sultan 19, 26, 33, 172
Euphrates 2, 9, 92-4

Faisal, King 95-7, 105, 110, 112, 120, 151, 156-8, 160-1
Fezzan 124, 125
France, French 3, 5, 9, 75-7, 80, 84, 86, 89, 92, 97-101, 103-5, 110-12, 116-18, 122-3, 125-6, 129, 131, 152, 164
Fortna, Benjamin 7

Galatasaray Mekteb-i Sultani 52, 75-7
Grand Vizier 5, 11, 13, 15, 19, 26, 30, 32, 35, 37-9, 43-4, 46, 48, 51-3, 76, 82-3, 94, 108-9, 129, 134, 143, 151, 153, 165, 172

Hama 39, 44–6, 98, 101, 111, 117
Hamidiye regiments 19, 37–8, 47, 50–1, 57, 94, 114
Harbiye, see Military Academy
Hawran 10, 44, 46, 98, 105–6, 109
Hijaz 1, 4, 11–13, 18, 35–7, 39–40, 42–4, 47, 49, 53, 60, 83, 91–2, 95, 124, 131, 166, 169
Homs 44, 55, 99, 130

Idris Sanusi, King 10, 126, 135, 140–1, 164
Iraq 10, 39, 45, 49, 95–7, 112, 129, 134, 140, 149–52, 155–61, 164, 172

Janissary 1, 6, 123, 172
Java 9, 52–3, 170
Jerusalem 18, 32, 35–40, 42–5, 81, 129, 134, 166
Jordan (Transjordan) 2, 111
Jouvenel, Henry 99–101, 103–4

Kabataş 19, 21, 26, 33, 128, 172–4
Kağıthane 24, 136
Kamil Paşa 5, 15
Karapapak tribe 40, 50
Kaymakam, local administrator 31, 50, 52, 58–9, 107, 110, 118, 126, 135–6, 138–9, 146, 155
Kologlu, Orhan 6, 136
Koloğlu, Sadullah 10, 44, 48, 58, 126, 128, 135–41, 163–4
Kosovo 51–2
Kufra 125, 131–4
Kurd 9, 37–8, 40–3, 45, 49–50, 57, 60, 93–4, 155, 166, 168
Kuwait 2, 52–3, 105

Land Reform 1858 91, 124
Libya 1, 10–11, 41, 44–5, 48, 53, 55, 58, 60, 81, 86, 88, 94–5, 123–6, 129, 134–6, 140–2, 145–6, 164, 170, 172

Mamuretulaziz, Elazığ 37–8, 40, 50, 55
Mansour, al-Kikhia 126, 128, 135, 146
Mansour, Omar Pasha 10, 20, 44, 48, 58, 86, 88, 94, 108–9, 126, 128–36, 141–2, 146, 163–4, 170
Mecca 10–12, 39, 44, 47, 76, 91, 95, 124, 136, 149

Mehmed Hamza 38, 155
Merhebi 10, 46, 113–14, 117–18, 120–2, 163–4
Midhat Paşa 2, 5, 150
Military Academy, Harbiye 2, 9–12, 27, 29, 32, 55–9, 86–7, 94, 105, 108, 137, 146, 163
Mosul 18, 31, 35, 37, 40–5, 49, 55, 60, 96, 158, 169
Muntafiq 10, 49, 149–51, 153, 155–6
Mülkiye. See Civil Service Academy
Münif Paşa 5, 11

Nablus 46, 55
Najd 97, 150–2, 157, 165

Palestine, Palestinian 94, 99, 101, 104
Parliament 10, 38, 80, 94–5, 113, 117–18, 126, 134–5, 141, 153, 155–7, 159, 164
Provence, Michael 6, 7

Recai Efendi, Hacı 7, 9, 31, 75–8, 82–4, 169
Rogan, Eugene 6, 32

Saadun 10, 39, 49, 129, 149–52, 155–61, 163–4
Sabah family (Kuwait) 52–3
San'a 36, 41, 171
Sanussi 124–6, 131–5, 140–1, 164
Shallash, Ramadan 9, 45, 92–105, 111, 122, 129, 163–4
Shammar tribe 26, 93, 96, 149–50
Süreyya Paşa 19, 39, 56
Suwayda 42, 101, 106, 109–12
Syria 1, 5–7, 9, 18, 35, 37, 39–47, 54–5, 58, 91–2, 95, 97–9, 101–5, 107, 109–13, 116, 120, 122, 129, 134, 164, 166, 172

Tahsin Paşa 26, 28, 48, 132, 143
Tanzimat 1, 3–5, 7, 11–12
Tekçe, Güngör 143
Tercüman-ı Hakikat, newspaper 14, 19, 29, 30–2, 39, 41, 43, 51, 83, 86, 94, 107–9, 145–6, 171
Thamarat al-Fünun, newspaper 171

Tigris 2, 171
Tripoli (Lebanon) 113
Tripoli (Libya) 11–12, 18, 31, 35, 39–40, 42–4, 48, 57, 59, 124–6, 131, 136, 141–2, 145
Tunis 123, 125, 136, 142

Vali-Governor 1, 2, 5–6, 8, 10, 12, 19, 36, 38–9, 41, 43, 45–7, 49–52, 60, 81–2, 91–7, 106–7, 110, 113–14, 116, 118, 126, 128, 131–5, 140, 142, 150–1, 156, 164, 166, 170–1
Van 37, 40–2, 49–50, 55, 155, 170

Yemen 1, 4, 11–12, 18, 26, 31, 35–6, 39–45, 47–8, 54–5, 57–8, 60, 124, 170–1

Zafir 48, 125–6, 141–3, 145
Zawra, newspaper 36, 171
Zühdü Paşa 15, 21, 37, 169

www.ingramcontent.com/pod-product-compliance
Lightning Source LLC
Chambersburg PA
CBHW062218300426
44115CB00012BA/2119